The Life and Opinions of the Rev. William Milne, D. D., Missionary to China

TO

DR. AND MRS. REED,

OF

WYCLIFFE CHAPEL,

AS

THE FIRST FRIENDS OF THE MILNE FAMILY,

IN LONDON;

AND

AS THE AVOWED FRIENDS OF CHINA,

THIS WORK IS INSCRIBED,

FROM POUNDSFORD PARK, WHERE IT ORIGINATED,

BY THEIR FRIEND,

THE AUTHOR.

THE

LIFE AND OPINIONS

OF THE

REV. WILLIAM MILNE, D. D.,

MISSIONARY TO CHINA,

ILLUSTRATED BY

BIOGRAPHICAL ANNALS OF ASIATIC MISSIONS,

FROM

PRIMITIVE TO PROTESTANT TIMES;

INTENDED AS

A GUIDE TO MISSIONARY SPIRIT.

BY

ROBERT PHILIP,

AUTHOR OF THE LIFE AND TIMES OF BUNYAN AND WHITEFIELD, THE EXPERIMENTAL GUIDES, ETC.

"The LORD said, I took thee from the sheep cote, from following the sheep, and have made thee a great name."—SAMUEL.

PHILADELPHIA:
HERMAN HOOKER—CHESTNUT STREET.

1840.

BV3427
M5P5
1840a

In Exch.
Columbia Univ Lib.

Wm. S. Young, Printer.

CONTENTS.

Chapter I.	William Milne's Early Life -	9
II.	William Milne's Missionary Spirit	32
III.	William Milne at Gosport -	48
IV.	Mr. and Mrs. Milne's Voyage -	81
V.	Mr. Milne's First Appeals from China - - - -	105
VI.	Mr. Milne's Reception in China	119
VII.	Mr. Milne's Visit to Java -	130
VIII.	Joint Labours in China - -	143
IX.	The Malacca Mission - -	156
X.	Miscellaneous Labours - -	199
XI.	Milne's Estimates of Chinese Character - - - -	219
XII.	Chinese Opinions - - -	228
XIII.	Missionary Events - - -	239
XIV.	Mrs. Milne's Death - -	263
XV.	The Widower's Closet - -	295
XVI.	The Mission Family - -	312
XVII.	Jewish Witnesses in China -	323
XVIII.	Apostolic Missions in Asia -	334
XIX.	The Asiatic Nestorians - -	350
XX.	The Syrian Mission Schools -	360
XXI.	The Origin of Christianity in China - - - -	366
XXII.	The Asiatic Prester John -	378
XXIII.	The Lamaism of Asia - -	388
XXIV.	A Voice from the Tombs of Morrison and Milne, to the Schools of the Prophets -	399
XXV.	The Syrian Churches in India -	414
XXVI.	The Opium Crisis - -	428

PREFACE.

HAD the Author known of any one in England, accustomed to write for the press, who had even the half of his own knowledge of Dr. and Mrs. Milne, he would not have become their biographer, notwithstanding all his love to their memory, and all his zeal for China. His health forbade equally, the excitement of living over again the days of his youth, and the research necessary in order to illustrate the Opinions of Dr, Milne on the ancient Christianity of China. The last was the chief difficulty: for our Ecclesiastical History does not even furnish a *clew* to the history of the Syrian Church in Asia, although she eclipsed both the Greek and Roman in numbers and purity, during the middle ages. The fact is, the Syrian Church had no influence on the Reformation: for Melancthon failed to enlist her patriarch against the Pope, and Luther, to establish her orthodoxy; and thus our historians took no interest in her ancient faith or fame. This created a *blot* as well as a blank in our literature; and he must be no ordinary scholar who can remove either now.

It is unnecessary for the Author to say, that he has not scholarship to be the annalist of this first and greatest Missionary Church in the world. He has done, however, in a small compass, all that he was capable of doing,—blended with the life of the *second* Protestant Missionary to China, graphic sketches of the Primitive and Nestorian Missions, which penetrated or skirted that mighty empire, " the Land of Sinim." Graphic is, perhaps, too strong a name for his sketches; loaded as they are with quotations in all styles. This appearance of *pedantry* was, however, inevitable. He would have been deemed visionary, apart from a host of vouchers. Besides, the list of historical authorities may furnish some future student with what the writer had not, a clew to the subject. His object is, however, to interest ordinary readers; and, therefore, he ought not to be tried for more than he attempted. He has not written for the learned, but for those who have read and thought less than himself about Asiatic Christianity. Whatever parade of learned names, therefore, meets the eye in this work, it is to prevent incredulity, not in order to gain credit for erudition.

To the friends of Missions, he would say,—This book presents, in the character of Dr. and Mrs. Milne, a *model* which may be held up to any young man or woman, who is contemplating Missionary work. It exhibits an *imitable* example, as well as one worthy of imitation. Such a book was much wanted. The Churches also do well to study the *influences* which formed the character of these distinguished Missionaries, if they would not send forth drones nor wasps into the field. Whatever, therefore, may be thought of the Author's opinions on this subject—and no one is at all responsible for any of them but himself,—the Churches will, to a certainty, hold up to all future candidates for Missionary work, the example of WILLIAM and RACHEL MILNE; and all proper candidates who study it, will, as certainly, look to their respective Churches for such friends as *he* found in Huntley, and *she* in Aberdeen.

R. P.

KINGSLAND,
1839.

MEMOIRS OF REV. W. MILNE, D. D.

CHAPTER I.

WILLIAM MILNE'S EARLY LIFE

"His decision of character rendered him an eminently devoted Missionary. Considering the disadvantage he laboured under, from the want of an early literary education, what he effected is *astonishing*."—Rev. Robert Morrison, D. D.

If Leang-A-Fa possess any susceptibility, he could not witness, unmoved, nor unprofited, the scenery of Kennethmont, in Scotland, where William Milne, his spiritual father, "followed the ewes." It is hardly either sublime or beautiful scenery; but there is enough of both in it, to make any one feel that a Shepherd boy, of even ordinary talents, who is out in all weathers, could not be utterly uninfluenced by it. William Milne certainly was not. I am not quite sure now, that I have stood *with* him upon the corner of the hill above Reeskhouse, when we were boys, admiring the hoary grandeur of "the Tap of Noth," and the silvery windings of "the bonny Boggie," in the valley between the hill and the mountain; but I remember well the mutual zest, with which we often talked of those scenes,

"O'er the hills and far away,"

when we met in England. We had both mused, as well as played, upon the same spots; and sat upon the same gray-stones and mossy hillocks, gazing at old Noth, the throne of the clouds; and at the ruins of old Reeskhouse, the castle in the valley. Our lips and hands had often been "as blue as blaaverts," with blackberries gathered amongst the same heather-knolls and etnach-bushes. Besides, these spots were dear to us both, as ground hallowed by the memory of our Pastor, Mr. Cowie, of Huntly, who sometimes preached and catechized in the neighbourhood; and by the labours of his elders, who often visited the Sabbath Schools in turn. We had thus been under the same teachers, although not in the same School; and retained an equal love to them. The Nathaniel-like spirit of John Leslie; the Ezekiel-like sublimity of Saunders Sievwright; the Paul-like shrewdness of William Smith, and the Jacob-like unction of James Cruickshank, had alternately awed and interested us. They loved us too, from the time they saw any thing hopeful about us: —perhaps, even before. This pleased us then, and it amazed us afterwards. We only thought of them then as the *best* men in Huntly, amongst many good men: but when we first met in England, we spoke of them as *wonderful* men; for we had found no parallels to them any where, in the same rank of life. We thus discovered, that our minds and character had been brought into contact with *genius* as well as extraordinary piety, although we knew it not at the moment.

I mention these circumstances distinctly, because I know the influence they had upon the mind of my friend. They gave, indeed, no romantic nor sentimental cast to his mind: but both the mountains and the men helped to render his young spirit thoughtful and solemn, when he began to read and pray amongst the sheep-folds. Even then, he felt that it was *sublime* "to sit on the brow of the hill, reading the lives of the Martyrs; admiring their patience and fortitude in suffering; and seeing them overcome their enemies, by the blood of the Lamb and the word of their testimony." He adds, "I longed that God would honour *me*, some time or other, thus to confess his name, and bear my testimony to the truth."

The expression, "*seeing* the Martyrs," in this record of his feelings, means more than even the vivid realization of their sufferings, which reading at the fireside can produce. He was reading amidst such hills and valleys as the Scotch covenanters suffered amongst:—for it was "The Cloud of Witnesses," not "Fox's Book of Martyrs," that awoke his emotions. He had thus around him, such lofty mountains as they had watched and worshipped upon, and such lonely woods and glens as they had been hunted in: and besides all this, the Christians he knew best, and loved most, were just such men in character and spirit as the holy men in "The Cloud of Witnesses." It was, thus, Cowie, Leslie, Sievwright, Smith, and Cruickshank, (his Pastor and Teachers,) he *saw* before him, when he peopled the wilds of Kennethmont with images of the Martyrs. He felt that these men would have been driven to the hills, and must have sealed their testimony with their blood, had they lived in the days of Peden and Cargill; and he believed that they *would* have died rather than renounce the covenant; and, therefore, as he loved them, he felt that he could be a Martyr in their company, or for their creed.

I analyze this fine enthusiasm, as it glowed in the breast of young Milne, because it will explain the mighty influence which the Scotch book of Martyrs had over the youths of Scotland, at the close of the last century. There were then, especially amongst the Seceders, Ministers and Elders, who were both the descendants and the living exemplifications of the old covenanters, in all that was thoughtful, devotional, and weighty, in their holy character. The late Dr. Waugh grew up amongst such men, and caught all their virtues, without any of their peculiarities. England saw in *him*, what the generality of the covenanters would have been, had they been treated as he was; and what many of their children became, when the Star of Brunswick arose. William Milne and myself recognised at once in Dr. Waugh, all that we had seen in Mr. Cowie, or dreamt of in "Maister Peden;" but all softened (it could not be sublimated) by the urbanities and polish of English courtesy.

It must not be supposed that young Milne's first associations with the scenery of Kennethmont were of this high order; nor "that from a child he had known the Holy Scriptures," or the holy men just named. He was proverbially a wicked boy, until twelve years old. Like Bunyan, he seems to have been a "lisping blasphemer and swearer;" so early was his "mouth filled with cursing." I did not know him then, nor can I fully account for such profaneness. It certainly was not common in the neighbourhood. To

"Curse or ban,"

was not the characteristic of the peasantry of Kennethmont. Minced oaths and low ribaldry were not uncommon; but daring profanity was certainly a rare thing. He said of himself, however, at his ordination, "I thought (then) that to invent new oaths would reflect honour upon my character, and make me like the great ones of the earth." I well remember too, that he was described by the neighbours as once "a very *deevil* for swearing." The only explanation of this, that I know of, is, that there may have been at Leith Hall occasionally, profane servants who had *graduated* in England, and whose *livery* made them "great ones of the earth," to a Shepherd boy,

"Clad in hodden-gray,"

and girt about with an undyed plaid: for other great ones than these *flunkies*, he had no opportunity of mixing with, so as to learn new oaths. He was, however, near the Hall, and close to a line of road where cattle dealers and drovers were frequently passing; and thus he may have been tempted to rival the worst. It was thus, not the voice of prayer nor of praise which first rung amongst the rocks and hills, as he followed his herds and flocks; but the voice of reckless impiety, or of ribald songs. His herding club, as was common with such boys, would often be flung with curses as well as fury, after a straying sheep or a rambling cow; and if he indulged any day dreams then of being great, they went no higher than to wear the Leith's livery, or to ride such a horse as Giggy of Buchain, the couper. These hints will throw some light upon his own narrative of his early life. "I was born in the parish of Kennethmont, in Aberdeenshire, in 1785. My father died when I was six years of age; and my mother gave me the education common to others in the same condition of life. As to that knowledge which is good for the soul, I was a perfect stranger to it myself; nor did others seek to impress my mind with its importance. The natural depravity of my heart began very soon to discover itself, by leading me into those sins, for the commission of which, my age and circumstances afforded opportunity. In profane swearing, and other sins of a like nature, I far exceeded most of my equals; and became vile to a proverb. I can remember the time (O God! I desire to do it with shame and sorrow of heart,) when I thought that to invent new oaths would reflect honour on my character, and make me like the great ones of the earth." This is very like Bunyan's account of himself. He often confessed with horror and detestation of himself, that when he was only a stripling, he had few equals in lying, swearing, and blaspheming God's holy name; all which became to him as a second nature.*

"Though I had a natural predilection for books, yet not, alas! for the book of God. I read it only when constrained, and even then with much reluctance and impatience. Though I learned by heart the Assembly's Shorter Catechism, and Willison's Mother's Catechism, yet this was more from a desire to be equal with my neighbours, and to avoid the displeasure of the Minister of the parish, whose presence I always dreaded as death, when he came round to catechise, than from any love to the truths which these excellent books contained." This, too, is like Bunyan. He says, "it was a kind of *prison* to me to hear persons read books of Christian piety. Religion was very grievous to me in those days. I could neither endure it myself, nor that any others should."† "Sometimes I used to say my prayers at

* Life and Times, page 11.   † Ibid, p. 8.

night, for fear of the evil spirit, from whose hurtful influence I supposed my prayers were an effectual security.

"I do not remember that any very deep impressions of divine truth were made on my mind for the first twelve years of my life, except once, when I was in my tenth year. Travelling alone in the middle of the day, between two corn fields, the idea of the eternal punishment of sin in hell, struck me with amazing force. My feelings on this occasion exactly corresponded to the language of the prophet, 'Who amongst us can dwell with devouring fire? who can dwell with everlasting burnings?' The thought filled me with horror, constrained me to pray for the *first* time, in the fields, and to form resolutions of amendment for the future. These impressions, however, appeared not to be accompanied with any spiritual change in the dispositions of the heart, as they soon wore off, and my vows were forgotten.

"The sinful propensities of my nature became stronger by indulging them; and many plans did I form, in hopes of rendering myself conspicuous, in the circle in which I moved, for the vanity of my mind, and the gaiety of my conduct. I foolishly imagined that, by the time I was sixteen years of age, I should attain great celebrity as a vain and trifling youth. God, however, (I desire to adore his goodness) had other and better things in reserve for me.

"About my thirteenth year a partial reformation was effected, to which the five following things contributed: 1. The reading of some religious books." On reading this, his colleague, Dr. Morrison, wrote— "See the advantage of religious tracts and books:

Yes, fill the world with these. If made waste paper of, (as some of them are, and will be,) even in that state, the scattered leaves of a Bible, or of other religious books, have been made, and will continue to be made, the means of exciting serious and godly thoughts, which bring the proud sinner's heart to mercy's throne."* "My attention was turned at this time to religious books more than ever before: I cannot tell the reason; perhaps to gratify a natural thirst for knowledge. The books I read were, 'Willison's Treatise on the Sabbath,' and 'Russell's Seven Sermons;' both of which made considerable impressions on my mind, and led me to prayer. 2. The example of two pious persons who lived in a family where I for some time resided; one of whom slept in the same room with me, and used to retire, at night and morning, for secret prayer. This I saw the propriety of, and, sometimes, imitated. 3. A secret hope which I entertained, of being saved by my prayers and reformation. Under the influence of this deceit, I obtained a false peace of conscience, which filled me with pride and self-confidence. 4. The dread of temporal evils; of danger in the night; and of being drowned in a small river which I had frequently to pass. (He had once a very narrow escape from drowning, whilst crossing that river in a 'spet.') 5. The representations which were given of the sufferings of Christ, by the minister at sacrament seasons. But as these representations seemed to move the animal feelings rather than to influence the heart, their efforts were short-lived." Sacramental addresses, in Scotland, are often very like Good-Friday sermons in England, vivid pictures of the mingled

* Canton Memoirs.

solemnities and glories of Calvary; and are brought out then, even in pulpits where the Cross is not a favourite subject.

"Soon after, I attended a Sabbath-evening school, which at that time began in our neighbourhood, where I became one of the scholars." These schools taught no one to read. That was not necessary in Scotland. Neither were they for the children of the poor exclusively; Mr. Cowie's Sabbath-schools embraced the young of all ranks in his flock, and were attended alike by all. Their chief object was to make us "mighty in the scriptures," by searching out, and committing to memory, *all* the proofs of any given point, in doctrine or duty. I feel young again, when thinking of these exercises! The number of proofs was occasionally incredible. It had begun to seem to me a *dream*, until I found it mentioned in one of Mr. Cowie's diaries, as extraordinary. He was accustomed to take a seat near the pulpit, whilst we stood in the front of the galleries. I see him now, "leaning upon his staff," with a scarlet handkerchief thrown over his head, and his eyes fixed on the ground. "I wept," he says, "all the time, often, to hear the boys bring so many proofs." Little did we imagine that the good old man was thus affected. We were trying to rival each other, and to make him look up with a smile to those of us who were the *last* to sit down. This will explain what Dr. Milne says about "the pride of knowledge," in the following narrative. "Here my knowledge of evangelical truth increased, and considerable impressions of its importance were made on my mind. My increase in knowledge made me very proud; but I was led to search the scriptures, and to pray. Sometimes

I used to walk home from the school alone, about a mile, over the brow of a hill, praying all the way. At this time I began the worship of God in my mother's family; and also held some meetings for prayer, with my sisters and other children, in a barn that belonged to the premises.

"Notwithstanding this change in my outward conduct, I fear that I was all this time acting under the influence of self-righteous principles: for I had never felt my need of Christ, in his complete character; nor had I, AS A SINNER, made any humble application to God, through Christ, for pardon and grace.

"At sixteen years of age, when, formerly, I had wickedly supposed that I should have my fill of iniquity, and see the accomplishment of my foolish plans, it pleased God, whose ways are a great deep, to remove me to a place where I had the privilege of conversing with pious persons, who embraced every opportunity of turning my attention to the concerns of eternity. Though I was a stranger to them, yet, knowing that I had a soul, they were concerned for my salvation. This was the case with one of them especially, who, though poor in this world, was rich in faith, and in whom the word of God dwelt abundantly. I used sometimes to go to his house, at the hour of prayer, when he and his family bowed the knee, and worshipped God, at the foot of their domestic altar. He was accustomed to make some remarks on the chapter read for the instruction of his children, and to prepare them for the solemn exercise of prayer: these interested me very much, and showed me a beauty in the word of God which I never saw before. He exhorted me to secret prayer, and to read pious books, which he and some others furnished me with, suitable to the inquiring state of my mind." (Burns' "Cottager's Saturday Night," is thus no poetical fiction. It is as true as it is beautiful. Indeed, it is not *all* the truth. I cannot identify the family which Mr. Milne refers to; but I know many a mud-walled and straw-thatched cottage in the district, where family worship was conducted thus every night, and often in the morning too.) "From this my enjoyment and pursuit of pleasure in the world were marred; and a beauty and excellence discovered in religion, which I had never seen in any past period of my life, and which led me to choose and follow after it as the only object deserving the chief attention of an immortal creature. As the family in which I lived were strangers to religion themselves, and derided all others who made it their concern, I was very disagreeably situated. The only place I found for retirement, where I could be quiet and unnoticed, was a *sheep-cote*, where the sheep are kept in winter. Here, surrounded by my fleecy companions, I often bowed the knee on a piece of *turf* which I carried in with me for the purpose. Many hours have I spent there, in the winter evenings, with a pleasure to which before I was a stranger; and, while some of the members of the family were plotting how to put me to shame, I was eating in secret of that bread 'which the world knoweth not of.'" This may seem romantic to those who are unacquainted with rural life in Scotland; but there was no sentimentality in it. He went to the sheep-cote, because he would have been disturbed in the barn, by his fellow-servants; and he carried a turf with him to kneel upon, because the floor was foul as well as damp. Besides, there was no *romance* about William Milne. It never even crossed his mind, that there was either any sublimity, or much self-denial, in kneeling before the Lord at night, amongst the sheep and lambs which he had followed by day. The recollection that David had done so, may have had some weight with him: but if it had, it was rather as an example than as a charm.

"My delightful employment at this time, being chiefly of a rural nature, afforded much opportunity through the day, for spiritual improvement. Books were my constant companions; and some of them made powerful impressions on my mind. A book, entitled 'The Cloud of Witnesses,' containing an account of the persecution in Scotland, in the reign of Charles the Second, gave me an exalted idea of the excellency and power of Christianity. Often have I sat on the brow of a hill, reading the lives of the Martyrs, admiring their patience and fortitude in suffering; and, seeing them 'overcome' their enemies by the blood of the Lamb, and by the 'word of their testimony,' I longed that God would, some time or other, honour me thus to confess his name, and bear my testimony to the truth. In this, there was, perhaps, more zeal than knowledge; more regard for the HONOUR of Martyrdom than PURE LOVE to God and his cause in the world. All this time, however, I knew but little of myself as a guilty and condemned creature. The book which God made use of more especially for convincing me of my depravity, sin, and misery, was Mr. Boston's 'Four-fold State,' which I read with the deepest attention. It conducted me into my own heart, discovered the evils which before lay hid in the chambers of imagery; the monstrous ingratitude to God, which had marked all my conduct; and the pollution of original and actual sin, with which my soul was contaminated. I saw that, as I was necessarily under the strongest and most righteous obligations to God, and had never for one hour of my life discharged these, but lived in unprovoked rebellion against the Author of my life, so I was justly under the curse of God's righteous law, and exposed to everlasting misery. 'What shall I give for the sin of my soul?' was *literally* the language which I used. To be condemned to toil for a thousand years, in the lowest drudgery; or to endure the punishment of hell for any LIMITED space of time, seemed easy when compared to ETERNAL WRATH, which I knew my sins deserved, and from which, for some days, I had but little hope of deliverance. To be transformed into a stone, or into one of the fowls of the mountains, which were often flying over my head, was what I sometimes wished, in order to avoid appearing before God in judgment, and to be freed from the danger of EVERLASTING punishment. My distress of mind was much increased by a mistaken notion of the doctrine of election, as I did not then see that the accomplishment of the purpose of God, with respect to the salvation of sinners, was intimately connected with the *use of the means of grace;* but supposed that the decree of God cut me off from the expectation of happiness in the world to come, and shut me up in gloomy silence, and 'fearful looking for of judgment.' This was so much the more distressing, as I saw that my own guilt *deserved* all this misery; and though I saw that God, as a Sovereign, had a right to choose whom he would, yet I saw that even the reprobate perish JUSTLY and RIGHTEOUSLY. 'But who can be *willing* to die the second death? and 'what will a man not give in exchange for his soul?' I could not endure the idea of being for ever left under the dominion of sin, and cast out from the presence of God; therefore I continued to pray, as opportunity served, *ten* or *fifteen* times a day, and said, 'who knoweth if God will return and repent, and leave a blessing behind him' on my poor and wretched soul? I attended meetings for prayer and spiritual edification; and the pious conversation of those who were with me, on the judgment to come, aided by the awful darkness and silence of *night*, made deep impressions on my heart, and tended to inciease my concern for acceptance with God, through Jesus Christ. God, in his gracious kindness, did not suffer me to remain long in this distress of soul, but directed me to those means by which I learned how even a vile and guilty creature, such as I was, might be for ever saved. There were two things which contributed to remove my perplexity and distress. One was a sermon of Mr. Boston's, entitled, 'The Believer's Espousals to Christ.' Here the offices of Christ, as mediator, were treated in such a convincing and encouraging way, as to produce a lively hope in my soul. The other was a sermon which I heard preached by the late Rev. G. Cowie, of Huntly, on a week evening, from Rev. xxii. 21. He expatiated on the free grace of God, through Christ, to the chief of sinners, with an eloquence peculiar to himself. He quoted those words from Christ's commission to his apostles, 'Go, preach the gospel to every creature,'—'BEGINNING AT JERUSALEM.' Then I was led to reason thus:—

If pardon and salvation were offered, 'without money and without price,' to those who had killed the Prince of Life, and thereby committed the greatest possible crime; then, surely that grace which could triumph over all THEIR guilt, and so richly abound where sins of the highest aggravation once abounded, may be extended to ME—pardon MY sins, and renew MY nature—heal and save MY soul. By these two things I was led to discover a glory and suitableness in the Gospel—as displaying the lustre of the divine perfections, and as preserving the honours of the divine law, while at the same time it conferred eternal life on the guilty sinner believing in Jesus. This discovery captivated my heart, and made me willing to devote myself, soul and body, to God for ever.

"Having an earnest desire of devoting myself to God, I was encouraged to do so, in the way of a personal covenant. I found this method of dedication recommended in 'Guthrie's Trial of a Saving Interest in Christ.' Judging this plan agreeable to the language of the prophet, that 'one shall say I am the Lord's, and another shall call himself by the name of Jacob,' &c., I determined to adopt it: and, having retired to a place surrounded by *hills* on every side, I professed to choose the Lord as my God, Father, Saviour, and everlasting portion; and to offer up myself to his service, to be ruled, sanctified, and saved by him. This was followed by much peace and happiness of mind, with earnest desires to be holy, with a determination to cast in my lot among the despised followers of the Lamb, and with a concern for the salvation of immortal souls."

This transition from the sheep-cote to a solitary and silent amphitheatre amidst "the everlasting hills," is both more and less sentimental than it seems. It was influenced by the example of the old Covenanters, and of the older Patriarchs. He imitated Abraham under the oaks of Mamre, and Jacob at Bethel, and John the Baptist in the wilderness, and the children of the covenant in Scotland, in thus placing himself *alone* with God, when he first pledged himself to walk with God. But this was not done because it was sublime, but because it was suitable. He never thought of how it would *tell* upon those who might hear of it; but only of how it would tell upon his own spirit at the time, and of how it would keep the memory of his solemn consecration for ever associated with calm, pure, and impressive scenery. And it did. The first sermon I heard him preach in London, was on subscribing with the hand to be the Lord's. He did not refer to his own covenant amidst the hills, nor did I know the fact then; but he made me feel that he had been, like myself, *alone* with God,—where God only was present.

"After this, I met with considerable opposition from my own relatives, on account of a change in my views; having found it necessary to leave the Kirk of Scotland, and join another body of Christians: not that I had any prejudice against it, for I was baptized and brought up in it, and would not have left it had I found the preaching in the place where I then resided equally evangelical and edifying as among those with whom I united. It was not, however, the difference between that preaching which was chiefly legal and moral, and that which is evangelical and spiritual, that induced me at first to dissent from the Kirk of Scotland; for my understanding, at that time, was scarcely ripe enough to discern it. But it was the very different effect which I felt produced in myself, and saw displayed in others by these two ways of preaching. When I attended on the ministry of those who were most evangelical, I felt myself disposed for prayer, saw the evils of my heart, and found the people spiritual and edifying in their conversation. Such I found not to be the case under that preaching which was chiefly of a moral kind. Being very young, and the only one in our family who had ventured to be thus singular, it was considered by some that I was under the influence of certain feelings, which were exceedingly dangerous, and which led me to act in a way that reflected on the piety and wisdom of my forefathers. But to die in peace, and have part in the first resurrection, were things infinitely more important, in my eyes, than the approbation of all that were related to me in the flesh, yea, than the applause of the whole world.

"Thus I continued for two years, endeavouring to follow the Lord Jesus, and to keep a conscience void of offence towards God and towards all men. Soon after this I renewed my dedication to God, wrote it down, and 'subscribed with my hand unto the Lord.' A year after I was received as a member of the Church of Christ at Huntly. Since that, to the present time, I have passed through many exercises of mind, and have had every day to lament, that I carry about with me 'a body of sin and death.' I have had many doubts and fears about my salvation. Many have been my backslidings; but I have endeavoured to look to Jesus alone for pardon and salvation; and though I have often, through the power of temptation and unbelief, been ready to cast away my confidence, and say, 'there is no hope;' yet 'by the help of God, I continue to this day.' My attainments in holiness have been, alas! few and small— this is the greatest burden of my soul from day to day: and, if I deceive not myself, there is nothing in the universe that I so much desire as *holiness* of heart and life—as conformity to Jesus in all things. I look on myself this evening as the CHIEF of sinners, and place my whole dependence for a complete salvation, on the righteousness and Spirit of Christ. O may I 'be found in him at last—not having spot or wrinkle, or any such thing.'" 1812.

Had Mr. Milne given the history of his conversion in Scotland, instead of England, he would have introduced the names of more of the friends of his youth than I have done, and connected it especially with the instrumentality of his father's friend,—good old Adam Sievwright, the basket maker. It was in his cottage he found a retreat from the company of the farm servants, in the evening. It is of him he says, "though poor in this world, he was rich in faith." It was at his family altar he first discovered the beauty and excellence of spiritual religion. The Reverend Mr. Hill, of Huntly, said truly in his sermon on the death of Dr. Milne, "the name of Adam Sievwright deserves, on various accounts, to be mentioned with much respect. He was one *chief* instrument of Dr. Milne's conversion, and ever after felt a deep interest in all his future steps."

I remember this meek, and lowly, and lovely Christian well. His mild eye, and the melting tones of his gentle voice, seem even now falling upon me. I see him yet at the "ingle-neuk" in his cottage, seated amidst his bundles of *sauchen waans*, (*willows*).

twisting a butter-basket, and talking about the glories of the Covenant of grace to young Milne! He set him to learn basket-making too, whilst like Aquila instructing Apollos, he "taught him the way of the Lord more perfectly." But one night, on parting, he put "Boston's Four-fold State" into his hands, with a solemn charge that it should be read prayerfully. It was so; but it stopped his basket-making, before he got half through *two* folds of the "Four-fold State." The good old man observed this, and asked him one day, "William, what has become of the basket now?" "O," he answered, "I have got *other* work to do now." The sight of his *lost* condition as a sinner plunged him into such despair, that he could not longer employ his leisure hours on the hills or at home, in any thing but reading or prayer. Just at this crisis, the venerable Cowie came unexpectedly to preach at Adam Sievwright's house; and took for his text, "The grace of our Lord Jesus Christ be *with you all!*" Adam used to say of that sermon, "Oh, but the Minéster had mair than usual *freedim* that nicht. Eh, sirs, it was a *saavoury* sermon!" So it proved. My friend's "captivity was turned like streams of water in the south." From that time, those who knew him best, and were oftenest with him, says Mr. Hill, testified that his progress was *visible* from week to week; so rapid was his growth in the life of faith.

Soon after this, he changed the place of his residence; but again, unhappily, into a family where God was not worshipped. He carried, however, his religion with him. He "confessed" the Saviour he had found, before all the household; and so wisely, that he won them over to establish family prayer,

Mr. Hill says, "both his master and mistress became, to all appearance, through his means, followers of the Lamb." He adds, "I have also heard of at least one person that occasionally visited that house, and was much given to swearing, who became so impressed with what was said to him, that he left off the wicked practice, and joined himself to the Lord." Mr. Hill, on stating these facts, in the funeral sermon, said to his hearers, "William was at this time young, poor, and amongst the meanest of the servants: but even a herd-boy, or apprentices, who know the Lord, may be the honoured instruments of plucking much prey from the soul-destroyer." I must add, that young converts, who do not try to do so at home, will never be *honoured* Missionaries abroad. The young man who will not say to his perishing neighbour, and do for the children of the poor around him, just what he would say and do for the heathen and their families, does not love souls exactly for their own sake, nor so well as his foreign sympathies seem to indicate.

William Milne did what he could at home. Indeed, it was by acting on the command, "when thou art converted strengthen thy brethren," that he caught the Missionary spirit. It was the spark of Sunday School zeal, which kindled the flame of Missionary enterprise in his bosom. He took a lively interest and an active part in the Scottish Sabbath-schools. They could only be conducted by men of *prayer;* and he gave himself to prayer. The following characteristic anecdote will illustrate what I mean. Going one night with a friend to visit a school, the road lay through a solitary glen which resembled the recess amongst the hills where he had consecrated himself to God. The scene recalled his vows. He paused and said, "I am afraid to enter on the solemn work of the evening without special prayer." The two friends knelt down together, and spent a considerable time in fervent wrestling with God. It was in this spirit he entered the schools; and the scholars both knew and felt that he was a devotional man. There was an air and an unction about him which revealed to them, that he had been with Jesus.

He also established winter-evening prayer-meetings, in the destitute corners of the parish; and with a few young men who were like-minded with himself went from house to house praying and speaking with the poor. He did not, however, allow these exercises to become substitutes for *secret* devotion. His maxim was—and he inculcated it upon his companions—"We must have time to pray alone. It will never do to separate secret from social prayer."

He had also the art of saying striking things in conversation in a striking manner: for although his appearance was not commanding, his looks were very expressive and searching. Being on a visit for some time at the house of a friend, where he found himself in his element, he fixed his eyes steadfastly upon him for some minutes without speaking. He wanted to express both his gratification and gratitude so that they should not be forgotten, nor yet savour of compliment. His friend asked, what absorbed his thoughts? "I was just thinking," he said, "that there are a goodly number here, with whom I should like to spend my *eternity*." This is well conceived and well expressed, for a shepherd lad! It was well-timed too. It is, however, illustrative of more than the power or the delicacy of William Milne's mind, when he was but a young Christian. It proves also that he had caught the spirit of a compliment, which was not seldom paid in the days of my boyhood to the preaching of Mr. Cowie. I did not understand my father or his friends, when they said of some sermons, "We could have taken an eternity of *siccan* thoughts and feelings, as we heard the day;" but I well remember the phrase, and the fact that it originated with a poor man who had listened to one of these sermons, although he could only get his head in at the kirk door, and had the rain falling all the time upon his neck. Indeed I am often compelled to ask myself, what must these sermons have been: for, although very long, they did not tire even the boys. They must, in fact, have laid hold even then of my spirit: for when I published my little work on "Eternity Realized," some of the good old folks at Huntly, forgetting that I was a mere boy when these sermons were preached, gave me credit for remembering the very *words* of Mr. Cowie. And I did, and do remember his *spirit* at that time! A child could hardly have mistaken that, it was so unearthly, rapt, and sweetly solemn! And then, it rivetted and irradiated so many manly and furrowed faces, that even children could not help feeling that there was a *spell* upon the spirit of their parents, which came down from the pulpit, stronger and stronger, as the sermon went on. O, these were "days of the Son of man," when even I, although not *ten* years old, felt something of the meaning of the words, "I was in the Spirit on the Lord's day, and heard a *great* voice, as the sound of a trumpet!" I indulge in these recollections, because in no other way can I give the reader a full *insight* into the forces which melted and moulded the originally stubborn spirit of the eventually judicious and devotional Dr. Milne. He would have been crabbed, if not conceited also, had he not come under the transforming influence of Mr. Cowie. That made his joy in believing, "both unspeakable and full of glory," and thus softened as well as sobered his temperament. Indeed, only a very *weak* man, whether old or young, could have been flippant or consequential in the presence of Mr. Cowie, when religion was the subject. In worldly affairs he was a perfect child: but when he spoke of " the mysteries of the kingdom" it was as true of him as of Job, that " the young men hid themselves in the shadow of their own shame," and the " aged laid their hand on their mouth." Even "Princes" like Jacob, who had prevailing power when wrestling with the Angel of the Covenant, "refrained from talking," and "nobles" of Israel, like Nadab and Abihu, "held their peace." " When the ear heard him it blessed him, and when the eye saw him it gave witness unto him!" His child-like simplicity in the business of life, added to this charm; it was in such striking contrast to the keen shrewdness, almost akin to cunning, which marked the bargainings of many. Neither William nor myself could overlook this. It turned any discernment we had, in the right direction. The " minister," we saw, erred always on the safe side, and was *transparent* in all his dealings. We laughed at his simplicity sometimes; but it secured our love, even when he *cheated* himself egregiously. One year, I recollect, he fattened and killed one of his cows, in order to sell cheap beef. The person who bought the fore-legs, brought back the largest bones, and asked if it was *fair* to pay for so much bone? The worthy minister gave *flesh* for it at once, as only fair.

CHAPTER II.

WILLIAM MILNE'S MISSIONARY SPIRIT.

In the beginning of the present century, Mr. Cowie's sphere was, perhaps, the only rural district in Aberdeenshire, where Missions to the Heathen could have come especially under the notice of a young Christian. The Kirk had not then been recognised the duty of spreading the Gospel, and any knowledge the Seceders had of the London Missionary Society, was confounded with their prejudices against the Haldanes and Rowland Hill. Mr. Cowie, however, knew better. Neither Rowland Hill's Episcopacy, nor Haldanes' Independency, could blind him to the merits of the Society or to the claims of the Heathen. He *sacrificed* both his name and his place, influential as they were, amongst the Antiburghers, that he might promote Foreign Missions, Home Itinerancies, and Sabbath-Schools. He threw all his mighty soul into the cause of universal Evangelization;—and that amongst souls capable of grasping a great object, and prepared to sympathize with it. I will not say, that none of the English fathers and founders of the Missionary Society led so many wrestling Jacobs to the throne of God on its behalf; but I will say, that none of them led on a *phalanx* of such "men of prayer" as Mr. Cowie called forth. They could do little else but pray for it; and therefore they often spent "the whole night in prayer." A world lying in wickedness, lay on their spirit, as "the burden of the Lord;" and its weight kept them down *long* before the Lord. They gave themselves but little rest, that they might "give Him no rest, until He arose to make Jerusalem a praise in all the earth."

I can scarcely credit my own recollections of the devotional habits of these men, although my own father was one of them, and they my best friends after his death. Indeed, it is only by referring to Mr. Cowie's journals, and by remembering Dr. Philip's estimates of these men, "mighty in prayer," that I can satisfy myself that I am not dreaming, when I speak or think of them. I was, indeed, too young to understand their devotional spirit, or to comprehend their solicitude about the Heathen. I understood only the fact, that something which they called "sweet communion with God," made them pray long and look very happy, and speak often one to another about Missionaries.

It was in this way William Milne became acquainted with the subject of Missions. Mr. Cowie's chapel was called the "Missionary *laigh* Kirk," even before the Antiburghers excommunicated him, and it retained that name for years. Even the Independent Ministers who came to preach for him, or to itinerate in our district, were always designated "*Missionary Ministers,*" by both the godly and the ungodly. Even conversion was called by the world, "turning *Missionary,*" and laughed at by a wretched *pun* on the word "machinery." William Milne was thus "born again," in the very *cradle* of Missions, in the vale of Strathboggie. His first nick-name, from the world, when he became pious, was sure to be "*mis-shinir.*" The very Sabbath-Schools had this name, even up in the Cabrach. Thus the church at Huntly was both literally and emphatically, a "Missionary Society." Its Pastor and Elders impressed a Missionary character upon all its movements, and its pious members carried this spirit into all the parishes (and these were not few,) from which they came up to worship at Huntly. This, as might be expected, was nobly sustained by Dr. Philip, when he settled at Aberdeen, and became the bosom friend of Mr. Cowie: then two kindred souls blended their hallowed fires upon the northern altar of Missions, and soon kindled prayer into *sacrifice*, amongst the young. No quarter yielded more or better Missionaries than Aberdeenshire.

It will not be wondered at now, that even a shepherd lad, when giving himself by an everlasting covenant to God, amidst the solitary hills, did it with a deep "concern for the salvation of immortal souls," as well as for his own confirmation in the life of faith. This will ever be a beautiful feature in his character, and an interesting fact in his history, but it can no longer create surprise. It was the natural effect of a religious education,—which made "concern for the souls of others," a mark of personal sincerity, and a help to growth in grace. He would have doubted his personal piety, if it had breathed no relative sympathy; just as he would have doubted his devotional spirit, if he could not have spent a whole night in prayer, now and then, in the sheep-cote. I shall never forget his surprise, nor that of some others, who were brought up amongst men who thus "gave themselves to prayer," when he was asked in England,—"what the Huntly-men found to *say* when they prayed all night?" This question almost tempted him to suspect the inquirers of knowing too little about *communion* with God. He wondered more at the habit of giving but a few *minutes* to secret prayer, than they did at the habit of devoting hours to it. The phrase, "*get to say*," grated on his ear! He had spent hours alone with God, and knew men who had done the same for years, where the difficulty was to know what to say first, and when words were the least part of the worship. He was thinking, not of what was said, but what was "unutterable," when the realizations of the Divine glory, and of the wonders of Redemption, and of the solemnities of Eternity, came over the spirit like entrancing visions; or, like a translation, carried it "out of the body, into the third heavens." He knew that the morning star had often found him where the evening star had left him, upon his knees before the Lord, utterly unconscious of the lapse of time. He was not the man, however, to judge the devotional spirit of others by what he himself had felt or seen. He soon understood the spirit of English piety, in all that distinguished it from Scottish. His only mode of arguing with those who wondered, "what his Scotch friends found to say," was to ask, with a winning smile, if they could not easily conceive how Dr. Waugh could spend a whole night in his closet? This appeal was unanswerable, by all who had ever worshipped with that adoring seraph; and it was not less so, when made in connexion with the wrestling prayers of Dr. Simpson, of Hoxton College.

These hints will throw some light upon his own account of the rise and progress of his Missionary spirit. The following is his own answer to the question—What induced you to devote yourself to the work of a Missionary of Jesus Christ among the Heathen?

"Rev. Sir, I am aware that the deceit of the heart will sometimes induce a man to consider himself called of God, to that for which he feels a partiality; therefore I desire to answer this important question with a due sense of the weakness of my own judgment, and with much consideration.

"I trust I speak the truth when I say, that I do not engage in it from any idea of my own sufficiency for it, nor from any notion that I have had an extraordinary call; nor from any hope that I have of ease or aggrandizement in the world.

"Not from any idea of my own sufficiency for it: for when I consider the nature of ministerial labours in general, and especially that of MISSIONARY LABOUR —the difficulty of parting with relatives and friends, —of studying a foreign language under the heat of a vertical sun,—of overcoming the inveterate religious prejudices of the Heathen,—of introducing among them a religion entirely new, and which condemns their own religion, yea, even the thoughts of their hearts,—the difficulty of preserving the life and power of religion in the heart, where there is scarcely any Christian society,—the mighty trust committed, by the Church, to a Missionary,—and the awful responsibility to God which attaches to his office,—when I consider all this, I exclaim, 'Who is sufficient for these things?'

"Not from any notion that I have had an extraordinary call to the work; for I neither heard any voice calling me to go to the Heathen, nor had I ever any *dream* that seemed to intimate my duty in this respect; nor did ever any particular passage of

Scripture come with *peculiar* force to my mind, from which I could gather that I ought to undertake this work. No. If these things are necessary to constitute a call, then I am not called.

"And, as I do not engage in this office from an idea of my own sufficiency for it, or from any notion of an extraordinary call, so neither is it from any hope of ease or aggrandizement in the world. Food and raiment, the benevolence of the religious world gives me reason to look for; but along with that I expect innumerable trials, and a life of hard and intense labour.*

"From the time that my own attention was turned to the things of God, I felt concerned for the conversion and salvation of others, especially for young people, for whose benefit I drew up a short address, for which my rural employment afforded me leisure. Even then I sometimes reasoned thus—'What, if in some future period of my life, I may have the pleasure of proclaiming to sinners this glorious Gospel, which appears so well adapted to the condition of man.'—The idea of the excellency of such a work made it desirable; but the sense of my own unfitness for it made me turn away my attention from it; so that for four years after, I had little thought of it, farther than that I would always have preferred it to any other employment. I had often read the 'Missionary' and 'Evangelical Magazines,' and felt deeply concerned for the coming of Christ's kingdom among the nations, and used to spend *hours* in the winter evenings in prayer for this desirable object. This, however, I conceived to be my duty as a *private*

* "A life of HARD and INTENSE labour," (although of short duration) and many "trials" he certainly had.—*Dr. Morrison.*

Christian; and never entertained the prospect of going to the Heathen myself, till about six years ago. One evening, walking with a dear friend, who is now entered into his rest, he told me that a brother of his, who, I am happy to say, is looking forward to the same work, had thoughts of becoming a Missionary of Jesus Christ. The following question was immediately suggested to my mind:—' Will this man's salvation be a greater wonder than *mine?* or can his obligations to the riches of redeeming grace be greater than mine, that he should desire thus to honour God, while I continue satisfied in a state of inglorious ease at home?' This I could not admit, for I was fully persuaded that none could owe more to Christ than I did. But then the question turned on this point of FITNESS for the work, and a CALL to it. Here I was constrained to pause, and was filled with much perplexity. I felt a desire for the work; but whether this arose from the vanity of my own mind, or from the Spirit of God, I could not tell. I dreaded the thought of rushing into the work, lest I should run unsent, and be only a burden on the Christian Church; and of staying at home, lest I should be declining an important duty, and consulting with flesh and blood. Some encouraged me to go—some were indifferent to it—and others against it.

"The means I used in this perplexed state were PRAYER, CONSULTATION WITH CHRISTIAN FRIENDS, and APPLICATION TO THE MISSIONARY SOCIETY.

"I set apart sometimes a day, sometimes part of a day, as circumstances permitted, as in the presence of God, to consider the nature and importance of this work, to examine my motives, and to solicit Divine direction. I often and earnestly prayed that God would hedge up my way, and not suffer me to go unless he would go with me; and that he would open a door for me in his providence if it were his will that I should go. When I considered that Jehovah knew the end from the beginning, and that I was under infinite obligations to be and to do whatever he saw fit, I was encouraged; and I said—'Here I am—thou, Lord, hast a cause to promote among men—thou canst promote it without me, but I am willing to go any where, and do any work that relates to the coming of thy kingdom in the world, if thou wilt make thy way plain before me; but if thy presence go not with me, carry me not up hence.'

"CONSULTATION WITH CHRISTIAN FRIENDS was another means which I used. I plainly told them how my desire begun—how it had been continued—what were my views of the work—what my difficulties. They had already an opportunity to judge of my talents, for I had been for some time engaged in teaching Sabbath evening schools. There were some difficulties in the way, arising from various circumstances; but the GENERAL voice was, 'that application should be made to the Missionary Society on my behalf;' which was done about four years ago by the Rev. Messrs. Morrison, of Huntly, and Philip, of Aberdeen. The result was, that a Committee of Ministers at Aberdeen was appointed to converse with me, and determine as they judged proper.

"They acted with that caution which became men feeling the importance of such a work, and concerned to advance the interest and honour of the Missionary Society. Having laid before me the parts of the work, and all things connected with it, they gave me a month longer to consider, and furnished me with farther means of information. During that time I betook myself again to prayer, read 'The Missionary Transactions,' 'The Life of David Brainerd,' and 'The Life of Samuel Pierce.' 'An Address to Young Men,' in 'The Evangelical Magazine,' for April, 1805, I found of much service.

"The conclusion to which my mind was brought, and the substance of what I wrote to Aberdeen, was as follows:—1. I have, through infinite and superabounding grace, the hope of dwelling with Christ in heaven; therefore I am under everlasting obligations to be entirely his, in body, soul, and spirit. 2. There appears something so excellent and glorious in the idea of creatures, so deeply corrupted by sin, so deluded with idolatry, being brought to form proper conceptions of Jehovah, to submit to the righteousness of Jesus, to observe, admire, and adore all the mighty operations of God, and make him the subject of their highest esteem; there appears something so *glorious* in this, that I cannot help desiring to be employed as an instrument to promote it. 3. As the Society wants Missionaries, and as my earnest desire is to serve the interests of the Church of God, I offer my services to them, willing to go forth to the ends of the earth, and to employ such talents as I possess, or may acquire, for the propagation of the Gospel. This was the substance of what I then wrote to the Committee at Aberdeen, who immediately sent word to me to prepare to come to England, which I did; and have gone through the regular course of studies at Gosport, under the care of the Rev. Dr. Bogue, my venerable tutor; to have sat under whom, I consider as one of the greatest blessings of my life.

"My sentiments this evening are the same; and if my Reverend Fathers shall be pleased to set me apart to the office of a Missionary, I am ready and willing to go forth the first opportunity. I am conscious of my own insufficiency for such an undertaking, yet truly DESIRE it. Though I love my native country, as is natural to all men, yet I have no anxiety about leaving it for such an object, but what arises from leaving a mother and three sisters behind. God, however, I hope, will provide for and take care of them. I love the object of the Missionary Society, and offer my life and talents for its promotion. 'Silver and gold have I none, but such as I have I cheerfully give.'

"I am convinced that exertions will be few, and success small, if the SPIRIT of the work be not preserved. Therefore I would desire to keep my own heart with all diligence, and walk closely with God; knowing that these are the most effectual means to maintain the spirit of a true Minister or Missionary of Christ.

"I resolve, should God carry me safely to the Heathen, and continue my health, to prosecute my studies, in order to attain a greater knowledge of the Word of God—to pay particular attention to the language of the Heathen; during which time, should there be any Europeans in the place, I wish to spend the Sabbath in promoting their best interests.*

---

* "This he did as long as he lived; but he sometimes doubted the propriety of deducting any time from his ministry to the Heathen; for after a man's whole time and strength are devoted to such duties as those of a Chinese Missionary, he will have to regret the defects of his preaching, and teaching, and praying To be lucid, and impressive, and convincing in argument,

Should it please God to spare me, to acquire the language with sufficient accuracy, I purpose to go from house to house, from village to village, from town to town, and from country to country, where access may be gained, in order to PREACH THE GOSPEL to all who will not turn away their ear from it: for I conceive that by the PREACHING of the Gospel CHIEFLY, the nations are to be converted. I hope to take advantage of the most favourable seasons for conversing with and preaching to the Heathen, and to use *similitudes*, as the Prophets did, in order to bring down the truth to the level of their capacity. I am resolved not to perplex them with things of 'doubtful disputation,' but to insist CHIEFLY on those grand principles of the Gospel, the faith and practice of which are essential to the salvation of the soul. I purpose, according to my ability, occasionally to publish and distribute religious tracts among the Heathen.

"As, however, the translation and distribution of the Scriptures form one great object of the Chinese Mission, to which I am destined by the Directors, I resolve to use every means to attain a more full and critical knowledge of them, in order to give the genuine sense intended by the Holy Ghost. For this purpose I would apply with all diligence to the original languages of the word of God, to weigh the force of words and phrases, and compare one version with another. I hope I shall be enabled to derive much advantage from the piety, learning, and experience of him (Dr. Morrison) with whom I expect

---

amongst a people of a strange language, and manners, and sentiments, that have no similarity to our early knowledge and association of ideas, is very difficult."—*Dr. Morrison.*

to be associated, whose counsel and advice I feel disposed to follow.

"As my object is entirely of a religious nature, I purpose to have nothing to do with POLITICAL matters, lest my ministry should be blamed, and its success defeated; but to 'be subject to the powers that be,' always seeking the peace and prosperity of the commonwealth. I wish to pay particular attention to the instruction of YOUTH, and to adopt those plans which are best calculated to convey divine knowledge in such a way as to interest and edify them. For this end, I hope to be able to take with me, and translate, some of those little, interesting, and useful publications, suited to youth, which abound in England and Scotland. Should my labours be so blessed, as that a church be raised, I shall endeavour to form it, and conduct its affairs, according to the word of God.

"As the money by which Missionaries are supported is the fruit of the labour of the *poor*, and of the abundance of the rich; and as it is the property of the church of Christ, I shall always consider it a matter of conscience to use it sparingly.*

---

* "This resolution is good, but it requires to be qualified and guarded. What money is for the *immediate furtherance* of the GOSPEL should not be used sparingly, in the publication and distribution of the Bible and good books; the best helps for acquiring a foreign language speedily, and well; teachers, dictionaries, &c. And money that tends to the preservation of a Missionary's health, by affording him wholesome and nutritious food and drink; and good air and lodging; and good medical aid; should not be spent grudgingly. Hard workers cannot be too well taken care of. Loungers, who study first their own ease and comfort, do not deserve the same treatment. No means for the conversion of the nations, that reason and Scripture sanction, should be left untried, from an apprehension that the property

"Depending on the grace of God, I would read the history, adopt the useful plans, and imitate the lives and labours of pious Missionaries of every denomination; especially I wish to WALK AS JESUS CHRIST WALKED, and to display the influence of the Gospel in my own temper, in the relation in which I may be placed, and in my whole conduct.

"Finally, as the success of all means depends on the power of the Spirit of God, I purpose to look up to him daily, by fervent prayer, for his blessing to accompany all my endeavours for the CONVERSION of the Heathen. The salvation of souls I look upon as the great end of my work, and would therefore wish to make all things bend to it, and to consecrate all that I have to the honour of Christ. In these ways I purpose to seek the object of my Ministry among the Heathen."

As this account of his *call* to Missionary work was given in England, at his Ordination, he could only name well *known* friends, when he enumerated his advisers. He was, however thinking, of John Burnet, of Huntly; a remarkable man, to whom he first opened his mind on this subject; and of Peter Smart, of Auchline, who seems to have invited him to the *first* prayer-meeting he ever attended. In a letter to Mr. Smart, he says, "I well remember the evening

---

will be used unsparingly. Let the property of the Christian public be faithfully, judiciously, and liberally employed for the best causes. And let faithful Missionaries be liberally supported. Call not their allowances charity or alms. Alas! do they deserve nothing of their brethren but fine speeches, and empty praises? What sacrifice does that disciple make who STAYS AT HOME and gives a little of his money, in comparison of the disciple who leaves father, and mother, and sister, and brother, and home, and gives HIMSELF to the work?"—*Dr. Morrison.*

you invited me to the prayer-meeting! Little did I think then, that this was to be one step towards the work in which I am now engaged: but God's judgment is a great deep. He is a sovereign God." How much Mr. Milne owed to John Burnet will be seen in the next chapter, when he poured out his heart on the death of his first counsellor. In the mean time, I cannot but again point out the incalculable importance of such men to the Missionary cause. This man was a flax-dresser, and had merely an ordinary education; but he was a man mighty in the Scriptures and in prayer; a man of deep thought and deeper feeling, and full of kindness. I was too young to comprehend any thing *beneath* the sunny brightness of his fine face, except the warmth of his heart, which drew me often to his side, in boyhood. But William Milne became acquainted with him, when he could appreciate him. They often walked and communed together whole nights, under both summer and winter moonlight, comparing their views and experience, and contemplating the state of the Heathen world. It was, therefore, John Burnet who fanned upon the hills at midnight, that spark in the bosom of William Milne, which was so readily recognised by Dr. Philip and others, as "fire from Heaven." I say, *midnight*, because they could only meet then. They had no other time at their command. Their interviews arose out of John Burnet's visits to the Sabbath evening School, at Kennethmont. When that service was over, the scholar conveyed his master down the Boggie side, as near to Huntly as he could, consistently with getting back to the farm before sunrise.

It was not, however, with John Burnet only, that

he communed thus. His interviews with him were but occasional. His chief communion was with Adam Sievwright. He often told him, pointing to the spot, that his first desire to go far hence unto the Gentiles arose whilst he was lying upon the heather, on the hill side, just above his cottage, reading the "Missionary Magazine." The good old man delighted, whilst he lived, to point out the very spot where William lay reading, weeping, praying, and longing for wings that he might fly with the apocalyptic Angel, to preach the Everlasting Gospel. "The desire never left him from that day," Adam used to say. I cannot point out the spot to my readers; but it is still well known. Mr. Hill, of Huntly, said in his sermon, "I have had the spot pointed out to me;" and exclaimed, "O, for the *zeal* that was there kindled!" That zeal, as we have seen, burned *where* it was kindled, although many attempts were made by his fellow-servants to quench it. They did all they could to draw him with them to balls, raffles, fairs, and other popular amusements; but in vain. Even when the Harvest-Home dance was at their own farm, and although the foreman pleaded with him to join them, he solemnly refused to be present even as a spectator. "I will not go," he said, "until I have got no work for Eternity!" He took care to have his hands always full of such work; and thus resisted such temptations, as old *Brook's* old woman resisted the devil, by saying, "Go away, Satan, for I am too *busy* to be tempted by you."

As Mr. Milne passed by some names, at his ordination, which were vividly present to his thoughts at the moment, so he glanced but slightly at the reception he met with at Aberdeen, when he first presented himself before the Committee of Examination, as a Candidate. Most of them were afraid, as Mr. Hill expresses it, *"that he would not do."* One Minister proposed that he should go out, if agreeable to himself, rather as a *mechanic* than a missionary. This suggestion being made to him, his answer was, "Any thing, any thing,—if only engaged in the work. I am willing to be a hewer of wood, or a drawer of water, in the Temple of my God." Thus, like Isaiah, he said, "send me," without waiting to know what would be the errand. It is an interesting fact, and it ought to have been introduced earlier, that the *first* chapter of the word of God which he committed to memory at school was the 6th of Isaiah. That splendid and solemn vision did not, as we have seen, lay any hold of his conscience in boyhood; but it is impossible not to see in his habitual awe of the divine holiness, and his love of personal holiness, when he became a Christian, that what laid hold of the boy's memory, had much to do with the formation of the *man's* character. Isaiah became one of his models through life. It is thus that *circumstances* call into play and power, in after life, truths which make no impression at the moment. Little did the old *Granny*, who taught William Milne to read, and set him the sixth chapter of Isaiah as a task, imagine that her curly-headed pupil would one day make Isaiah's example his own guide in the ministry, and his own standard of character. Even to himself it must have appeared almost a dream, when he compared his first recital of Isaiah's words, with his subsequent application of them, especially when he said, in reference to China, "Here am I, send me!" This little anecdote will imbody to more eyes than my own—the boy trudging to school in winter with a *peat* for the schoolmistress's fire under one arm, and his Bible under the other, repeating to himself, "In the year that king Uzziah died," &c.

CHAPTER III.

WILLIAM MILNE, AT GOSPORT.

When he came to Aberdeen, in order to sail for London, I was, perhaps, the only person in Dr. Philip's Church, who had known him from the time of his conversion; and as my hopes and wishes were similar to his own, we had much confidential intercourse. How I envied him! How gladly I would have gone to Gosport with him, to sit at the feet of Dr. Bogue! I had then begun to read about China, and to try to spell out the meaning of some of its hieroglyphics. The hierogliph for friendship,—two pearls of equal size and lustre, I pointed out to him at the time, as a fine emblem and a fit model for us. We resolved to be friends.

Let no one laugh at the gossip or the egotism of all this. It had something to do with William Milne's first introduction to Miss Cowie, who afterwards became his wife. He had, of course, Dr. Philip's far better introduction. Still, I was very intimate with the Cowie family, and often called Miss Cowie a *Chinese* lady, because she wore her nails so very long. She had also to listen to all my rhymes and reasonings about China; and they were not few. Indeed,

I carried all my juvenile discoveries and designs to her. She had thus to listen also to whatever I knew or thought of Mr. Milne. She knew also Dr. Philip's high opinion of him. Accordingly, she made him a present of some neckcloths, before he sailed.

All this had no conscious influence on either of the parties, at the time. There was no design in it. Her kindness to a Missionary, was a matter of course; and he was too humble to think of her then, and too much absorbed with the prospect of study to waste a thought on marriage. They met and parted, without the shadow of an idea that they would ever meet again. She did not cease to hear of China, however, when he was gone. It was my favourite theme, and she was my chief auditor and oracle. Our conversations, however, had no reference to Mr. Milne. Indeed, they could not; for he had never dreamt of China as a sphere of labour, nor had any of his friends thought of it in connexion with him; and certainly I had no reference to him, whilst I continued to call her the Chinese lady. All this, however, was remembered by her afterwards, and playfully called my *"prophecy"* when she was about to become Mrs. Milne.

On his arrival at London, Mr. Milne was welcomed into a Scotch family, (Mr. Conn's) who were friends of Dr. Waugh's. He found in Mrs. Conn "a mother in Israel;" and in her circle, much of what he had seen at Huntly. Dr. Waugh won his heart at once; and he soon found himself at home with the Conn's. Some of his early letters to them, from Gosport, are now before me, and revive my recollections of their Scotch kindness: for I shared it too, soon afterwards, along with my friend Dr. Morison of

Brompton, when like Mr. Milne, we were "strangers in a strange land." He was welcomed, too, I think, by Mr. and Mrs. Taylor, of Hoxton; a family in which he found a fine union of Scotch and English piety and hospitality.

I mention these Students' *homes,* because they are hallowed in the recollections of all who entered them. They did much good also to the cause of Missions. Would there were more such *homes* in London now, to cheer the hearts of Students, who feel themselves bewildered strangers, or mere boarders, in our mighty Babylon! Sure I am, that the *living links* thus created between the hearts of young Missionaries, and old families, were conducive to the happiness of both, and had a powerful influence upon Missionary character.

On his arrival at Gosport, Mr. Milne was delighted with the reception which Dr. Bogue gave him. He had seen that venerable Patriarch of Missions at Huntly, if I may judge from my own recollection of Dr. Bogue's visits to Scotland. One thing is certain,—he had heard enough of him in the North, to be well prepared to venerate him, and to expect much profit from him. And he was not disappointed. He counted it "one of the greatest blessings of his life" when he could well judge of great blessings,—"to have been under his care."

On entering the academy he made a request to Dr. Bogue, which must have pleased him. It could not, however, *surprise* him; knowing as he did both the state and character of the Church at Huntly. The request was, that the Doctor would so apportion his studies as to leave him a whole *hour* every day for prayer on behalf of dear Huntly. This, whilst it revealed the pupil's spirit to the tutor, would appear to Dr. Bogue just as *natural* in one of Mr. Cowie's sons in the gospel, as any ordinary request. None of *his* spiritual children ever forgot his Church, wherever they went. Very few may have consecrated an *hour* daily, or even weekly, to intercede for it; but still fewer neglected to pray for it. So much was that Zion loved by "this and that man" who "was born there."

This is a deeply instructive fact to all Churches, which endeavour to raise up Missionaries. The young man who cannot forget nor cease to pray for his spiritual birth-place, will keep around himself so many vivid and hallowing associations with the scene and the society, that his own *character* will be as much benefited by praying for his native Zion, when he is in a foreign land, as that Zion must be gratified and edified by knowing of his fond and fervent prayers for her welfare. It is not every church, however, that can lay such *hold* upon the heart of her sons or daughters as to make sure of their prayers. A young man who has not *reason* to remember his own *Zion* "above his chief joy," is not to be *calculated* upon, for either eminent or steadfast piety, much less for prudence as the Pastor of a mission-church, whatever may be the apparent strength of his principles, as a Missionary candidate. No man's principles are independent of his early religious associations. If the latter are not both pleasing and holy, and so much so that the heart can fall back upon them in the hour of depression, and be thrown back upon them in the hour of temptation, the former will neither work nor wear well, in a land where "all things are against" them. It is, therefore, very questionable whether any young man, whatever be his spirit, whose *chief* associations are with a University or a College, should ever be sent into a *new* Mission, or placed *alone* in any Mission. His College testimonials, however high, will have no inspiring or restraining influence upon himself, when he has no one around him who can appreciate learning. Even the memory of his Tutors and Fellow-Students will not help his principles much, when he stands alone amongst the heathen, unless his Father's house, or the house of the God of his Fathers, be very dear to his heart. It would, I am fully aware, be a very delicate thing to question a young man, as to the number and strength of the *links* which either his own home, or the House of God, has thrown around his heart: but still, it is the fact, that the Missionaries who have done most and best, are those who had the sweetest associations with the church they came from, and with their home-fireside. The churches are solemnly bound not to overlook this result, which experience has made so striking. They, not a Missionary Society, must throw the *spell* upon the spirit of Missionaries. They alone can become a *relative* conscience, which, like his own personal conscience, will speak without prompting. A society can only invest him with office, and give him its confidence; and all he can give to a Society in return, is his own confidence. He cannot fall in *love* with it, except as an abstraction; and the love of abstractions, however beautiful they may be, is neither very warm nor lasting. It should, therefore, be both the aim and effort of the churches to *endear* themselves to every young man they select for foreign service. They can do so; whereas, no Society can throw unspeakable charms around the routine of its duties, in accepting and sending forth Missionaries. There must ever be a *business* aspect about the intercourse of the executive with candidates.

I will not apologize for this digression, long as it is. Future candidates for Missionary work will *study* as well as read the life of Dr. Milne; and as his character was formed by the influences of the Church he came from, and cannot well be imitated apart from influential friends, I deem it a sacred part of my duty to make him create for young men of his own spirit, such friends as Mr. Cowie created for him. Then, like Dr. Bogue, Tutors and Boards will be able to calculate upon their Students. But this subject will come up again, in the course of this chapter.

"Whilst a student at the Missionary Seminary, Gosport, Mr. Milne drew out a few rules for his conduct, and formed resolutions to regulate his thoughts and actions; they are here inserted as illustrative of his character. Some of them are his own; others are copied."—*Dr. Morrison.*

RULES OF CONDUCT, AND RESOLUTIONS.

January 1st, 1810.

I. AS TO MYSELF.

1. To spend a little time thrice a day for meditation, prayer, and reading the Sacred Scriptures, and some devotional book.

2. To spend some *extraordinary* time every three months for the state of my soul and work.

3. To spend some time on Saturday night, from eight o'clock, in religious exercises for myself, and relations, and friends, in Scotland.

4. To attend as many prayer-meetings as I can, for the benefit of my soul.

II. FOR STUDY.

1. Not in general to spend above *six* hours in bed.

2. To make *eleven* and *five* the hours of rising and going to bed.

3. To endeavour to spend about *fourteen* hours in study and devotion, the rest at victuals and recreation—walking twice a day for my health.

4. The different parts of the day to the studies, as they will best suit.

III. TO OTHERS.

I. To treat my tutor and fellow-students with respect.

II. To receive reproof or remarks on my conduct and performances with meekness—even though harsh and unreasonable.

III. To endeavour to observe, in giving reproof, not to offend, but to profit.

IV. To endeavour, by conversation and otherwise, to be useful to my fellow-students.

V. To endeavour to be useful to all.

1. In my preaching, to aim at the conversion of souls, and the advancement of grace in saints.

2. In my conversation with men, when I meet them in this place, and in the places where I go to preach, to endeavour to be a pattern.

3. To go out once or twice a week into different

houses to perform family worship, and give suitable exhortations. N. B. This I have reason to believe was not wholly in vain.

4. To endeavour to awaken and promote the spirit of religion by correspondence. In order to this, to keep a little book for noting materials for correspondence.

5. To keep some account of my matters, sermons, progress, and correspondences.

6. Not to be too forward nor positive in stating my sentiments—pay due deference to the sentiments of others. To avoid partiality, keep myself, first, that I may not offend others, second, that, not being engaged in controversy, I may the more easily find out the truth.

7. To read my diary and these rules every Saturday night. N. B. Some of these could not be kept, except one were always in the same place.

CONSIDERATIONS AND RULES.

Gosport, July 12th, 1810.

I. Consider, O my soul, for what end thou art in this place. Let not thy thoughts fix on it as the scene of thy rest or labours; but what shouldest thou pursue as thy only end?

II. How shall I best conduct myself when I visit the sick, and when I visit others; either to pray with the former, or to drink tea, &c., with the latter?

1. Do not make these visits long, lest I weary the people and neglect my studies, or fall into unprofitable conversation.

2. Never enter into any dispute, or into conversation, about the character of any absent person, unless to answer some good end.

3. Endeavour to turn the conversation to something profitable.

CONSIDERATIONS RELATIVE TO A PROFITABLE CONVERSATION IN COMPANY.

Gosport, August 23rd, 1810.

1. Consider, O my soul, that, perhaps, some in this company may be lying under the wrath of God. Should I not do something for such?

2. Some may be acting inconsistent with the gospel, and although I know not, yet, if I am spiritual, something may drop which will reach them indirectly.

3. Consider that, perhaps, some of the company may be halting between two opinions, and waiting for the sanction of thy example to determine them in some things; but *wo* to thee if thou doest or sayest any thing which will encourage to evil, or to a lukewarm profession.

4. Some in this company may be beginning religion,—tempted, wounded, or persecuted, and discouraged. Should not something be said which has a tendency to counteract these evils?

5. Consider what views thou didst have of those ministers who did not converse *profitably* in company—avoid this evil.

6. Some who are sitting around me at tea, or dinner, &c., may be near to eternity: perhaps this may be the last company they will ever be in.

7. What, if this be the last opportunity I shall ever have of doing good?—am I improving it? What, if the chilly hand of death should, in the midst of this company, stop the springs of life? What, if the

hour of thy departure should come in this place—art thou suitably employed?

8. Would Jesus and his Apostles; would Brainard, Whitefield, &c., have been HERE in THIS company? Would they say what I am saying, or do what I am doing? N. B. Perhaps, my soul, God has gathered this company together to give thee an opportunity for usefulness. Also, I may be sure that my being IN THIS company will tend to answer some end, either to HARDEN or RECLAIM; to DEADEN or to quicken, to do good or evil.

Gosport, January 1st, 1811.

Resolved not to copy many of my letters.—

1. Because I can write double the number to others.

2. Because it would take too much of my time.

March 2.—Resolved, that, in general, when circumstances will permit, that I will attend to secret devotions *before* supper.

CONSIDERATIONS BEFORE PREACHING.

March 10th, 1811.

1. Remember, O my soul, that thou art now to plead the cause of Christ, therefore be fervent.

2. Remember, that some who shall hear me to-day will, perhaps, be in heaven or hell before another opportunity, therefore be faithful.

3. Some are remarkably ignorant, therefore be very plain.

4. Some are captious, therefore be cautious.

5. Some, perhaps, are beginning, tried, tempted, desponding; therefore seek to direct them.

6. What, if I never preach again? therefore be as

serious as if I were going from the pulpit to the bed of death.

This outline of his Rules deserves to be well studied by all Missionary Candidates; and it will convince the friends of Missions, that there is *discipline* in the Colleges, which thus set young men upon such self-scrutiny and watchfulness, as well as upon such close application: for I quote it as a *specimen* of what prevails, and not as an exception; and twelve years' constant attendance at that Committee of the Missionary Society, which superintends the case of Students, warrant me to bear this public testimony to their general character and habits, in all the Colleges employed by the Society. This fact ought to be known also by all Candidates, who may come from any of the Universities. They will be examined and judged according to this standard of piety and prudence, whatever may be their College testimonials, or their talents. Young men with more literature than piety, or with less grace than knowledge, have no more chance of passing the Missionary Board than dolts or dreamers have of *success*. "*Sticket* Licentiates" from the North, may as much save themselves the trouble of applying to be Missionaries, as *stupid* shopmen or mechanics in the South; for little *piety*, and little *sense*, are equally thrown over-board, by all societies now. And who can wonder?

How successfully Mr. Milne studied, and won confidence, at the Missionary Seminary in Gosport, may be judged from the single fact, that Dr. Bogue selected him to be the Colleague of Dr. Morrison, in China. The President could not have paid either of his pupils a higher compliment. Both parties felt this when they met, and whilst they lived; for although Dr. Morrison and Dr. Milne were not alike in the details of their character, they were emphatically "kindred spirits" in the great elements of it. Those who knew them both best, admired most their natural adaptation.

It will be seen from the Rules which Mr. Milne laid down for himself as a student, that he "resolved not to *copy* many of his Letters." He did, however, copy some of them, and happily I possess the volume of his manuscripts which contains them, and have the permission of his sons to use it for this work. One of these Letters will confirm what I have said of his first introduction to Miss Cowie. It is addressed to the Rev. George Burder, then the Secretary of the Missionary Society. "I have no views at present of forming any marriage connexion: and if I shall have any afterwards, I shall think it a great privilege to have the counsel of the Directors on a matter of such importance."—*Gosport*, 1809.

This Letter contains also a sentiment highly characteristic of his spirit:—"I am willing, for I think it exceedingly right, to enter into a personal responsibility for *repaying* the Directors the full expense of my education, if upon grounds unreasonable, or unsatisfactory to them, I shall decline going abroad: for although I have no idea of changing my mind, yet as I am a sinful and changeable creature, I cannot *say* that I shall not. I pray the Lord to keep me from such falls; and I hope He will, for his own name's sake."

In a Letter to his Mother, of the same date, he says, "I like this place very well, and my employment better. Mr. Bogue is a Scotchman, and a very able divine and faithful preacher—I have been sent out twice to preach. I hope you will not spread that abroad, unless to particular friends who would 'help together by *prayer* for me.' I love the work with all my heart; but I feel myself unworthy of it, and unfit for it."

How jealously he watched the influence of both his new studies, and new associations, upon the *tone* of his piety, appears from a Letter to his second Pastor, the Rev. Mr. Morrison, then at Huntly, as the successor of Mr. Cowie. "I find the truth of what you warned me of,—that it is very difficult to maintain a lively sense and impression of the TRUTH on my heart, in the midst of study. I found a remark of Dr. Owen's very true, that a person may be often speaking of religion, and yet have a very *barren* soul. I have frequently reflected upon a remark of Mr. Cowie's, that the ranks of Professors will be *thinned* on that day when the secrets of all hearts shall be made manifest! I look to you as a Father for counsel. I find by experience, that it is not change of place nor employment that increases a Christian's spirituality of mind; but fresh, and confirming, and sanctifying discoveries of the greatness and glory of the Truth. How are matters at Huntly? We preach; but I am ready to think, that most of us would be but *light metal* amongst the good people at Huntly and Lesslie. I am ashamed to say, that we wrestle too little to be otherwise? I think old Christians, who have seen the piety and talents of those who have been instrumental in making "Jerusalem a praise," would weep, if they saw us; like the men who laid the foundation of the second Temple. O, that the Lord of the harvest may thrust forth *right* men! Would not James Skinner be persuaded?"

This extract is full of Mr. Milne's real character; which was judicious, discerning, and highly devotional. The Mr. Skinner named in it *was* drawn forth into the field of Missions. Mr. Milne appealed to him thus: "I earnestly wish, Brother, to see you at Gosport in three months; for the harvest is great, and the labourers are few. There are millions in India and *China* perishing for lack of knowledge. Brother, think more of this subject. Think of that promised period when Christ shall come in a bright cloud, with all the holy angels, and millions of the heathen washed in His blood!"

This extract contains the *first* reference to CHINA, which occurs in Mr. Milne's early Letters; and then he saw it only through the medium of India, as many still do. He soon came, however, to look at India and all other places through the medium of China, and to feel most for the land where souls are numbered by hundreds of millions.

This sympathy with distant and vast nations did not divert his attention from the small villages of Hampshire. The laborious student during the week was a laborious itinerant on the Sabbath; a *home* Missionary, before the "Home Missionary Society" called the Churches to their *first* relative duty; and whilst his chief encouragement "to speak the Word to the ignorant people" within his reach, was, that "the *prayers* of the good people of Duncanston (some of his old friends in Scotland) were following him into the villages." It is delightful to trace in his letters at this time, his vivid recollections of "the praying people" of Huntly, Duncanston, and Lesslie, and of his old Sunday School. "I am every Sabbath *with* you, *in* the School, though absent in body;" he says, "I hope their prayers follow me! Give my love to them." 1809.

The memory of such friends is invaluable to a young Missionary. It is a kind of *second* conscience to him, both whilst in College and when abroad. A young man is much to be pitied who has come out of a circle in which there are no *commanding* Exemplars of devotional spirit, holy character, and heavenly-mindedness! Indeed, unless he has much "root in himself," he is in great danger of *withering*, both whilst studying the classics, and when he becomes a translator. The Churches should think of this, and take care to bring the sweet influences of their most devotional Members to bear upon every young man whom they wish to be a Missionary. He is not fit for that office if he is not *fonder* of them than of any other class whatever. His partiality to the *literary* Members of the Church is not worth a rush, as an element of Missionary character, if the Enochs in his circle be not dearest to his heart.

It is hardly possible to ascribe too much to the hallowed influence of Enochs, upon the spirit and character of Mr. Milne. He never forgot them in England, nor when in Malacca. Whilst at college, the memory of their beautiful holiness, and warm-heartedness, followed him like his shadow. It kept him saying to himself habitually, "I would have Holiness to the Lord written on my soul, body, talents, and time; and a *wall-fire* of Love to God around my spirit." 1809.

In 1820 also, he wrote thus concerning such Fathers, Brethren, and Friends:—"Wherever the Missionary goes, a deep reverence and filial love for men of this character will ever go with him: their *silver locks*—the image of their person—their fatherly solicitude—their faithful reproofs—their wise counsels—their fervent prayers—will often rise up *fresh* in his recollection." Thus at both the commencement and close of his Missionary life, Mr. Milne kept around his spirit, as a cloud of witnesses, the image and example of all the holy men and women who had won his esteem. Whoever had much *worth* in his circle, had much *weight* on his character. I shall often have occasion to illustrate this fact, in the course of his history.

In aiming at this high mark, he did not confine his musings to the dead and the distant friends of his youth. He sought also the acquaintance of his most devoted fellow-students, and especially of those who were training for foreign service. When any one of them was ill, he tried to enter into all his fears of being unfitted for Missionary work; and then to lead him far into "the manifold wisdom of God," in such dispensations. And when any one was about to embark, he had always a parting letter ready to *slip* into his hand, of this kind:—"Methinks the following Texts are as much addressed to you, as if proclaimed in thunder from the clouds of Heaven, by the royal mandate of the Captain of Salvation,—'Keep nothing back; declare the whole counsel of God; be strong in the grace which is in Christ Jesus.'" 1810.

The following lines were addressed to a German lady, who went out to Mr. Albrecht's station in Africa, that year:—"Seek thy happiness in God, and the burning sands will *smile* around thee. Keep thine eye fixed on the glory set before thee, and thy mind will be lively in thy work, and increase in self-denial, and thus rise superior to difficulties. Think often on the incarnation, atonement, intercession, and reign of Christ; this will make thy faith strong; thy holiness abound, and the Heathen very dear to thee."

It was not to Missionaries only he made such appeals. He endeavoured to interest the very poorest of his old friends in Scotland, on behalf of the Kingdom of Christ. Some of them were "rich in faith," and he drew largely upon their faith, by presenting to them enlarged views of that kingdom. He called upon them to believe that what Christ died and lives for, "is a work infinitely dear to him: a work to which all the gifts of Nature and the blessings of Providence are subservient; a work, for which thrones, dominions, and powers, if they oppose it, will be tumbled into the dust; a work, which the cattle on a thousand hills, and all the gold of Peru and Mexico; yes, and the designs of Hell itself, must unite their influence to farther." 1810.

Such were the spirit-stirring appeals which the young student circulated amongst his native hills! His zeal did not expend itself, however, upon great public objects. He blended with these pleadings for public spirit in reference to the world at large, beseechings and thanks for attentions to his old Sunday Schools along the *strath* of Boggie. He wrote letters to his sisters, full of truth and love, illustrated by extracts from his favourite authors; and sent messages of counsel and caution to such of his old companions as had been drawn or enlisted into the Aberdeenshire Militia; and challenges to such of us as he accounted faithful, to "come to the help of the Lord against the mighty." To myself he wrote with great caution on this subject. His first letter to me, from Gosport, in 1810, runs thus:—"Abound in the duties of the closet, and seek spirituality in them. Seek to fill up the station you are *now* in, to the honour of God and the comfort of his people. Seek his direction concerning what we have spoken of. Pray, above all things, that He may not suffer you to have your *own* will, unless it be agreeable to His will. Pray that He may open or shut the door for you, according to His own will, and that He may bring your soul to be *satisfied* with his will. Pray for me, dear Brother, that I may have grace to think for God—to speak for God—to write for God—to live only and die only for God. May this be *your* portion also! O, Spirit of Truth, seal Eternity and Judgment upon our hearts, that we may not walk about *idle* in Creation! Remember me kindly to the Members of the Committee who examined me." This message to the Committee was as much a lesson I wanted then, as that in the more personal appeals. That Committee consisted of Professor Bentley, of the University of Aberdeen, and some of the principal clergymen of the city; and their *first* opinion of him did not please me. They did not discover his talents until he *prayed* before them. He was, indeed, a *rough* diamond, when brought from the hills of Kennethmont, in the "Sunday *claithes*" of a Shepherd lad, before learned Doctors in a University town: but even then, the sparkle of his eye, and the form of his head, and the shrewd curl of his lip when he smiled, ought, I thought, to have given

"The world assurance of a man."

They saw, however, nothing in him, until they saw him upon his knees before Him, who "looketh not on the outward appearance, but upon the heart." Then, to their credit, they saw through him, far enough to send him back to the hills, to reconsider his designs. This, I thought, was but a *cold* reception. He judged more wisely; and I felt that he had done so, when he sent *kind* remembrances to them all. At his ordination, he said of them truly, "they acted with that caution which became men feeling the importance of such a work, and concerned to advance the interest and honour of the Missionary Society."

In the Spring of 1810, Mr. Milne heard of the death of one of his first and best friends at Huntly, and appealed thus to those who, like himself, owed much to, as well as enjoyed much from, the visits of that remarkable man,—" Alas, what painful news saluted my ears across the intervening space of 600 miles; John Burnet is numbered with the dead! How little is the value of saints known until they are no more! How shall this loss be made up to Huntly and the Church? This is a very *speaking* dispensation! We have good grounds to think that these words proved his death—for they have been the death of all the saints,—'Father, I will that they whom thou hast given me be *with* me where I am, that they may *behold* my glory.' But let our souls penetrate within the veil, and may we not suppose our friend saying,—'While I lived in yonder world, I was clogged with a body of sin and death. It drew many a sigh from my heart. It gave me oft an errand to my *barn* in Huntly to complain to my God at the throne of grace. Often did it hinder me, whilst travelling between Huntly and Inch (to teach in the Sunday School, and exhort in the Fellowship Meeting.) But now the body of sin is taken away altogether. I am a wonder to myself! When on earth, I often thought I should never see God. But now, I see him, and am like him! And I shall be *ever* with the Lord; and the constant manifestations of the Divine Glory will keep my soul always in frame for the songs of Eternity! This degree of holiness I sought for on earth, but found it only in heaven. O, to Grace, how great a debtor!' "

From this vantage ground within the veil, Mr. Milne came down, as it were, into the midst of the Prayer-meeting at *Carnhill,* saying with tears, "Brethren, I have more need of your prayers than ever! Allow me to say, that the work I am engaged in *is your own.* It is *your* Lord's vessels which I have to carry! Who is sufficient for this work! O, that He may say to me as to Isaiah, 'Thy sin is purged, and thine iniquity is taken away!' I want more grace to think for God—to write for God—to speak for God—to live for God; for great things are upon the wheels of Providence, with respect to the heathen."

The man whose death thus affected Mr. Milne, I knew as well as a *boy* could know a profound thinker. Thought was throned upon his brow; not in gloom, but in light full of glory, when he spoke. His majestic countenance, when lighted up in the Sanctuary, sometimes took my eye off from the Preacher for a moment. I liked, too, although I knew not why, to enter into his *heckling* house, when he was alone. He was a flax-dresser, and worked alone; and thus could work and talk at the same time, when any of the boys of the Sabbath School crept to his side. One day as I stood watching him, whilst the *tow*, and *pob*, and dust were flying off from the heckle, and the flax becoming like a skein of fine silk in his hand, he said to me, "What does all this teach you? What do you see in it?" I saw only, that he saw something good in it; for his ruddy face was rosy with smiles. "You know," he said, "old father Frazer, from Inverness, who is now visiting Mr. Cowie. He says wonderful things, you know, to every body. Well; when he was standing where you are, he took a handful of that coarse stuff, and held it out to me, saying, 'Can yourself put that tow and pob into the bonny flax again? You have heckled it out: heckle it in again, John Burnet?' 'I cannot, I said: and *wudna*, if I could.' 'Weel,' he said, 'when Grace heckles a sin out of your heart, O dinna, heckle it in again. Once out, keep it out.' Now, my Laddie,—mind father Frazer's advice!" It is nearly forty years since John Burnet gave me this lesson. O, that I had acted upon it as well as I remember the time and the place of it! I mention it, that the following tribute of Mr. Milne's to the memory of this great and good man, may be appreciated: "He was justly dear to me! I often conversed and walked away the silent hours of slumber with him. In him, I could place confidence. To him, I *first* made known my desire of being a Missionary! He always listened, and seemed interested in my case. But now—I must see him no more, till time shall cease, and nature die! O, my soul, hear the loud language of this dispensation, and follow his unaffected piety, and prepare to meet thy God. He died in triumph, you say: but forgive me, if I say,—O, why did you not send me some of his dying words? I hope some one will have compassion on me in this matter, and send me these as soon as possible."—*Letter to the Rev. Mr. Morrison.*

This is another illustration of the hallowed influence of *Enochs,* upon the mind of a young Missionary. And the inspiration did not expend itself in pathetic letters, or in solemn musings. The young friend of John Burnet, worked whilst he wept thus. About this time, the Rosshire Militia were stationed at Gosport; and as he found amongst them some pious men, he formed them into a class, and set them to form a congregation. This measure was so successful, and his preaching so useful, that very soon Dr. Bogue preached to them, and admitted *fifteen* of them to the sacrament. Prayer meetings also multiplied amongst the soldiers; and were occasionally so impressive, that the men did not separate until three or four o'clock in the morning. Mr. Milne says of some of these solemn meetings, "I feel *translated* to Lesslie;" meaning that they reminded him of his old devotional friends. He also set apart a portion of his time every day, to converse in his own room with the soldiers who were under serious concern for their souls.

When Mr. Milne wrote this account of his military mission, he had himself preached to this regiment "forty-four times." He also united with his fellow students in preaching to the Invernesshire Militia at this time; and all this, without slackening or failing in his studies.

About this time, the success of the South Sea Missions well nigh won his heart to that quarter of the world. Mr. Bicknell and *Tapioe,* from Otaheite, were then in this country; and he seems to have conversed with them frequently. Tapioe interested him deeply. He dwells, indeed, in his letters, upon the fact, that his native convert was so affected by translating the Saviour's words to Thomas,—"thrust thy hand into my side,"—that he could scarcely eat for some days. This lively sense of Immanuel's condescension commended itself to Mr. Milne's taste. It was in keeping with his own "whole nights in prayer;" when he himself first discovered the glories of the Lamb. He was equally delighted with Tapioe's answer to some one who coolly asked him, "Do you love Jesus?" "I wonder," said the convert, "that you speak of him with so little concern: I cannot think of him without weeping." These traits of character were perfectly intelligible and attractive to Mr. Milne. All this was in his own line of things. So was the following fact. "I asked Tapioe, what he prayed for?" "To get the *stone* out of my heart," he said, laying his hand upon his breast. He says, he will build a Chapel and a School for the Missionaries; when he gets home, if we will teach ten, who may teach other ten, and thus increase knowledge in his country." '"His people," he says, "will lie down and sleep under a cocoa tree without fear," whilst waiting for the Sabbath at Chapel.

There is so much of this kind in Mr. Milne's letters at this time, that there can be no doubt of the leaning of his mind to the South Seas then. And who can wonder? He was, however, silent, notwithstanding all the fascinations of the scene. He allowed them to affect his heart, but not to influence his choice, whilst he was only in the first year of his studies. And students do well to imitate him in this silence, whatever they may feel, now that Mr. Williams has rendered the Polynesian islands *magnetic.* Young men who can endure fiercer climates, and grapple with harder languages, ought not to commit themselves, at the outset of their studies, lest they give up to an island, what was meant for a continent; or to a tribe, what would move an empire. The following letter, addressed to a friend who was *thinking* of Missionary work, will show how Mr. Milne judged: "Dr. Bogue desires me to press it on you. But what shall I say?—Take a map of the world, and spread it before your eyes. Take your Bible in one hand, and your pen in the other. Look over the different countries one by one, and under every one you find without the Gospel, write, *' This is under the curse! Where no vision is the people perish!'* When you have gone over them all, add them together: and, brother, what a number of countries you will find in this awful state? What myriads—supported and surrounded by God—are yet ignorant of him; deriving their strength from him, and yet exerting it all against him; living on his bounty, and yet without one grateful thought to the giver! The effects of sin are felt by them, but the designs of grace are hid from them. They are pining in their wounds, but have no one to show the healing balm, nor to say 'the Lord that healeth thee!' They are in prison, and have no one to say 'Come forth!' Look at these things, and let your eye affect your heart."

Mr. Milne's own heart became affected at this point of his appeal—and for the *first* time too, so far as I can judge—with the state of China. The map and the myriads, made him forget Tahiti. "Suppose yourself, my brother, wafted to CHINA, to Hindostan, or to some of the populous heathen countries —could you continue to follow the *plough* any longer! If you saw multitudes, multitudes, multitudes, flocking to an Idol's temple, with offerings of fruits and flowers, and some with the fruit of their body for the sin of their souls, would you be able to keep *silence*, and not declare that Jesus by one offering, hath for ever perfected them who are sanctified?" This appeal fell upon his friend like the mantle of Elijah upon the ploughman of Abel-Meholah, Elisha, the son of Shaphat: "he left the oxen, and went after him" to the school of the prophets.

As the preceding letter was written at Dr. Bogue's request, it was, perhaps, also shown to him before it was sent off to Mr. Skinner. Be that as it may, however, Dr. Bogue brought China fully under the notice of Mr. Milne, immediately after, and warmly urged him to become the colleague of Dr. Morrison, at Canton. I have now before me the original sketch of the letter which, in consequence of this application from his revered tutor, Mr. Milne wrote to the Directors; and as this rough draught was evidently written during the *tumult* of his spirit on such a proposal, I prefer it to the revised form of the communication.

Gosport, June 9th, 1811.

" *To the Directors of the London Missionary Society:*

"Rev. Fathers and Brethren,

" Grace and peace be multiplied! I contemplate with pleasure that wise Providence, which brought me under the patronage of your society, and feel grateful to God and to you for placing me under the care of my worthy tutor, for whom my esteem in-

'creases, the more I know of him. I have had frequent conversations with him, respecting the future scene of my labours in the service of the Society. He has uniformly given it as his *decided* opinion, that I should go to Canton, to assist Mr. Morrison. I am really at a loss what to say: the object of that mission is so great; the requisite qualifications so many, and the responsibility so awful! When I consider the vast utility of putting into the hands of that immense population, the words of eternal life, and the wisdom of Mr. Morrison, I am inclined to go. But when I view the difficulty of the language—the aptitude necessary in learning it—and my own want of that aptitude, I shrink from the thought, and say to myself, surely, if God had designed me for such a station, he would have given me more advantages in *early* days! My knowledge of the language is very superficial. I have had only about twenty months to attend to them. From which, I am led to think that I should be of small service in such a mission as China, and that Mr. Morrison would be greatly disappointed in me. He will expect an *adept* in languages. Notwithstanding, I do not feel *averse* to go there, should you wish it. Had you a station less arduous, or one where I could begin to preach as soon as I land, I should prefer it. Not that I am unwilling to encounter difficulties, nor for the sake of ease; but from a consciousness of my own inability for a station, where an assemblage of talents is essential to the success of such onerous work. But should you fix on me I am willing to go, and make a trial of the strength of the Lord God. From the opinion I have of the judgment of my worthy tutor, and the reverence I have for your judgment, I leave it, under God, to your decision. I would not choose for myself, Lord, thou knowest! Guide the decision of the Directors for bringing thine own decree into effect, and send me where thou knowest me to be best fitted to promote the interests of the Society.

"Pardon, gentlemen, the liberty I have taken in stating my sentiments freely, and without ceremony. I am, though the meanest, the willing servant of the Society. W. M."

There is a note to this letter, intended to qualify a little what he says of the results of his *twenty months'* study of languages: "Although I cannot justly charge myself with negligence, yet I can assure you, I have not made that progress which you would wish, and some might expect. Still, I must acknowledge, it has been *greater* than I at first expected." It was very great, all things considered. Few ever made so much progress in so short a time, who had no elementary instructions before entering an academy; and although he did not remain at Gosport another twenty months, he was a respectable linguist before he left. This will be easily believed in reference to the classics, when it is remembered that Dr. Morrison said of his progress in Chinese, "that few had been so rapid: his attainments in the difficult language of this great empire were eminent."—*Life,* Vol. 2, p. 160. Such, indeed, was his *tact,* as well as his power of application, that it proved a snare to his patience when he began to teach others. Even Dr. Morrison suspected that he "held the rein too tight" at the Anglo-Chinese College; and he himself allowed that he may have done so. "Our method of study and application may have appeared hard, as I make it a uniform rule, except in extra cases, to insist on lessons being thoroughly learnt, before proceeding to new ones;—so I think there may have really been some ground for thinking the mode of instruction too strict and rigorous." *Ibid.* p. 148. This is going far forward in his life for proof of his scholarship at Gosport: but in no other way could I explain to the reader the conduct of either Dr. Bogue or the Directors, in selecting Mr. Milne for China, at so early a period of his collegiate course. It would have been *folly* in the case of students in general, who had entered College as he did, ignorant of the grammar of even his own language. But the fact is, he had not only a tact for acquiring languages, but his intense application to them was as prayerful as the waiting of the disciples for the Pentecostal gift of tongues: he "continued in supplication and prayer" for "power from on high." He also entreated for the prayers of his most prayerful friends, that he might succeed in his efforts. It is delightful to find him telling "poor saints" in Scotland, who had never heard of Latin, Greek or Hebrew, excepting the inscription on the cross,—how fond he was of the learned languages, and how useful and beautiful they were!

Mr. Milne's position as a student in England, destined to be a missionary to the heathen, gave him some weight and influence with the small farmers and the poor tradesmen, whom he had associated with whilst he was a servant. He knew this, and wrote long letters to some of them, although the *postage* was heavy. He did right! A letter from *England* had a charm in those days. It was a distinction, too, to a poor man. The village postman himself walked more erect when he had a London letter or two in his hand. Even the postmaster was all courtesy when an inquiry was made for a letter with the Gosport post-mark. Mr. Milne did not forget this. He remembered also how high his own heart beat, when he received his first letter from London. He was not afraid, therefore, of giving offence to an old acquaintance, by even a *double* letter. And that he was not afraid of offending by speaking *home-truths,* where he thought them wanted, the following extracts from such correspondence will prove.

To one old friend he writes,—"Few, I suppose, were ever more intimate than we have been. You had a right, if any man had, to hear from me. Do not impute delay to coldness of affection. I feel that I love you. I have just now been *praying* for you in my poor way. I return you my sincere thanks for all your kindness ever since we first met at the prayer meeting. I love my work. O that I may love it for Christ's sake, and not from any inferior motive! I generally preach three times on a Sabbath. I know you will think this too soon. Yes; and if you knew all my ignorance, you would be confirmed in your opinion. But time flies, and souls are perishing! Now, my brother, how is it with you? Has Christ the chief place in your heart? You will not be *angry* with me, I am sure, for saying that I have been sometimes afraid that the world was too much in your heart. I hope you will look into this matter. Love to you, makes me say so. I have not seen such a marked and visible difference between you and the men of the world, in the family, the field, or the market, as there ought to be. I have not seen, in some instances, that decided attachment to the friends of Christ, which I think should have been shown. But I have gone far enough on this part of the subject.

"How is Mrs. S.? Is she living to Christ, or the world? Is she seeking to be holy, humble, meek, and heavenly? These are excellent qualities in a wife; especially in a mother. Give my best respects to her, and tell her I hope to eat bread and cheese in her parlour yet, and talk with her of heaven and the way to it.

"How are the *lambs*, which God has given you to feed? Are you both wrestling for their souls' salvation?

"How is your *mother*, and your sister Anne? Tell them that I hope they are still seeking more of the mind which was in Christ, and longing to be delivered from a sinful heart.

"How are your *brothers*, James and William? Tell them that I am afraid they are lovers of the present world: but that I pray their hearts may be turned from it.

" How are your *servants*, and who are they? Do those who ' fear God dwell with you?' Do you teach them? Will they have reason to bless God for leading them into your family? Do you give them books to read, and allow them time, and encourage them to seek Jesus? Give my love to any of your servants who know me, and say that I hope they will serve Jesus, the best master.

"Remember me to your sister Margaret, and her husband. Are they searching the Scriptures, as for hid treasure, and looking for the coming of Christ.

"What is *Alexander* doing? O, tell him to seek the Lord whilst young; for many die in youth!

"How is *Margaret* M.? Has she got a good husband? Is he kind to her, and she obedient to him? O, tell her from me, that no Christless or graceless soul shall see heaven! She used to say she would walk a good way to hear me preach. Well, if I am spared, I shall see if she will be as good as her word: I suppose you will allow me to preach in your *barn*, if ever I return?

"How is G. and his partner? Give my respects to them. I hope the work of God is going on in them.

"Now, brother, I must be done. I often think of the time we spent together: some of it for good, and some to little purpose! May we be humbled! As Meikle says, 'We must be *crucified* to the world, or *cursed* with it.' Pray for me. May you and yours be presented before the throne without spot, and with exceeding joy!"

This is a fair specimen of Mr. Milne's solicitude and fidelity, in the case of those of whom he stood "in doubt;" and it shows how deeply he had studied their character whilst amongst them, and how well he remembered their chief snares afterwards. Nor was he less mindful of those friends whose piety was eminent. He often says to some of them, "I should think myself highly honoured to sit at your *feet* and learn." He well might, although sitting at the feet of Dr. Bogue! And yet, he could "stir up even their pure minds, by way of remembrance," without seeming to counsel them at all. To one "mother in 'Israel," whom I well remember as a pattern of the beauty of matronly holiness, and whom every one thought ripe for heaven, he says, "I would just observe—although it be not *necessary* for you—that your years will not be many now, and that there is yet much to do in order to be meet for the inheritance of the Saints in light. For, O how solemn to appear before infinite Majesty, and to have the beams of Divine purity darted on our naked spirits, in all their effulgence? How will our views of God, of sin, and of our ourselves, change in many things, and be enlarged in all things? But how sweet to hide in the righteousness of Christ, and take a *peep* into eternity, without overwhelming consternation! I have no doubt many of you who are mothers in Israel, bear unworthy me on your hearts at the Throne. This consideration often humbles me in the dust: for 'what am I, O Lord!' It also fills me with *love* to the saints, and makes them so very dear to me, that I think I could *kiss* their feet, were they even like Lazarus. The Lord sanctify *you* wholly, soul, body, and spirit, and bring you to the grave like a shock of ripe corn, in full age."

To one of his young friends, a school-fellow of my own, who had been long ill, he wrote thus:— "Grace and peace be multiplied to you! How wonderful, yea mysterious, are the dealings of God with his people! Truly, they are a 'great deep!' But the wheels of Providence are moved by the hand of love, and keep the path of infinite wisdom with the greatest exactness. Every *turning* brings something new and important to some of His friends, whether prosperity or pain. And why not pain? It is from Him whose love and wisdom exceed a *Seraph's* penetration. He, as one observes, brings by a Divine chemistry, good out of evil, sweet out of bitter, heaven out of hell. He has long held the cup of affliction to your lips. I hope it will make your flesh *fresh* as a child's. O, seek deliverance from *sin!* It is the curse of the universe. If you are able, write to me. A letter from you might bear the title, 'From the *dead* to the living.'" This last expression reminds me very forcibly of the influence which *Mrs. Rowe's* Letters had, at that time, upon not a few of Mr. Milne's young friends, in and around Huntly. How often some of us read them under "the auld beech tree," beside the older Castle Gordon, by the light of both the rising and the setting sun! Some of us wandered even by *moonlight* amongst the deep and winding shrubbery of "the meadow braes," almost conversing with the dead, and planning letters from them to rival Mrs. Rowe's. Mr. Milne knew our early habits, and tastes, and associations; and although he had no great sympathy with our sentimentalities, he respected our intense love of solitude and reading, and endeavoured to give them a *devotional* direction. And they had need of this—for some of us hated special prayer almost as much as we loved reading. We communed, alas, far more with nature than with God, and oftener with dead poets than with living saints. We venerated, however, the wrestling patriarchs of the village, and felt keenly at times that Milne had more of their devotional spirit than we possessed. We knew, also, that he was happier than we were, even when our romantic musings were most spiritual.

CHAPTER IV.

MR. AND MRS. MILNE'S VOYAGE.

When the time of Mr. Milne's embarkation drew near, Miss Cowie arrived in London, where many were prepared to welcome her; and especially the family of Thomas Wilson, Esq. Drs. Waugh and Bogue also vied with each other, in showing how much they respected her. The venerable patriarchs treated her as if she had been the Rachel of Jacob, the Phœbe of Paul, or the Mary of Bethany. It was not *sympathy*, however, that they manifested towards her. She needed none of that from any one. Her heart was too much affected with the wants of China, to think of her own sacrifices for that land. She *gloried* in her mission! And yet, there was nothing unfeminine in her character or spirit. No forwardness, flippancy, or ostentation. She was equally calm and cheerful; resolute and modest. Her spirit was in fine keeping with the perfect symmetry of her pensile frame and features. Her person was exactly the *temple* for her soul, and her will evidently lost in the will of God. Drs. Waugh and Bogue saw and felt this, and treated her accordingly. They felt, also, that they were sending a rich blessing to Mrs. Morrison, as well as giving a treasure to Mr. Milne, in thus sanctioning and honouring the object of his choice. And Mrs. Morrison found in Mrs. Milne "a friend indeed." They verified, when they met, the Chinese hieroglyph for friendship; two pearls of equal size and purity. I was often reminded of this, whilst Mrs. Morrison was in this country for the restoration of her health, and resident at Liverpool with her parents, Mr. and Mrs. Morton. She was then often in my family and flock, and never at my fireside without pouring out her warm heart in Irish benedictions upon Mrs. Milne. And these were not confined to my house. She told all her friends of "the guardian angel" she had found in the wife of her husband's friend and colleague. Her children, too, then very young, spoke of mamma's friend in raptures.

These facts, although out of their proper place, will prepare the reader to enjoy the history of this excellent woman; especially as it is from the pen of her husband. It will be found in a future chapter. In the mean time I may be allowed to say, that the only occasion on which I ever saw her agitated or disconcerted, was, on her arrival at church to be married. I had taken her there exactly at the hour: but Mr. Milne had not arrived. He had to come from the west end of London to Shoreditch; and some accident happened to the coach by the way. Half an hour was thus lost. This alarmed her for his safety. It also delayed the marriage of another party who had come with us. However, just as I was about to run off to make inquiries, Mr. Milne arrived, and all was right. We returned to the house of her cousin, Mr. Cowie, in Hoxton, from which the party went to Ilford, in Essex, on a visit to Mrs. Pates, one of the sisters-in-law of Mr. Cowie, of Huntly. There we parted to meet no more on earth; but pledged to meet often in spirit at the Throne of Grace.

On the 4th of September, 1812, Mr. and Mrs. Milne sailed from Portsmouth, for the Cape of Good Hope. Their voyage will be best described by the following letter, which Mrs. Milne addressed to Dr. Morrison, of Brompton, and myself, on her arrival. We were then fellow-students at Hoxton College.

"11th *January*, 1813.

"My dear Friends, .

"In a few lines I sent to Cousin by the first opportunity since I arrived at the Cape, I promised to send *you* or *them*, by the next conveyance, some extracts from my journal; and likewise what I have seen and heard since I came to this place. As far as I recollect, I sat up in bed and wrote you a few lines after we were under weigh, on the morning of the 4th of September. On the afternoon of the 6th, (Sabbath,) saw the last sight of English land: heaved a deep sigh at the sight of it, and the recollection of the many dear friends I left therein,—not to see them any more till the last trumpet shall sound to call us to judgment, and when we must all appear. O that it may be, to " be ever with the Lord, and to enjoy his presence for ever and for ever." But on recollecting the work I had the prospect of engaging in, I was made to rejoice that I was accounted worthy to make this small sacrifice, of leaving my native country, and many who are dear to me, to endeavour to promote His cause who gave his life a sacrifice, I trust, *for me.* 14th: We parted convoy off Cape Finisterre, in company with two other vessels: we steered a S. W. course. We were frequently put in alarm by the sight of strange sails. Three times we were prepared for action; but when the ships came up with us, they all proved friends. Our ship was but poorly manned, so that all the male passengers had their stations appointed them, —Mr. Milne's was in the *cock-pit*,—in case of an action taking place. At one time we were under such alarm that the ladies and their servants went below into the steerage, and got their *mattresses* placed around them to save them from the shot. I remained on deck to see the issue. The first land we saw after we passed Cape Finisterre was the Canary Island. The Canary birds were flying around us, they were so very tame. In the afternoon saw the peak of Teneriffe towering its lofty head above the other mountains which are around it, and showing its summit above the lower clouds. On the morning of the 3rd October, saw the Island of *Salt.* There were three vessels lying taking in salt:—two Americans, one Portuguese. The Americans, on seeing us bearing down on the island, and supposing we were an English ship of war, gave themselves up for lost. Could perceive no vestige of vegetation on the island. The mountains are stupendous, and more barren than any I ever saw in Scotland. There are two families and one hundred negroes residing on the island, who take charge of the salt pans. Salt and wild goats are all that are to be got on the island, except turtle, which are to be had in abundance on the beach;—part of one was sent us by one of the Americans. We had two days' soup of it; but for my part, I would have preferred a dish of *Scotch broth* to it. One part of the turtle tastes of fish, another of flesh, and another of fowl.

> Here rocks alone, and trackless sands are found,
> And faint and sickly winds for ever howl around.

Next day we were between the islands of St. Jago and Mayo. At the latter place we intended to have stopped to take in fresh water; but the wind being fair, we did not stop, as it would have detained us the greater part of two days. At the island of Trinidad there is one rock, the end of which represents the gable of a *church*, with a gentle declivity toward the other end. At the bottom of this wall there is a large cavern, where the sea enters and has a free passage through part of the rock. At the back of this rock there is one much higher, in the form of a bee-hive. At the other side there is another, which represents a tower. At a little distance from the former there is a fourth, which attracted my attention still more than the others. It would appear it had once been a solid mass; but now it is cloven asunder, and represents a Gothic arch. Indeed, the scene altogether represents the ruins of an old castle, with all its towers and battlements. I took a rough sketch of the island, as we sailed nearly round it. The captain, with some of the passengers and crew, intended to go on shore to see if they could find fresh water; but just as the boat was lowering, a heavy squall came on, when, had they been betwixt the island and the vessel, they must have perished. Saw no more land till the 31st, when we saw the lofty Cape Mountains. On the morning of the 1st December we stepped on shore, praising God for his great goodness to us while we were on the mighty deep. As to our opportunities, Mr. M. preached once every Sabbath, and taught six boys belonging to the ship three or four times a week. They committed to memory several passages of Scripture, hymns, and catechisms. Two that could not read,

I taught. As to our *society*, they were all polite people, and treated us with every mark of respect. You may suppose a number of curious farces occurred amongst so many passengers (being fifteen) in so long a voyage; which might be mentioned in conversation, but not in writing: however, we maintained the greatest friendship with them all the time. Our provisions were very good, but rather short toward the end of our voyage: and no wonder, when five passengers were taken on board at Portsmouth, and one at sea, after the ship's stores were laid in. The weather upon the whole was very good: we had several squalls, but only one gale, which lasted twenty-four hours. We were taken *aback* all in an instant, while the ship was in full sail, and going at the rate of from nine to ten knots an hour; the ship lay almost down on her broadside, till such time as her sails were taken in, when she righted again. This happened at two o'clock in the morning, when we were all in bed: trunks, boxes, and crockeryware, were flying in all directions, and the greatest consternation amongst us for some time: but, blessed be God, no one was hurt, neither did the ship receive any damage. During our passage, I saw sharks, whales, and flying-fish; one of the latter we caught; they are very small, and taste like fresh herrings. Our health during our voyage was good, except eight days that I kept my bed, and the tooth-ache that Mr. Milne was troubled with for some time. As to the way we spent our time, it was for the most part in each other's company, in some useful study or conversation. We are just as happy *a two* as ever you saw; the smile of sympathy and love is ever on our countenances toward each other, and I am sure this will give you and all friends pleasure. On our arrival at the Cape we were welcomed by kind friends, under whose roof we find a comfortable dwelling. Met with many pious soldiers from our own country, who refreshed our souls much after being so long deprived of Christian society.

"Mr. Milne had a severe illness since we arrived, which I mentioned in Cousin's letter, which was sent by the "Porposs," enclosed in a packet to Commissioner Gray, Portsea. I have been well ever since I came here; the climate is not so hot as I expected. This month is one of the hottest (in general;) but the oldest persons that I have conversed with say they never experienced so much cold at this season of the year. The houses here have no *fire-places*, so that I cannot enjoy that comfort that *you* know I was so *partial* to. The Cape is a clean, pretty little town, situated at the bottom of stupendous Mountains; one is called the Lion's Rump, another the Lion's Head, a third, the Table Mountain, which in common is covered with a cloud for a table cloth; the others they call the Devil's Hills. A few days after our arrival the military were drawn up round the Lion's Rump to fire a *feu de joie*, in honour of Lord Wellington's victory. The cannon belonging to the regiment of artillery lying here, were drawn up by a number of horses to the top of this hill; their fire was answered by the batteries, which are placed round the bay. You cannot think what a grand effect the roaring of the cannon had among the surrounding mountains. I have been a day's journey into the interior, on a visit to the *Moravian* Missionaries, at Gravenskloof. We left the Cape at five in the morning, and at eight made a hearty breakfast on the ground at the foot of the Blue Mountain, where many of our countrymen lie buried till the morning of the resurrection, who were lost at the intake of the Cape. We sung ' *Crown him Lord of all*,' on Africa's wild plain. The greater part of the roads to this place are through deep sand. I was much struck with the *whiteness* of the sand. I saw mountains of it as white as snow; and beautiful flowers, such as *we* nurse, in flower pots, growing on them; also several land tortoises. We met with a hearty welcome and good entertainment from the Missionaries and their wives. At eight in the evening the bell rung, when the Hottentots assembled to perform their evening devotions. You may judge what were my feelings when sitting in the midst of a congregation of Hottentots; many of them dressed in sheep-skins. Seemingly, many of them possessed the grace of God. Next day we went through a number of their huts, and, by a few words of Dutch, that we had gathered, and the help of an interpreter, we conversed with them about the love of Jesus, &c. They, with their eyes streaming, and their black hands lifted up, expressed their gratitude to God, for ever thinking of them, or sending Missionaries to instruct them. Their huts, although mean, are in general clean. They sleep on sheep-skins. A garden is attached to every hut, which they keep in good order. On the morning we left them, after commending each other to the grace of God, a great many assembled at the door of the house, and while we were getting into our wagon, they sung a hymn, expressing their thanks for our visit, and praying for our success. I left these places with a heart filled with gratitude to God, for what I had been permitted to hear and see of the power of his grace on the heart of these poor Hottentots, that were once little superior to the *brutes of* the field, and exclaiming, *Who would not be a Missionary?* The children have made great progress in education; some of the girls sew tippets, children's caps, &c. I bought a white veil of their working, that I shall be proud to wear. On our way home they killed a serpent about four feet long, the cobracapella, one of the most venomous. The earthquake which happened here about three years ago, hath been the voice of God to many, who date their convictions from that period, not only in Cape Town, but through the colony. I trust we have seen the dawning of a great day in the Cape. Mother Smith, whom you no doubt will recollect to have heard of, is the most extraordinary woman I ever heard of, or met with. I will treat you with a short account of her. She is in her 64th year; she has been a truly pious Christian this many years; she possesses a dignity and solemnity in her appearance peculiar to herself; notwithstanding she has as much life and energy, as if she were in her 16th year. She was, I think, for two years at our Missionary Station, at Bethelsdorp, when Dr. *Vander Kempt* settled there. Since she returned to the Cape, she has been the Missionary's *director*, along with two or three old ladies. She teaches the slave school twice a week; once a week she preaches to more than 200 slaves; and, in general, there are more than half that number of free people, some of them very genteel. I have heard her preach. The whole service is in Dutch, and conducted in the same manner as in Scotland, only she is clerk as well as parson; she has a fine voice. Her address is pointed, serious, and powerful; her eloquence is great, and her action natural, lively, and graceful; her application is superior to most ministers: she sat all the time except in prayer,—then she displays such fervour of soul, that she seems as if she would pull down heaven into the hearts of the poor slaves. Mrs. S. is greatly beloved by the slaves, and by all ranks of people; indeed, she is looked upon as an oracle. God, by a long train of dispensations, has prepared her for this extensive usefulness. She has been twice married, and has lost both husbands, and ten children by death. See! out of the eater comes forth meat! She is the same in private as in public, just as it were on the border of glory. But, my dear friends, my paper is nearly covered with one thing or another, so that I must draw to a close, begging you both not to neglect an opportunity of writing to us. I long very much to hear from you, and other dear friends at Hoxton.

"I remain yours, in the best of bonds,
"R. MILNE."

I introduce this letter at full length, not so much for the information it contains, as for the *cheerful* spirit it breathes; which will prove to parents who may be called upon to resign a daughter, that she may be thoroughly happy as the wife of a Missionary, if she herself love Missions as well as her husband. I have now before me a letter of Mrs. Milne's, written on the same day to her friend Mrs. Andrew Taylor, of Aberdeen, which will throw still more light upon this fact. "I often think of one thing that my dear Mrs. T. used to comfort me with,—that I should be a happy woman in getting *such* a husband. She is a true prophetess! I am a *happy* woman. I should never have been cast down had I known what was in store for me;—I mean, so kind, so tender, so affectionate a husband!" It was not herself only who said, that they were "just as happy a two as could be seen." Mrs. Morrison, who best knew their domestic life, used to say, with great emphasis, "They are such a happy couple!" Dr. Morrison also says, "They were much attached to each other, and lived happily."

Mr. Milne's letters from the Cape, although numerous and long, pass over the voyage as a trifle. "Being at sea," he says, "is not half the terrible thing I used to think it. It is not much more formidable to me than taking a walk or a ride into the country to see a friend. We have not, however, had much bad weather." Whilst at the Cape he occupied some of his time in trying to ascertain enough of the state of *Madagascar* to enable him to put questions concerning it, at the Isle of France, where he intended to land, for the express purpose of planning a new Mission to the Malagash.

He took a deep interest also in the Malays and Hottentots at the Cape. On visiting the Malay burying-ground, "one day, he found," Mrs. Milne says, "an old man praying on the grave of his child; now with his hands hanging at his side, and anon covering his face, whilst he cried in a sing-song tone, 'Alé, Ela, La, Ei!' He could speak a little Dutch. Mr. Milne asked him, 'Can you read the Koran?' 'Yes.' 'Why pray over the dead?' 'I think it good. The Koran says it is good.' 'Do you worship Mahomet?' 'Yes.' 'You should worship God only; Mahomet is but a son of Adam, as you or myself.' 'But my religion says, worship Mahomet. Jesus

Christ was a good man, but Mahomet is a better!' 'Poor thing,' Mrs. M. adds, ' what a delusion!' "

Of the pious Hottentots, Mr. Milne says to his friends in Scotland, "the sight of their worship would have done you good: perhaps it would have made you ashamed of yourselves to see their devotion. They sing so sweetly the same tunes which are sung in Scotland!"

The day before he left this interesting people, he wrote thus:—" We saw the Rev. John Campbell go away to visit the Missions. This journey will take him eight months; for he has to accomplish the whole of it by wagons drawn by oxen. I rejoiced to see this Missionary expedition fitted out in the ancient style of patriarchal simplicity! They have to pass through immense deserts, where the sand flies like snow, and where there is but little water. I think the *Bible* will be sweet to them! They will undoubtedly know what those words mean,—'a vast howling wilderness.' I trust, also, that they will taste the sweetness of that passage,—' The Angel that was with the Church in the wilderness.' I have passed through two of these deserts (though small,) and they are covered with rushes, flowers, and brambles, and infested with snakes, tigers, and other wild animals. There is not, however, much danger, if the party keep together, kindle fires in the night, and have their arms always ready."

After a voyage of forty days, Mr. and Mrs. Milne arrived at the Isle of France. Its immense heathen population and immoral Popery affected them deeply. "We were grieved," he says, "to see the place so given to wickedness, and none seeking to awaken them. Fine Missionary field! I sometimes conversed with the people in French, and gave away tracts. We found, however, among the British residents, a few pious souls: but they are as rare here as white crows. One soldier, from Aberdeenshire, spent three days in going about searching for me. He visited us often, and took leave of us on the beach with a sorrowful heart."

They now sailed for China in the same ship which brought them to the Mauritius; and, as usual, he preached every sabbath on board, although only eight or ten of the crew understood English. "Last voyage," he says, "we had a young man who could interpret to Moors, but he has left the ship. It is hard to be surrounded by about forty who would hear the Word, and yet I cannot speak it! I know not their language, and it is not possible to learn it on a voyage. This is one of a Missionary's trials; but it will give vigour to his application in learning the language of the people amongst whom he may live." I quote this paragraph that Missionaries may imitate Dr. Milne at sea. Perhaps I may be allowed to say to them here,—that they cannot please sailors more than by taking a hearty and open interest in their improvement. I speak from experience, although I have never been at sea. During some years, I preached regularly to sailors in Liverpool, and never with more pleasure. Any Minister will gain their respect and confidence, if he will throw himself upon their honour, and show himself their friend. Being unable to preach much on board, Mr. Milne spent his time chiefly in studying Chinese, from an elementary work, by Dr. Marshman, of Serampore; and with such success, that his old fears gave way not a little. In a letter to a friend, he says, "Whether

I may succeed, must be the decision of a future time, but, at present, I think a person of even moderate capacity, with habits of close study, may acquire it in far less time than is generally supposed." This, be it remembered, is the opinion of a close student. It is, therefore, interesting to find him saying, whilst he had no teacher, "As to the elementary part, the Chinese language is the richest in the world; but as to the oral part, it seems the poorest of all languages, there is so little variety of sound."

During this voyage he felt the dull uniformity of being, "far out at sea," so much that he was rather glad when "some awful thunder filled the mind with solemn thought." Occasionally, he was glad also to "fish for sharks and dolphins," although the latter were "always fortunate enough to escape death." But whilst thus amusing himself, he was studying the crew, that he might counsel the Master. This he did in the following paper, which he respectfully handed to the captain:—

RULES FOR SHIP-MASTERS.

In order to the proper regulation of a crew,—

1st. No correction should be permitted to be given without the knowledge of the master; because there are many young officers who delight in this way to show their authority over the poor men.

2d. Never permit any one to be made a fool of by the rest, because it breeds many quarrels among the men.

3d. Never correct a drunken man, it is all lost on him.

4th. Recollect your men have the same feelings with you.

5th. Keep a small library of different kinds of books, in various languages, for the use of the men.

6th. Try to persuade those who have parents, or wives, or poor relatives, to save part of their pay for their use, and also to write to their friends frequently.

7th. Encourage some one who is able, to teach the others reading, writing, arithmetic, and navigation.

8th. Encourage all to live in the fear of God.

Another subject, which deeply engaged his attention during the voyage, was—a Mission to MADAGASCAR. That *martyr-mission* forms a part of his history. He collected, whilst at the Mauritius, from French books, and from the conversation of persons who had resided in Madagascar, the principal facts upon which the enterprise of the Missionary Society was afterwards founded. Indeed he drew out the original plan of that Mission, and submitted it to the Directors, who inserted it at the end of the first "Travels" of Mr. Campbell, of Kingsland.

But whilst these things diversified his pursuits on board, nothing diverted him long from his grand object, preparation for his Chinese Mission. And as he could not do much at the language of the people, he studied closely their character and opinions, from his books on the subject, which seem to have been select, although not numerous. Dr. Morrison said of him to the Bible Society, when he sent home an account of his death, "Few have made such rapid progress in a comprehension of the opinions of the Chinese, which he studied assiduously, for the purpose of conveying the truths of the Gospel to their understandings and hearts."—*Life*, Vol. ii. p. 160.

He prepared himself for this keen and minute observation of their nationalities, whilst at sea. There, he asked himself, what ought I to know of this people, in order to teach them what I think of Christ and salvation? He pursued this question in all directions, until he fixed all the chief points on which accurate information was essential; and thus he knew what to look for when he landed. He prepared, if I may be allowed the expression, twenty-one cells in his memory, which he resolved to fill, as he might have opportunity; and from the day he landed, until the day he died, it might have been as truly said of him to the Chinese, as Burns sung of Grose the antiquary,

"A chiel's amang ye, taking *notes*."

A very different kind of notes, however. They were upon the following points:—

QUESTIONS RELATIVE TO THE RELIGION AND MANNERS OF THE CHINESE.

1st. Have they generally the idea of *one* supreme Being; or do they suppose that there are two or more beings who divide the government of the world between them?

2d. What ideas have the Chinese of the efficacy of sacrifices? Do they connect with sacrifice the idea of *atonement* for sin? Do they speak of a mediator?

3d. What virtues or power do they suppose idols to possess and exercise?

4th. What are their ideas of the number and power of evil spirits; and have they any notion of *good* angels? Do they speak of apparitions?

5th. What are their sentiments of the metempsychosis, and of the sufferings of souls in purgatory? Do their *pictures* serve to explain their sentiments on this subject?

6th. What influence do they suppose the *stars* to have on the constitutions, tempers, and fates of men?

7th. What do they say of the Divine decrees?

8th. Is the Chinese *ritual* large; and what may be considered as its prominent parts?

9th. Has the worship, in Chinese temples, any resemblance to the Jewish ritual; or to any of the institutions of the gospel? If so, how can the *resemblance* be accounted for?

10th. Have the Chinese any day, either weekly or monthly, which they set apart in a more solemn manner for the worship of their gods; and have they any public religious instruction?

11th. What is the nature, design, and degree of that worship which the Chinese pay at the *tombs* of their ancestors? Do they suppose that their deceased relatives have power to confer favours, or deliver from dangers?

12th. Wherein do they suppose the *happiness* of the spirits of good men, in the other world, to consist? Do they expect a resurrection?

13th. What reasons can you assign that the Chinese empire has continued, for such a long succession of ages, under a government, the radical principles of which are the same?

14th. Is *sorcery* practised to any extent?

15th. Do they suppose that *heaven* is the Deity?

16th. Is there any difference between the worship which they pay to heaven and that which they pay to shin? Have you ever heard or read of any estimate of the *number* of their deities?

17th. Does the practice of confining the feet of female children prevail universally, or generally, in China? From what did it arise? How is it effected? What is the design?

18th. What particular ceremonies are there observed at the burial of the dead; for example, as to place of interment, removing the body to a distance, feasts and offerings, prepared and presented?

19th. Are the coronation ceremonies grand; and wherein do they consist?

20th. What is the sense of the Chinese laws in regard to those who *fail* in business; and what is the common practice?

21st. Is slavery allowed by law; and how?

This document shows more of the character and compass of Mr. Milne's mind than any one I have yet produced. Still, it is only a large specimen of his inquisitive and discriminating power. We have seen already how minutely he looked into men and things, that he might judge for himself. This cast of mind, when well balanced by prudence and spirituality, is invaluable in a Missionary. "Any fool can ask questions," it is said. He is no wise man, however, who cannot ask questions; and no uneducated man certainly could have asked these questions.

It is difficult to say, whether a Missionary who has no curiosity, or one who has too much, ought to be most avoided by societies. A very inquisitive man, may prove a very inefficient evangelist, now that Literary and Scientific Associations are wise enough to welcome information for its own sake, and candid enough to treat Missionaries as they do other travellers. This may prove a snare, where strange flowers, fossils, or antiquities abound.

On the other hand, however, an incurious Missionary is sure to turn out an uninteresting preacher. No mind will keep in healthful play, nor in holy energy, long, which has no taste for the daily observation of men or things. It is only an everlasting learner, that will be an everlasting teacher, either at home or abroad. The churches should remember this fact, both in selecting Ministers and Missionaries. At home, indeed, it is hardly possible to sink into a mere solemn drone, now that penny Magazines "meddle with all knowledge," and make science child's play, and history household words: but abroad, he who cannot create knowledge as well as preach the Gospel, will soon become a drone. He who cannot study the *people,* at least will not study *for* them with much effect, nor with lasting pleasure. Besides, it is *cruelty* to himself to set down a merely well disposed young man upon a lonely island in the Pacific, or in an interior desert of Africa. In such a sphere, a mind without energy and intellectual resources, will eventually sink or wither. Paul himself kept up the healthy action of both his mighty mind and his *inspired* piety, by trying how far Grecian and Roman customs could be turned into legitimate illustrations of truth and duty. Much of his spirituality lay in the habit of converting every thing into its own substance; and at no point or stage of his apostolic career, do we ever find him trusting his piety to its own vitality. It was evidently not for "bread alone," nor merely to be an example of industry, that he worked at tent-making in Corinth.

He had not work enough for his *head* there at first, and therefore he employed his hands; and thus kept his heart right with God. A man of less piety or a Missionary of less zeal, would have sat down and wept, and thus weakened the "little strength" he had.

Having given some prominence to the inquisitive *turn* of Mr. Milne's mind, it is only fair to himself and the subject to add the rules by which he hallowed and regulated his curiosity.

REGULÆ STUDII.

1. Never to spend time in seeking to know that which cannot be known by the utmost labour in this life; and which, in half an hour may be fully known in eternity.

2. Never to spend time in seeking for that which, when attained, cannot serve the interests of rational beings, and the glory of God.

3. Whatever knowledge or talent is attained, let it be devoted to the service of God, and the interest of the Gospel."

Such were his pursuits and spirit during his voyage to Macao; which was both short and pleasant. As he approached the shores of China, and caught glimpses of that mighty empire and the adjacent islands, he saw at once the vantage ground it afforded him for renewing his appeals to his friends in Scotland, on behalf of his mission. In doing this, he wisely identified his wife with that mission. Almost all his letters begin thus:—" We now stand on the borders of China, and turn round to salute and bless you, over the ocean, in the name of the Lord."

He knew well how welcome their *joint* letters would be at home; and wrote many. Not a few of these are now before me: but it would be injustice to him, were I now to state, that the first and longest letter he wrote whilst off Macao, was to the mate of the vessel. Not all the engrossing interest of the new scene, nor all the pressing claims of old friends, could divert him from the immediate duty of trying to win the soul of a young countryman of his own, whom he was not likely to meet again in this world. His letter to him contains *twelve* quarto pages. A few extracts from it will show how thoroughly he could concentrate all his soul upon winning *one* soul, even whilst he was impatient to land, and aware of the impatience of many to hear from him.

"My dear sir,—As we are about to part, probably to meet no more in this world, I take the liberty of expressing the best wishes of my heart for your future welfare. As you are a countryman of mine, I feel that interest in your welfare which is natural for one Scotchman to feel for another. As you are an *immortal* creature, I feel that concern for your soul's salvation which a Christian ought to feel."

"Your situation at sea, as an officer, though respectable, is not considered favourable to morality and religion. Ignorance and profaneness abound. But the man who commits sin in order to be like his neighbours, acts a part as foolish and dangerous as if he were to cast himself into the sea, after the example of one deprived of reason and hope." The letter then appeals to all the young man's recollections of the truths of the Gospel, as these are laid down in the assembly's catechism. It then furnishes him with a list of useful books commended, thus:—

"Boston's Four-fold State. (He was a Scotchman.) Reverend John Newton's life. (He was for some time an officer of a ship.) Parke's Travels, will entertain you much in leisure hours. Guthrie's Geography is an excellent work. Buck's Anecdotes is a very amusing book. You may easily find them in England, perhaps, in Bengal. I beg your acceptance of Baxter's Call; it has been useful to many.

"I am concerned not only for your salvation, but also the improvement of your mind, and for your respectability in society. As you have already risen to the condition of an officer, there is little doubt but that, by proper attention, you will soon rise to be a master;—a most important charge! Tyranny and cruelty in a Captain will most likely meet punishment from the hand of God, by the hand of a rebellious *child*, in this world; and due punishment in the next, it certainly will meet. Write often to your parents. They will be glad to hear from you. It is a *cruelty* not to be described, to trifle with their feelings, by neglecting, as some do, to write."

These specimens of this letter are introduced here not so much for their own value, nor as an illustration of the writer's spirit, but to suggest to young Missionaries the duty and beauty of doing with all their "might, whatsoever their hand findeth to do," whilst at sea, and on parting with the companions of their voyage. Dr. Milne will be able to meet this officer at the judgment seat, without a blush of shame or fear.

It will be recollected that the crew of the vessel were chiefly Moors, to whom he could neither write nor speak. He therefore took the more pains in instructing the few who understood English. These, he made his *mission*, until he stepped ashore at Macao.

It is hardly possible to forget here, how differently the *Jesuits* in general felt and acted when they reached the shores of China. Xavier's tomb on the island of Sancian, had more attractions for them than the souls in the ship. When father Premare and his ten Missionaries came to Sancian, they stole off in haste to the sepulchre of their saint. "We spied," he says, "a pretty large stone standing upright; and the moment we read the Portuguese words, '*a qui foi sepultado S. F. Xavier*,' we *kissed* the sacred earth several times. Some of our countrymen (Frenchmen) watered it with their tears. Then the first transports of zeal being over, we raised just such a tent as Xavier had died in. In fine, we sung Te Deum, with the litany of the saint; and began to pass the most delightful evening that can be enjoyed in this world."

"How exquisite are the pleasures which are felt, when men, on occasions like this, interchange their fondest thoughts and feelings! We are going, (says one,) upon our Apostleship in that very place where Saint Xavier concluded his. He could proceed no farther into the vast empire of China, whereas we have free access into it. What may we not hope to achieve there for God's glory, under the auspices of a saint, who was able to open the gates of this empire to us?"

"'He died here (says another) after having converted whole nations. But shall we be so happy as to make a *similar* end?' "We afterwards sung the litanies of the blessed Virgin. During another pause, we said over our *beads*, and renewed the praise of the Saint: and these orisons were intermingled with discourses which had all the *merit* of prayers.

"We then enumerated the virtues of the Apostles of the East; and then I found myself deficient in them all. One of the Fathers remembered the night when Ignatius watched in the church of Montserrat before the image of the Virgin, at the time he was about to devote himself to God. We called our Vigil at the sepulchre of an Apostle, '*Notre nuit d'armes*.' (The readers of Don Quixote need not be reminded that, by the laws of chivalry, knights had to watch their arms a whole night before they could wear them. This was their probation.) Whilst we were employed with these reflections, day broke upon us; and we celebrated mass on the anniversary of St. Francis Borgia. The stone of the sepulchre was the basis of our altar, which was erected on the very spot where Xavier was interred. After the masses, we sung *Te Deum* again, and kissed the ground a *hundred* times. Then we all reverently took up a little portion of the earth, to preserve as a sacred relic; and returned, singing the praises of the saint whose spirit we endeavoured to inherit." Premare and Bouvet, with their companions, were the first Frenchmen who played the fool in this style at Sancian. Indeed, with the single exception of Carrocio, an Italian, they were the first Jesuits who did so. They were not, however, the last. How this *foolery* would have grieved the spirit of Francis Xavier! He himself, indeed, would have been almost as superstitious at the tomb of an Apostle: but the apocalyptic angel did not shrink more from the worship John was about to offer, than Xavier would have spurned such homage. Dr. Milne studied the character of Xavier, when he lost his RACHEL, and placed him *high up* in his list of "Eminently Good Men."

CHAPTER V.

MR. MILNE'S FIRST APPEALS FROM CHINA.

It has already been stated that Mr. Milne identified his *wife* with himself in the mission. This doubled at least the interest of his letters to many; and to none more than to the churches of Aberdeen and Huntly. The first letter he wrote in Dr. Morrison's study, at Canton, was to Dr. Philip, then of Aberdeen, who had been Mrs. Milne's pastor. It begins like all the rest: "We now stand on the borders of China, and turn back for a moment to bless you in the name of the Lord! During the whole of our voyage, we both enjoyed good health; and a degree of spirits, which nothing but the goodness of God, the importance of our object, and our domestic happiness, could have supported. We are now *far* from you, but can never forget you. An old writer speaks of the *Cotus*, an African plant, which, whoever tastes, instantly forgets his own country, with all its sweets. This plant we have not yet met with. We love you all, and love our country; and yet we had much rather be where we are. We have not repented coming out; and we have every reason to bless God that we came out together.

"Shortly after our arrival (at Macao,) I was obliged to go to Canton. The Portuguese bishop and clergy, in their zeal for the *dying* church of Rome, prevailed on the governor to send me away. The governor, however, permitted Mrs. Milne to remain in Mr. Morrison's house;—they cannot send him away, because he is in the service of the East India Company. But for this, he would have been sent off ere now; for all the blindness and intolerance that ever reigned in the darkest ages of Popery, exists in Macao. Every day in the week seems a feast or a fast day. The bells are the most religious I ever heard, for they ring on every occasion, day and night.

"In Canton, on Sabbaths, I have feasted on *Rutherford's* Letters. They contain much that is excellent; and often strike home like thunderbolts! I value them not the less, I assure you, because they were written in *Upper Kirkgate*, (the street in which Miss Cowie had resided,) in Aberdeen. Were the venerable *prisoner* there now, he would find Christian charity twenty degrees higher than it was in the time of his banishment. I suppose he never thought that the familiar hints which dropped from his pen then, woul do good to a *half-banished* Missionary in China! But that which is written in the *closet*, as well as that which is spoken in the *ear*, is often 'proclaimed on the house-top.'

"This is a *vast* benighted country; we stand on the borders of it, like men on the banks of the vast sea; we see only a little, and dare not venture in but an *inch* or two. The city of Canton is like the New Jerusalem only in one thing; that *strangers* are not permitted to enter. I have once peeped in at the gate; and I hope yet to enter. A few days ago, I went to the top of a little hill to view this land; (I trust it is a 'Land of Promise!') My thoughts were, 'O that God would give this land to the churches, that we, their Messengers, might walk through the length and breadth of it, to publish the glory of His salvation! Mr. Morrison says of the Chinese, that, generally speaking, they have all the cunning, deceit, and intrigue of the French, without any of their good qualities. I think them exceedingly corrupt in their morals. They are a civilized and industrious people; but their land is *full* of idols!"

It is easy to conceive how a letter of this kind—alternately cheerful and solemn, playful, and pathetic—would interest Dr. Philip and his church on behalf of China. Such *natural* appeals to the churches they went out from, would win for Missionaries far more sympathy, prayer, and co-operation, than any studied advocacy or stilted eloquence could command. Those who have read the letters of the Jesuits from China, to their friends in France, will remember their utter want of all natural sympathy with *home*, except on the single point of the *national* glory. In all other respects, they are almost *heartless*. And even this is not their worst feature. Many of these letters palliate the vices, whilst they exaggerate the miseries of the Chinese. It will prepare the reader to appreciate Dr. Milne's appeals; and it may suggest to some young Missionary a useful lesson, to illustrate this distinction. When *Premare* addressed his first appeal to Le Gobien, in 1700, he coolly said, that "Such Europeans as settle in China, and are eye-witnesses of what passes, are not *surprised* to hear, that mothers kill or expose several of their children; nor that parents sell their daughters for a trifle; nor that the empire is full of thieves; and the spirit of avarice universal. They are rather surprised that *greater* crimes are not heard of during seasons of scarcity. If we deduct the *desires* so natural to the unhappy, the innocence of their habits would correspond well enough with their poverty and hard labour." Thus, the *moral* question is almost blinked. Accordingly, it is on account of the wretchedness of the poor, he exclaimed, " O, if I could only teach them to sanctify their *miseries*, by setting before them a God, suffering for their sakes!" (Let. Edit.)

Not thus did Mr. Milne write. In a letter to an influential English family he says, "Every species of crime abounds here, except cruelty to parents. In the treatment of aged parents the Chinese are very exemplary. I have been in their temples. These are similar to Romish cathedrals. The worshippers bow often before idols, great and small. Incense burns continually before these dumb idols. In every house and boat there is an image, which is worshipped several times a day. Perhaps some professing Christians should *blush* when they hear this! Just at this moment drums are beating, bells ringing, music playing, to delight these drowsy gods and to keep them awake and attentive." All this shocked the *Protestant* Missionary. A century, before, however, Father Bouvet, and a party of French Missionaries, almost rivalled the Chinese in idolatry at Sancian. In a letter to Father De la Chaize, confessor to the King of France, in 1669, he says, "We cast anchor almost within musket-shot of that sacred spot where St. Francis Xavier was buried. Having testified the reverence we bear to that holy Apostle, by several bows and prostrations, in both the *Chinese* and European manner, we sang *Te Deum* to thank the great Saint. This ceremony concluded with a *triple salvo* of all our boxes, patteraroes, and small arms on board, with acclamations, '*Long live the King!*' The whole ceremony *delighted* the Chinese, and gave them a very favourable opinion of our nation!"

I make no apology for introducing these *contrasts* into this work. They will explain more than Mr. Milne's *personal* dread and hatred of Popery. They will also create wonder that any of the Chinese could have caught glimpses of the LAMB SLAIN, which, in spite of all the mummery of Popery, won their hearts, and led them to lay down their lives for Christ. They will also prepare us to review the Chinese and Japanese *martyrology* with jealousy as well as sympathy. This, as we shall see, Dr. Milne did, and held the balance with a very *equal* hand, although his dread of Popery led him at this time to oppose Catholic emancipation. He actually wrote thus to the Directors of the Missionary Society. "Whether my banishment from Macao to Canton will give any *weight* to "Catholic claims," the British public will judge as soon as you inform them of this circumstance."

In a letter to a circle of zealous ladies, on this subject, he says, "If we had you here we could find you plenty of *work*, but little room; for this people do not favour European ladies. The angry Bishop and Clergy, afraid of their tottering Rome, have driven me away from my wife to Canton. They have permitted her to remain with Mrs. Morrison: for they do not dread so much harm from the ladies as from *male* heretics. What think ye? Will it be termed *revenge*, if I say that I shall try to bring their fears upon them? Well, if it should, I cannot help it. I am determined to try; and if I succeed I shall not think I have done wrong. I shall make a bold push to get *into* China, in spite of them." "Our *purses* always bring you to mind. They have never been empty since you gave and filled them. We have always something in purse, much in Providence, and all things in promise. From the shores of China we salute you over the ocean!"

To an aged "Zacharias and Elizabeth," he wrote thus: "Distance does not displace such kind friends. We send back over the ocean our compliments, our prayers, and our thanks. We begin now to feel some Missionary trials; but they are not very heavy, and we both bear a part: for although I am chiefly aimed at, yet my dear *Rachel* and I are so perfectly united, that I believe she takes the weightiest half of the burden. China is a land full of idols; a land of darkness and spiritual death! Here we have none of "the shepherds' tents" beside which you feed; none of the assemblies of the faithful! But we do not repent coming out. God has been better to us than our hopes by far. Trust in the Lord, ye *London* believers! We are not destitute of all the means of grace, although we have few of a public kind. We need, however, your prayers; for to keep up the spirit of religion in the soul amongst blinded Heathen is not very easy.

"I am anxious to hear of you both. Sometimes I think Mr. I. is gone home, and now safe and warm 'in Abraham's bosom.' Let us strive to have our path perfumed with the *graces* of the Holy Spirit;

then it will yield a goodly fragrance, when we sleep under the clods of the valley.

"It would be the joy of our souls to tell amongst the Heathen, that the Lord Jesus reigneth; but we can scarcely *lisp* the glorious tidings in their tongue as yet. Now and then I scatter a few seeds, which, perhaps, may not all be lost."

Mr. Milne's first letter to his mother and sisters blends some fine appeals for China, with the finest expressions of his *home* sympathies and recollections. It is too long to be introduced here as a whole. So are all his letters at this time; for he could do little else at Canton but write whilst he was, as he says, "nearly as much alone as in a cloister." I ought to have mentioned earlier, that before he left Kennethmont to study at Gosport, he built, and chiefly with his own hands, a house for his mother. I had forgotten this interesting and characteristic fact, until I found in the letter I am about to quote, the question, "do you still live in the house which I built?" My venerable friend Mr. Campbell, of Kingsland, said to me the other day, with no small triumph in his looks, "I have preached in that very house, sir; and remember well, looking up to the hill side where the shepherd lad lay reading about the Heathen, and praying to be sent to them. I see the place now!" This little anecdote will explain the spirit of the following extracts:—"The farther I remove from you, the more I seem to love you. Of all earthly relations, none but my *wife* can be dearer to me than she who brought me into the world, and those who sucked the same breasts with me. My dear partner too loves you all nearly as much as I can do. O, what a blessing she is to me!

I wish my dear sisters may be as well appointed in husbands as I am with a wife!

"The people here are all heathens, they worship idols. I have seen them offer sacrifice to the *devil*, of whom they are much afraid. They think that a sacrifice will induce him not to harm them. Some of their idols in the temples are twenty feet high. They need bells and drums to *awake* them to hear their worshippers' supplications." The God of Israel is not like unto them. He slumbers not, nor sleeps!. The Chinese worship *four* times oftener than Christians pray.

"Living here is very expensive to the Society. It grieves me much to be at such expense. I hope it will not amount to the half soon. My *Moonshee's* wages would support you all: and yet there is no possibility of helping it now. The *heat* is very great, and servants must do almost every thing. I feel that my body is not very *strong*, although I have good health. I am apt to study too hard. I must take care."

"I begin to read the language of China, and speak and write a little, though I have not been three months here. It is very difficult, and very peculiar; but I hope soon to be able to speak of God's salvation to his people. The whole of the New Testament is translated, and will soon be printed. This will rejoice the heart of *north* country Christians. I preach on Sabbaths to some few English and Americans at my lodgings. This, I suppose, is the first *English* preaching that ever was at Canton.

"Perhaps I may be able ere long to send Mamma and sisters a trifle, to show that I have not forgotten the *fifth* commandment. O, how I should like to take care of *you*, dear mother, in your declining years. My *Rachel* would nurse you as she does me. I long to hear whether you have experienced a *change* of heart, and whether you seek your *all* in Christ! I pray, particularly on Sabbaths, that your hoary head may be found in the way of righteousness, and that my dear sisters may be led into the truth. A covenant God be with you all!

"Are you still in the house which I built? How do you get on for money? Do you get regularly the *five* pounds, through, from me? What persons are particularly *kind* to you? Is the *school* continued with you? Is there any thing I can do for you? Are any of my aunts, uncles, cousins, pious? What changes are there among my particular friends? Are any of the people of Cults and the Brae become pious? If health be spared, I propose to write to the *five* churches;—Huntly, Lesslie, Catrach, Aberdeen and Banff, by the next opportunity."

It will be seen from the abrupt transitions in these letters, that I do not possess the originals, but copy from the rough notes of Mr. Milne's letter-book. I do not regret that, so far as the illustration of his *character* is concerned. First thoughts, and first words, in letters, are often the best, and always show the man most truly. The following extract will show how Mr. Milne wrote to men of education and rank. It is from a letter addressed to the secretary of government at the Isle of France. He had preached to the *slaves*, when he touched there on his voyage to China; and the government had published some remonstrance against his conduct, injurious to his character and Missionary intentions. He saw the bearing of this upon his own designs for

Madagascar, and upon the position of other Missionaries; and remonstrated, in his turn, with equal courtesy and courage.

"Honoured Sir,

"When I parted with you, you expressed a wish to hear of my proceedings (in China.) I should be ungrateful, did I not embrace the first opportunity of gratifying, to the utmost of my power, one to whose kindness I am so much indebted. I have little new or interesting to communicate, having been so short a time in this country. I was obliged to leave Macao by the bishop and clergy, that their consecrated island might not be defiled by a heretic! This is the same spirit, though now restrained, which kindled the flames of Smithfield for Ridley and Cranmer,—men whose *shoes* I should have been honoured to carry.

"When I came to Canton I hired a factory, and have applied to the language with all my heart. It is Herculéan labour, and requires all the energies of the mind; but I hope to master it in course of time.

"I have sent six parts of the New Testament; translated by Mr. Morrison, to the Mauritius Bible Society. The whole is now printing, and will be ready about the close of this season. If you would esteem a complete copy of the Chinese New Testament as a curiosity for your library, I beg you will inform me, and one shall be sent.

"I am still of opinion that the letter published, by order, in the Government Gazette, about my addressing the slaves, did much *injustice* to my character, and intentions. I know that this was not intentionally done; but as both his Excellency and yourself were convinced of the falsehood of the reports,—

which malice alone could have raised,—I hope the letter will not be suffered to stand in the records of Government. This, my dear sir, is a piece of justice which I *claim* from you, whose heart would be grieved to permit any word to stand which reflects dishonour on the innocent. I send you a copy of a notice (on the subject) for the Gazette, entreating you to have the goodness to see that it be published.

"I return you many thanks for the interest you took in my object whilst I was in the Mauritius. I beg that my dutiful remembrances may be presented to his Excellency, the Governor. I hope you will continue your favour to the Mission. I rely on your goodness for all this. It would, however, ill suit the character of a *Missionary* to close a letter without dropping a hint on the subject of religion. Your situation, honoured sir, is one of much importance, although it has, no doubt, many trials and perplexities. But earth is not the *portion* of the soul. Time hurries us on to eternity. A good conscience is worth millions of worlds. None can be truly happy without a pure heart, a holy life, and an interest in the salvation of Christ.

"About three months ago, not fewer than 30,000 persons lost their lives in China, by a great overflowing of water, occasioned by an earthquake, it is said. The pride of the Mandarins, and the servility, intriguing, and covetousness of all classes of the Chinese, seem beyond description."

Mr. and Mrs. Milne had received, whilst at the Cape, much kindness from the chief judge of Bengal, John Herbert Harrington, Esq., and from his lady, who were there for their health. This they did not forget in China. Mr. Milne seems, from his notes, to have written very fully to that gentleman on the subject nearest to his heart—the state and prospects of China; but his letter-book contains only the *heads* of the information, introduced thus:—"Your Christian friendship and benevolence lay us under many obligations. We have a lively remembrance of them, and of your worthy lady, in our prayers. It gave us great joy to hear that her health and spirits were much improved, and that you were both about to return to India. There, we trust, your lives and influence will be employed for the honour of God and the good of mankind, in some form or other." This letter, like all the rest, refers to the *difficulty* of the Chinese language. Let it be remembered, however, that Mr. Milne had not spent three months at it, when he could both read and write a letter. I have now before me specimens of his writing at the time, and the characters might be from metal types, they are so neat. The celebrated *De Chavagnac* did not make such progress at first. In one of his letters to *Le Gobien*, he says, "As to the language of this country, I can assure you that no one would take the pains to learn it who is not heartily concerned for the advancement of religion. I myself have employed *eight* hours daily, for these *five* months, in copying dictionaries. I am now qualified to learn to read; conning over the characters, and spelling them like a child, with a linguist."

Having quoted *Chavagnac*, it is only fair to say, that, like Milne he was much shocked by the *vices* of the Chinese, as well as by their privations. "The spirit of usury is such amongst them," he says, "that nothing but the *special* grace of Heaven could lead them to restore the ill-gotten property, in order to be baptized." "The corruption and depravity of their hearts form an equal hinderance to their conversion. They never scruple to commit the most enormous crimes in secret, provided they do but keep up a virtuous exterior. About a fortnight since a *Bonze* came, and desired me to instruct him. He promised to submit to whatever I enjoined; but, no sooner had I set before him the purity God requires in a Christian, and our law, which is so holy as to forbid an impure thought or desire, than he replied, "If that be the case, I shall never turn Christian!" Yet he was perfectly sensible of the *truth* of our religion." The worthy Father had many disappointments of this kind; and as such will occur again to our Missionaries, it may be well to record one or two. "The Chinese are so *madly* prejudiced in favour of their own country, manners, and maxims, that they cannot imagine any thing, not Chinese, to deserve the least regard. They will confess that all things in Christianity are august, holy, and well grounded; so that one would suppose they were coming over to us: but so far from this, they coldly answer,—Can any good thing be produced out of China? Your religion is not in our books. Is there any truth unknown to our literati?" It was Chavagnac who first showed the literati of Nanchang a universal map. "They searched long for China; and at last mistook one of the hemispheres, embracing Europe, Asia, and Africa, for it. I let them go on in their error for some time. At last, one of them desired me to explain the *names* in the map. There, I said, are Europe, Asia, and Africa. (America they thought too large for the rest of the earth.) There is Persia, India, Tartary. 'But where is *China*,' they all cried. '"Tis in that *nook*,' I said; 'and these are its limits.' Words can never express the astonishment they manifested: they gazed on each other, saying, '*Ciao te kin;*' it is very small!"

Mr. Milne, it will be recollected, felt a deep interest in Mr. Campbell's exploratory Mission to Africa, when at the Cape. He did not forget it when in China. One of his first letters was to Mr. Campbell; and its history is remarkable. It is thus endorsed by Mr. Campbell himself:—This letter came from China in the "William Pitt, East Indiaman." She was supposed to have struck upon a sunken rock, about 150 miles off the coast of South Africa, and all on board to have perished, as none were ever heard of afterwards. The loss of the ship was known only by the lid of a box, and a parcel of letters wrapt in wax cloth, being driven ashore at Algoa bay, 500 miles N. E. from the Cape of Good Hope. This was one of the letters in that bag, and was forwarded to me whilst in Africa." There is nothing peculiar in the letter itself, but its *cheerfulness*. It begins thus: "Though I am so much fatigued with writing, that to hold the pen, or even to sit, is a burden, yet I must let you see that I can still write English, although rather clumsily. I hear you go on speedily in your African discoveries. It will be an act of the greatest charity to let me have two or three sheets from you, on your return. You will have much to tell the world! I sent you an account of Madagascar, and some thoughts on the plan of a Mission to that Island; and also of one to the Mauritius. I hope they came to hand. If I can collect any thing worth reading, I will write to you."

CHAPTER VI.

MR. MILNE'S RECEPTION IN CHINA

Dr. Milne will be now, chiefly, his own biographer. No one can regret this, when I state that the following narrative of his labours was drawn up at the request and under the supervision of Dr. Morrison. This is a pledge for both its accuracy and modesty. I leave it therefore to make its own impression; part of which will be, that I have not given my friend credit for more piety or talent than his own pen sustains, nor for more missionary spirit than his labours evince. I have taken no liberties whatever with his narrative, except to illustrate it here and there by anecdotes, or subsequent events. He introduces his autobiographical sketch thus:—

"The difficulty of writing with impartiality any narrative in which the author himself has acted a part, and where he in a manner becomes his own historian, is universally confessed: I now begin to *feel* this difficulty.

"Few men like to interweave their own errors, weaknesses, and foibles, into their narrative; and, whatever a false modesty may have taught them to say or to write, there are perhaps in reality, but very few who would cheerfully hold up their *partners* in any work, to the view and respect of the public, where they evidently see that such an exhibition will throw themselves into the shade. All men who act from principle (and who is there that does not at least wish it to be supposed that *he* acts thus?) conceive that their views, plans, and line of conduct are upon the whole right, and, in as far as they can see for the time, *better* than any other they could adopt; hence, it is hardly to be wondered at, if they sometimes speak and write of them in terms which strongly imply *self-approbation*. When a man writes a narrative in which his own opinions and actions form part of his materials, it may be a question whether in referring to himself, he should speak in the *first* person or in the *third*, whether he should say, "*I did*," or "*he did.*" To condemn the former, as displaying vain egotism, would be no less improper than to commend the latter as a proof of retiring modesty. In writing in the third person, a man perhaps stands a better chance of escaping severe criticism: while he who writes in the first person, enjoys some advantage of going on with more *facility* in his subject. Believing both methods to be equally good and equally fit as a medium to display either vanity or modesty, according to the state of the writer's mind, I have therefore, in what follows, not been at all scrupulous about the matter, but have written in the first or third person, as they chanced to occur to my thoughts at the time. If the reader think, that in any instance I have overstepped the bounds of modesty, and done *more* than justice to myself, I request he will ascribe it to a principle which is very common to man, perhaps inseparable from his nature;—namely, *a desire to be thought favourably of, by mankind.*

" To return from this digression. The expense of my journey to London, as well as a considerable part of the preparations for it, was borne by the Aberdeen Missionary Society. I ever felt my obligations to the Directors of *that* Society, for their great kindness, both in their official and individual capacity. The correspondence of several of these worthy men, often proves refreshing and instructive to me in these Heathen lands. While at Gosport, I pursued my studies with as much assiduity as my bodily strength would admit. I began with scarce any hope of success; but resolved that if I should not be successful, it should not be for want of application. The first intimations of the Society's wish to appoint me to the Chinese Mission, were received with surprise and fear; but having no predilection for any particular place, I referred the decision to the Directors; hoping that Divine Providence would overrule their determination for my own good, and that of the cause which I wished to serve. It has since often proved a source of satisfaction that, by a voluntary act, I put the decision *out* of my own power. Having gone through the usual course of studies, and being fortunate enough to obtain the approbation of my tutor, to whose paternal kindness I ever feel deeply indebted, I was ordained to the Gospel Ministry on the 12th July, 1812. On the 4th of the following September, I went with Mrs. Milne, who was also from the North of Scotland, on board of ship at Portsmouth, to sail for the Cape of Good Hope. At the Cape we met with some of our old friends, and experienced much kindness from the Christians there. We were introduced to John Herbert Harrington, Esquire, who, together with Mrs. Harrington, were on a visit from Bengal; these worthy persons showed us great kindness; and have ever since continued their benevolent attentions both to our family and work." (This early and influential friend of missions, was induced to return to India for a few years with Lord Amherst, after having retired from office, to spend the evening of life at home. That evening he was disappointed of: he died just as he came in sight of England again.) "We next sailed by way of the Isle of France, where, at the request of one of the Directors of the Missionary Society, I employed myself in collecting information relative to the Island of MADAGASCAR, to which the Society was about to send a Mission. A small pamphlet was compiled partly from French books met with there, and partly from the verbal communications of those who had resided at Madagascar. These imperfect hints were afterwards published at the end of the Rev. John Campbell's book of Travels in South Africa. It was intended that I should visit that island, if a convenient opportunity offered, which was not the case during our stay at the Isle of France. On the 4th July, 1813, we arrived safely at Macao, and were most cordially welcomed by Mr. and Mrs. Morrison." Thus briefly is his voyage to China told: and thus easily is it made, too, now. It was not always thus safe to sail to Macao. Father Avril, who discovered an overland route to China, says that, "of 600 Missionaries who had sailed from France to China, only one hundred arrived: the rest perished by sickness or shipwreck." (*Avril's Travels.*) "I commenced the study of the Chinese language, under the same impressions as those with which I had begun my studies at Gosport. I had an idea that the language was extremely difficult (an idea which I have never yet seen any reason to change,) and felt convinced that, for a person of very humble talents, great diligence, undivided attention, and continued perseverance were requisite, in order to his attaining, after long application, as much knowledge of it as would enable him to be of *any* service in the cause of Christianity.

"I therefore resolved that, in as far as it should please God to give bodily health, I would labour to the *utmost* of my strength, and not be discouraged if my progress should be very slow. I began under more favourable circumstances than my fellow-labourer had done. I had the aid of Dr. Morrison's writings on the Chinese language, of his experience acquired through a period of six years, and hoped to enjoy his personal instructions for a considerable time. But, on the 2d or 3d day after I began, a verbal order was sent from the (then) Portuguese Governor of Macao, commanding me to leave the settlement in eight days; which was shortly after followed by another message, ordering me to go on board a vessel that was then going out of Port. It was in vain stated to the Governor, that I would pledge myself to leave the place in the course of one or two years, after acquiring some knowledge of the Chinese language. No, the order to depart must be obeyed. This measure was considered by some disinterested persons, both of the English and other factories, as very inhospitable and ungrateful. They reasoned thus: 'Mr. Milne is a subject of Great Britain—a country that is spilling its blood and wasting its treasures, to preserve the integrity of the kingdom of Portugal; moreover, he has infringed none of the local regulations of the Portuguese in this place. Hence, it can hardly be considered honourable to refuse the ordinary rights of hospitality to any subject of an allied country. But Mr. Milne, it is supposed, has some religious object in view, which it is feared, may prove detrimental to the interests of the Church of Rome; therefore the zeal of the Catholic clergy is awakened against him. Still, whatever his ultimate views may be, he has not yet appeared in any other capacity in Macao, than that of a British subject; and when it is considered how ample a toleration, and how many privileges the Catholic clergy enjoy in England, and in the British possessions in India, it cannot be viewed as an equitable proceeding to deny a temporary residence to an individual who has perhaps not the wish, and certainly not the power, of doing any thing against the Romish religion on its present footing in Macao.' Such were the views which some gentlemen who acted a friendly part on this occasion, had of the subject. Whatever their own particular sentiments of religion, or of Missionary efforts, were, is another matter. They viewed this measure rather politically than religiously; and some of them were not backward to use their influence to obtain a revocation of the order. The kind attention of the chiefs of the Dutch and Swedish factories, and of several gentlemen, in the English factory, on the occasion, laid me under many obligations. It was necessary, however, for the time, to remove. I accordingly left Macao on the 20th July, (Mrs. Milne being allowed to remain with our friends,) and went in a small boat to Canton, where I remained the ensuing season; enjoying that hospitality among the *Heathen*, which had been denied in a Christian colony! Not having been long from my native country, and having generally met with kindness in the colonies which we passed on our way out, I no doubt felt more at being driven from Macao, than a person who had seen more of strange countries, and passed through more of the varieties of life, would have done. Afterwards, when reflecting more maturely on the subject, I saw that there was reason to make every possible allowance for the conduct of the government of Macao, and to put as favourable a construction upon it as it would bear. I was aware that the Governor did it not from personal ill-will: his official situation probably rendered it prudent to listen to the voice of the church." (That church could treat some of her own Missionaries in this style. In 1704, D. Fontaney had to vindicate the Jesuits to the confessor of the king of France, for their harsh treatment of the French Missionaries, on their landing at Macao. The Frenchmen did not find the Portuguese free from the spirit of jealousy or rivalship.—*Locker, Vol. 2, p.* 180. Even Ricci and his colleagues were denounced by the Portuguese as spies and traitors, when they landed at Macao. See *Le Compte's China, p.* 359. Thus, commercial as well as sectarian rivalry, had something to do with Portuguese jealousy from the first. Brotherhood at Rome is not a security for brotherly kindness abroad.) " Here it is but just to acknowledge that, subsequently, I was permitted to return to Macao, when my affairs required it; and that I never after met with any farther impediment from the government or from the people; on the contrary, the kindness of several respectable Portuguese families deserves my hearty acknowledgments. For some time I continued labouring at the language in Canton, with but little assistance, till Dr. Morrison came up with the factory, when I enjoyed the benefits of his tuition for about three months.

"Not considering myself a competent judge of the

methods proper for acquiring the singular and difficult language of China, I resigned myself *entirely* to his direction; a measure which I have ever had the *highest* cause to be satisfied with. He suggested the importance of laying aside, for a time, almost every other study, and spending the whole strength of body and mind in one pursuit, viz., that of the language. The whole day, from morning till late at night, was accordingly employed in Chinese studies. My other pursuits were laid aside for the time; even theology, and the critical study of the sacred Scriptures, for which a peculiar partiality had always been felt, were scarcely attended to above an hour in a whole week. This sacrifice appeared at first exceedingly *hard* to make, but the advantage was afterwards experienced. Three other suggestions of the same gentleman, respecting the study of the Chinese language, I shall here mention, partly to testify my obligation for them, and partly for the consideration of those who may in future study Chinese. He remarked that, in learning a foreign language, he thought a person should at first attend much to the *colloquial* dialect, because when he can once ask a few questions, and is master of a few constantly recurring phrases, he will then be able to derive benefit from the instructions of a native teacher, and also be daily gathering something from what he hears in conversation.

"Again, it was observed that, from the nature of the Chinese language, it seemed to be of importance for the learner to commit *much* to memory. The practice of the Chinese themselves strongly confirms this remark.

"Finally, he advised that, in reading, particular

attention should be paid to the character. A few characters should every day be written and carefully analyzed. These suggestions I found of great service; and when the urgent necessity there is for commencing the work of instruction among the Heathen as early as possible is considered, I think an attention to the first three of these remarks will early and amply repay their labour, while a rigorous adherence to the last remark, namely, a careful attention to the *character*, will in course of time secure a degree of correctness which is very essential in writing on sacred subjects.

" On the 14th October, 1813, our daughter Rachel Amelia was born; she was baptized on the 23d January, 1814.

" While in Canton, it was necessary for me to hire apartments, generally called a factory here, which, though small, cost 500 Spanish dollars for the season. To a person without the ordinary commercial prospects which bring most foreigners to Canton, and who was supported by a benevolent society, this sum was large; but there was no means of avoiding it.

"Being then incapable of doing any thing in the Chinese language, and as there was no public religious instruction in the English language in Canton, I preached in this " hired house " on the Sabbaths, during that and the following winter, to those from the different foreign factories and ships who chose to attend. Dr. Morrison had a Sunday lecture in Macao, for the benefit of those who wish to avail themselves thereof.

" Here I would again detain the reader, while I remark that the Chinese, however opposed to the

Gospel themselves, yet never *object* to foreigners using the religions of their respective nations whatever these may be. On the contrary, men who seem to regard no God, and treat with contempt every kind of religion, *sink* greatly in the estimation of the sober-minded. The foreign commercial establishments in China are considered the representatives of their several countries; and to leave them totally destitute of religious ordinances, and of public teachers, tends to diminish their *national* consequence in the eyes of the Chinese; and not, as some have foolishly thought, to lessen the suspicions of that people. Independent, however, of any political consideration, the fact that the several factories are without Christian ordinances, and that there are several thousands of foreigners, English, Americans, &c., professing the Gospel, for three or four months annually, during the time the ships are in China, entirely destitute of Christian instruction, will not be viewed as a light matter by the friends of truth, morality and religion. The effect of those instructions which our countrymen receive from their respective clergymen and pastors at home, is often lost in the contaminations which reign around them while abroad; and many of them die in China without any one to administer salutary instruction and consolation in their last moments! It is earnestly to be wished that the different Christian nations which trade at Canton, particularly England and America, from which the greatest number of persons annually come, would seriously consider this, and speedily adopt suitable means for the removal of so great an evil. One or two Christian ministers of exemplary and consistent character, who would value a situation more for the opportunities it affords of doing good, than for the prospect it holds forth of raising them speedily to wealth and independence, would be exceedingly useful among the Protestant foreigners in China. Christians are not the proper objects of a Missionary's labour, neither has he time to spend in their instruction: that belongs more properly to ministers who have a fixed charge. I would gladly provoke the Churches in England and America to this 'work of faith and labour of love;' and hope their choice of agents for this important service will fall upon men of piety, learning, and dignity of conduct—men who, while they are free from those useless peculiarities which would disgust persons of rank and education, will consider it as a duty cheerfully to attend the *hammocks* and sick beds of poor illiterate sailors—men whose conduct will command respect, reverence, and affection, do honour to their character as ministers of Christ, reflect credit on the Protestant faith in the presence of its enemies, and tend to draw forth the esteem of the Heathen around them.

"Dr. Morrison, some time since, suggested the importance of this idea to some clerical persons in America." (Happily, Dr. Morrison lived to see his suggestion acted upon, and to have American colleagues at Canton.)

As Mr. Milne mastered the Chinese language soon, and thus partly *disproved* his own opinion, I may safely add to this chapter the original form of his opinion. "To acquire the Chinese is a work for men with *bodies* of brass, *lungs* of steel, *heads* of oak, *hands* of spring-steel, *eyes* of eagles, *hearts* of apostles, *memories* of angels, and *lives* of Methuselahs!

Still I make a little progress. I hope, if not to be master, yet to gain as much as will suit the purposes of a Missionary. Every sentence gained I value at the rate of a *dollar;* so that should I gain 10,000, I shall not consider myself poor!" MSS., 1814.)

CHAPTER VII.

MR. MILNE'S VISIT TO JAVA.

" Dr. Morrison had now, by his own individual labour, brought the translation of the New Testament near to a close; it was finished and revised in the end of 1813. Though he did not consider the work as laying claims to perfection, yet the completion of it was viewed as constituting an *era* in the Chinese Mission. It was an event which every good Christian ardently wished for; and, as a commencement to the work of evangelizing China, it was a most important attainment. The news gladdened the hearts of many thousands of Christians at home, who offered up their most cordial thanks to God, for his goodness in preserving the translator's life to finish the work, and their most fervent prayers for its success. The translator was never elated with his work; yet he felt grateful to the author of his being for making him thus far instrumental in serving the cause for which he left his native shores; and his colleague deemed himself happy in reaching China, just when the second volume of the sacred oracles was ready to be put into the hands of the

Heathen. Dr. Morrison had, as already noticed, brought out with him from England a manuscript containing the Acts and some of Paul's Epistles, which had been at a former period rendered into Chinese, by some Catholic Missionary. These he found of much assistance in his first efforts to communicate Christian knowledge to the Heathen; and he frequently derived assistance from them in course of the translation. He deemed it right publicly to acknowledge his obligations to his *unknown* predecessor, the author of the MS., which was done in a letter addressed to the Committee of the British and Foreign Bible Society. Dr. M. was not ignorant of the efforts that were making in Bengal by the members of the Baptist Mission, in the same cause; nor is any thing here said with a view to disparage, or throw a veil over, the highly useful labours of so meritorious a body of men. On the contrary, Dr. M., from the beginning, thought that the labours of several individuals, instructed by different native teachers, would ultimately contribute to the progressive perfection of a translation of the Divine oracles into Chinese. He hoped that the harmony of the Gospels (by the Catholic Missionaries,) and several of the epistles, as well as a Chinese teacher, all of which he had before procured for and sent to them, would contribute in some degree to the progress and perfection of their version."

The candour of all this is delightful! It was not, however, always reciprocated! The church of Rome ought to have said something of her claims when this statement was given to the world. Morrison and Milne told all they knew of her Chinese translations. If, however, *Le Compte* is to be credited, her Missionaries translated the entire Scriptures into Chinese. He says expressly, that the translation was *completed*, although, he adds, "it would be rash imprudence to publish it now." The Pope forbade the use of a Chinese Missal: did he interdict the Scriptures too? This subject will come up again.—*Le Compte's China*, p. 391.

"About this time, Dr. Morrison heard of the good effects of his tract, on 'The Redemption of the World,' in reforming a native Chinese of vicious manners, who had, in early life, been educated as a Roman Catholic. This encouraged him to hope that his labour, though carried on under very unpromising circumstances, would not 'be in vain in the Lord.' Many thousand copies of that small publication have since been widely circulated among the Chinese. The fruits do not immediately appear; but 'the word of Jehovah shall not return to him void; it shall prosper in the thing whereunto he sent it.'

"As Mr. Milne was not permitted to remain in Macao, and could not, without some danger of attracting the attention of Government, continue in Canton all the year round, it became a question, what was the most proper course to take. After due deliberation, it was resolved, that, as the New Testament and several tracts were finished, an edition of them should be printed; and that he should go through the chief Chinese settlements in the Malay Archipelago, and circulate them as widely as possible. The objects of this tour were:—

"1. To circulate the New Testament and tracts.

"2. To seek a quiet and peaceful retreat, where the chief seat of the Chinese Mission should be fixed; and where those important labours, which could not be carried on to great extent under a persecuting government, might be pursued without interruption.

"3. To make such memoranda of the Chinese population, circumstances, &c., as might in future assist to direct the operations of the Mission with regard to the means proper for spreading the Gospel among them.

"4. To inquire what facilities existed in Java and Penang for printing a volume of *Dialogues, Chinese and English,* compiled by Dr. Morrison, with the view of assisting his junior brethren in the acquisition of the Chinese language. These were the principal ends of the proposed tour. The books resolved to be printed and circulated, were—New Testament, 2,000; Tract, 10,000, Catechism, 5,000. Total 17,000.

"To carry these through the press, at a time when the jealousy of the Chinese government was feelingly alive to every movement of foreigners, was a work attended with no ordinary anxiety. Happy Britons and Americans!—ye know not the anxieties which despotism occasions. Though the servants of God have no reason to be appalled by the fury of the oppressor, because there is an arm that can restrain the wrath of man, yet it is in human nature to feel solicitude. However, it pleased God, under whose control are all the movements of human society, so to order it that the whole impression was carried through, and suitably disposed of, without exciting the public attention.

"When the printing was finished, the greater part of the edition was placed under Mr. Milne's care, for distribution among the Chinese emigrants in the places already named. He had then scarcely learned the rudiments of the Chinese language, as he had not attended to it above six months; more than a third of which time he had laboured under great disadvantages, being obliged to *fag alone* without the assistance of his senior brother. He of course felt his extreme inadequacy for a work in which a much greater acquaintance with the colloquial Chinese was necessary. To be so early deprived of the tuition of Dr. Morrison, to whose personal kindness and pious counsels, he was no less indebted, than to his attainments in Chinese literature, was very painful to him. It was, however, a great ease to his mind to leave his family under the kind care of Mr. and Mrs. M., and in the midst of some benevolent persons, whose attentions were ever ready and abundant. At Dr. Morrison's suggestion he had committed to memory the volume of Dialogues, formerly mentioned, and copied over both it and the grammar, which labour he found of exceeding great service afterwards—he had begun to read in the more easy colloquial books, and could write the character imperfectly. With these very inadequate qualifications, and with a teacher who knew not a single word of any language but his own, he set out on his tour; resolving to do the best he could; and hoping that, by the divine blessing, the service which he was going upon, would contribute its quota to the establishment of truth and righteousness in the earth. The advices and judicial counsels of his faithful friend, proved exceedingly useful; they were often adverted to during his absence in the islands.

"After having, with two gentlemen who were in the same boat, narrowly escaped seizure by a Chinese war-boat, he went on board the ship 'James Drummond,' bound to Java, by way of Banca. She was carrying 450 Chinese emigrants, who were landed at the latter place. While on board, twenty-five copies of the New Testament (perhaps the *first* complete copies of the Chinese Testament ever disposed of,) and many tracts were distributed among these poor men who were going abroad in search of their daily bread." (Both Morrison and Milne can *afford* to let me say, that *Corvinus*, in 1315, published his Tartar version, in China: Moshian says, "in a beautiful form." I have read somewhere of a *Gothic* one found in the interior, by a Jesuit. The family to whom it belonged would not sell it for any money. They called it their "*Thesaurus.*" I regret that I cannot *name* my authority for this fact, at present.) "In this service he had the assistance of a fellow passenger, W. S. D. Esq., son of the Rev. Dr. D., of Rayne, North of Scotland, whose obliging manners and intelligent conversation rendered the passage very agreeable. This gentleman introduced Mr. Milne to the kindness of several official persons on their arrival in Java; and has ever since continued to manifest to him and his family, a degree of benevolent and friendly attention, which deserves their warmest acknowledgments.

"At Banca, where there is a considerable number of Chinese employed chiefly in the tin mines, some New Testaments and tracts were distributed, and others left under the charge of Captain, (now Major) Court, the resident, who afterwards caused them to be circulated at the different mines. This gentleman manifested much politeness towards Mr. Milne, for which he ever felt grateful.

"On the 10th of March, the vessel arrived at Batavia. Mr. Milne, being an entire stranger, lodged in one of the taverns of that *unhealthy* city for sixteen days;" (it is very much improved since;) "after which, by the kindness of the government, he obtained lodgings at a little distance from town, in a more pleasant and healthy situation, and near to two gentlemen whose kindness, together with that of their families, he can never be sufficiently thankful for, viz.: the Rev. Professor Ross, of the Dutch reformed church, and the Rev. W. Robinson, a member of the Baptist Mission in India. Many agreeable hours were spent in their company, after the fatigues of the day, in going from house to house among the Chinese, were over. Before leaving China, he received a letter of introduction from J. T. E., Esq., chief of the H. E. I. Company's factory, to the Honourable Sir T. Stamford Raffles Lieutenant-Governor of Java, who, in the most handsome manner, afforded every facility to his objects. Governor Raffles viewed every judicious attempt to spread the knowledge of Christianity as tending to improve the state of civil society, and to render Governments prosperous and stable. Hence, he furnished Mr. M. with the means of travelling at the expense of Government, through the interior and eastern parts of the island; and proposed to afford him facilities for visiting Pontiano, Sambas, and Banjermasin, on the island of Borneo, where many thousands of Chinese are settled. The war with Balli and at Maccasser, and other circumstances, prevented any attempt being made to carry this last proposal into execution. Arrangements, however, were made before Mr. M.'s departure from Java, for sending Testaments and tracts to those Chinese colonies.

"When Mr. Milne began his journey to the interior and eastern parts of Java, the Governor gave him letters of introduction to the residents, and principal British Officers and Native Princes in the settlements through which he had to pass:—who all uniformly treated him with kindness, and rendered him every needful assistance. Before leaving Batavia, he sent round by sea, several boxes of books to the chief eastern ports; and took some large packages in the carriage in which he travelled, for circulation in the small Chinese settlements in the hills, and along the road. He visited all the chief towns, (except Djocjo-carto,) and villages on Java, where the greatest number of Chinese reside; and circulated among them the New Testament and tracts. From Java he passed over to the adjoining island of Madura, on which there are also several Chinese settlements; and where the word of God was also circulated. On his return from the eastward to Batavia, he narrowly escaped shipwreck. Had the vessel been detained at sea sixteen hours longer, all that were in her must, according to human probability, have perished, as she sunk in the roads, the morning after they left her. The good hand of God saved him from this, and several other imminent dangers to which he was exposed in the interior. While at Batavia, he had occasional slight attacks of fever and ague, but was mercifully preserved from that devouring disease, the Batavia fever, which has swept off its tens of thousands, and which proved fatal to W. Robertson, Esquire, a medical gentleman, who had travelled in company with him a considerable part of the journey to and from the eastern settlements.

"While on Java, and other islands, he used his best endeavours to put the books committed to his care into the most proper channels. Though they were generally well received by the Chinese, yet immediate good fruits could not be looked for.

"The tracts and books must be followed by the preaching of the Gospel, before their full effect be known. It is also a very possible case that some of them may have been destroyed—some of them neglected—some of them never read—some of them sold for gain—and some parts of them but very imperfectly understood; yet he was not discouraged by any, or all of these considerations. For he thought that if *one-tenth,* yea, *one hundredth part,* should in course of a century to come, answer the great end proposed, the heavy expense which the Christian public had been at in preparing, printing, and circulating them, would be more than amply repaid. He hoped that some of his three brethren who had just come to Java, The Rev. Messrs. Kam, Bruckner, and Supper—the last of whom fell a sacrifice to the Batavia fever in the close of 1816, would study the Chinese language, and follow up the distribution of the written word, by oral instruction; and that the Missionary Society would soon appoint others to labour in that important island, for the conversion of the Chinese. As Java has now reverted to the King of the Netherlands, it is sincerely wished that the *Dutch Missionary Society* may also adopt some measures for the same purpose. The first establishment of Christianity in the Molucca Islands, the translation of the whole Scriptures into the Malay, and the composition of several excellent theological pieces in the same language, will continue, as long as history can preserve records, as imperishable monuments of the pious industry and extensive erudition of Dutch divines; and of the liberality of that Government which bore the whole expense. The faithful men who did the work, have long since gone to their reward—but their labours remain—'Divine Providence has commanded devouring time to respect and spare them' for the instruction of future generations, and as facilities to future labourers.

"The Dutch Christians in Batavia manifested much kindness to Mr. Milne; and gave him encouragement to hope that some of them would, in their several stations, use means to impress the truths of the Gospel upon their Chinese neighbours. It is hoped, that they will now, when Providence has replaced the reins of Government in the hands of their country, come vigorously forward to occupy the ground which is so effectually within their reach. Those engaged in the Chinese Mission will rejoice if they can do any thing to farther their efforts in so good a work.

"On the 4th of August, Mr. Milne left Java, and on the 11th, arrived at Malacca, where he was employed till the 18th, in the same manner as he had been on Java. He had an introductory letter from Governor Raffles, to Major W. Farquhar, the Resident and Commandant, who behaved in the most kind and generous manner to him, affording every assistance to the work in which he was engaged. Mr. Milne had taken a Chinese printer with him from China; and in addition to the books brought with him, he had printed at Java and Malacca, a translation of the 1st of Genesis, 1800—Tract, 300—Hand-bill, 1,000—and farewell address (the last only of his own composition.) As the season for returning to China was pretty far gone, he was obliged to give up all idea of proceeding to Penang, as was originally intended; but found means of forwarding some Chinese Testaments and Tracts to that island, as well as to Rhio, Bintang, Tringana, Siak, and other places where Chinese were settled.

"On the 5th September, 1814, he again reached China, and was in great mercy restored to his friends. In the relation of his tour, there was found much ground for thankfulness to God; and some reason to hope that his being formerly prohibited to remain in Macao, would, contrary to the design of the authors of that prohibition, "turn out for the furtherance of the Gospel."

These grateful and respectful references to Sir Stamford Raffles were cordially reciprocated by that highly intelligent and philanthropic gentleman. In saying this, I do not refer chiefly to the public testimony he bore to the character of Dr. Milne, but to the manner in which he spoke of him in private, whenever the subject of Missions was introduced. I had opportunities of knowing this, whilst he was visiting his cousin, Dr. Raffles, at Liverpool; and have this year compared my recollections with those of my old friend, who says, that his Cousin's private letters to him are even more explicit than the eulogiums I heard from his lips.

"The farewell Address, written by Mr. Milne at this time, was translated after his death by Dr. Morrison. I preserve it, as a specimen of his spirit.

"TRANSLATION OF A FAREWELL LETTER TO THE CHINESE ON JAVA.

"*A general address to the respected people of the* TA-TSING *Dynasty, who dwell in Pa, (Batavia) and in other places (on Java.)*

"BENEVOLENT ELDER BRETHREN,

"Peace, prosperity, ten thousand blessings, and all the good which you desire.

"Your younger brother, intending to visit other ports, presents this parting token of respect, but his eyes will constantly look towards you; his heart, always ruminating, will remember you, and resolves to pray, that the Deity may bless you, your children, and your children's children, to ten thousand generations.

"Your younger brother thinks, that the Maker of the heavens and the earth is the one only true and living God, and there is none else.

"The past, the present, and the future, are fully known to God. He rewards goodness, punishes wickedness, and can do all things.

"The gods who have not made the heavens and the earth cannot endure as the heavens and the earth, (that is, must perish;) but the true and living God will exist externally. He made and nourishes all men under heaven, and will judge all. When we sit—when we sleep—when we speak—and when we think, God observes all.

"No man can at any time see God; therefore no man understands his form.

"All human beings under heaven have often sinned against God, and deserve to suffer his displeasure. But God, being merciful and gracious, sent his only son Jesus into the world to practise virtue, and to redeem them from their iniquities, in order that all who repent of their sins, and trust in Jesus, should obtain eternal life in heaven. Those who do not receive his doctrines, but work iniquity, must go down to hell, (that is, earth's prison) and suffer undefined punishment.

"These are the doctrines of the holy books which your younger brother has presented to you, his respected friends.

"These books teach men about the affairs of ancient times, concerning the character of men of the present age—the happiness and misery of the life to come—the temple of heaven—and the prison of hell.

"Some parts of these books are, perhaps, not easily understood at present; but pray to God to unfold them—every day read a little—perhaps some person will come to explain them to you—then you will be able to understand.

"Remember what the Sages have said,—

'Do not blot or destroy good books.'

"Brethren, this life is temporary. Still things under the sun are vanity; therefore do not set your hearts upon them.

"While we live, the riches of the world have their use—when we die, they are altogether useless after death: we cannot carry away a single Wan (that is, none at all.) Seek God's gracious favour; deal justly with all; let not the rich greedily oppress the poor, nor the poor discontentedly complain of their lot; for both rich and poor must shortly die.

"Parents, teach your children to read the sacred book—to write—to trust in Jesus Christ—to venerate the aged—to discharge filial piety to you—to love their brothers and sisters—to pity the poor, and do good to all men—then all will be well.

"Your younger Brother
"ME-LEEN,
"Bows and pays his respects.
"*Batavia*, 19th day of the 5th moon of the 19th year of Kea-king; or July 5th, 1814."

CHAPTER VIII.

JOINT LABOURS IN CHINA.

"In the month of April, 1814, during his colleague's absence in the islands, Dr. Morrison published a small tract, containing a general outline of the Old Testament history. The creation, the deluge, the descent of the children of Israel into Egypt, and their deliverance from thence, the giving of the law and other principal events down to the coming of the Messiah, are briefly noticed, and interspersed with quotations from the sacred volume, teaching the unity of God, the end of sacrifices, &c.

"In the same month a small collection of spiritual songs or hymns to be used in the worship of God, was sent to press. Most of them were originally prose translations made by Dr. Morrison, from the Scotch version of the Psalms, and from the paraphrastic hymns of that Church, from Dr. Watts' hymns, and the Olney hymns, by Cowper and Newton. From prose they were turned into verse by Dr. Morrison's Chinese assistant and his son. As poetic compositions, they perhaps do not excel, but they contain the most important matter for Christian edification, and are capable of being sung in congregations and families. Dr. Morrison employed his assistants in this labour on the Sabbath days; hoping that by turning their attention to divine subjects, some good effects might be produced on their own hearts, while preparing materials of usefulness to others.

"(On the 17th April, 1814, John Morrison was born; and baptized on the 1st May.)

"The chief part of the edition of the New Testament, noticed in the preceding section, having been circulated in the islands of the Archipelago, and on the border of China, it was thought necessary to prepare the way for another. The former edition was printed in a large octavo size, in conformity to the most respectable editions of the Sze-shoo and other Chinese classical books. But for a book of this size, much paper is required; hence it becomes very expensive. This consideration induced Dr. Morrison to think of a new edition in a duodecimo size.

"1. Because it would be less expensive than the octavo edition.

"2. Because, in the present state of China, it was desirable to multiply sets of blocks. One set could be easily destroyed or lost. If there were two or more sets, the chance of preserving the work and extending its usefulness, was greater. He had often contemplated, not to say the necessity, but the propriety, of removing from Canton to Penang, or Malacca, where he might enjoy more liberty to pursue his work with an easy mind. In that event, he was desirous of leaving a set of blocks in the hand of some bookseller in China—casting, as it were, this bread of God upon the waters, in hope that it would be taken up by some one making the voyage of life, and perishing for want of wholesome food.

"Here we may also remark, that the prospect of gain arising from the sale, might induce the bookseller to print, and dispose of the sacred volume; and the success of any book in leading men to the knowledge of God, does not depend on the *motive* of the circulator. It is, indeed, devoutly to be wished, that the sale of the holy Scriptures should become an object of *gain* in China; nothing would so effectually ensure their speedy and extensive circulation. A thousand sets of blocks, (were so many wanted,) prepared at the expense of the Bible, or any other Society, and given gratis to individuals, who would diligently employ them for their own pecuniary advantage, would be most usefully bestowed. Millions of persons, to whose abodes we cannot penetrate, would be accessible to them; and, instead of an individual agent or two, thousands of volunteers would shortly offer their services. If pious Christians, or Missionaries, could always be obtained for the circulation of the Divine Oracles, it would be doubtless preferable; but as that is not uniformly the case, such instruments as can be got, should be employed; for the *days are gone,* (may they never return!) when men, hoodwinked by ignorance and superstition, supposed that every thing which did not pass through official, consecrated, and clerical hands, must necessarily lose its effects in the instruction and salvation of mankind!" (These days seemed gone, when Dr. Milne wrote; but now they seem to be returning. They are returned, so far as the great body of the clergy are concerned. Whether the *laity* of the Church of England will abet the insolent bigotry of the high priesthood, now that it out-herods the Pope, remains to be seen. Another laity, however, and "a more excellent priesthood," laugh it to scorn, as a mere political *mania*, which will defeat itself, and cover its authors with shame.)

"3. Because an edition of this size would be more portable than the former. This is an object that deserves attention in every useful work, and particularly where the state of the Government is such as to render great caution necessary in the circulation. Mr. Milne several times met with Chinese, whose only objection to the New Testament was its size. Had it been smaller, they could have taken several copies into the interior provinces, with less difficulty than they could take one. The 12mo edition is not a pocket size, but an approximation to it; and the mode of printing in China, will admit of the whole being printed in a pocket size whenever it may be wished. The Chinese have several books of this character, which they call Seu-chin, that is, a *sleeve-gem;* probably from the circumstance of their frequently carrying in their sleeve, valuable articles which Europeans usually carry in their pocket. To have the whole Scriptures in Chinese, in an edition of this size, is a desideratum, they would truly be a *gem* in the sleeve!" (Dr. Morrison says, "The Romish Missionaries published a kind of BREVIARY in this size, and with this title." They would have published the *Missal* also in Chinese, and used it, too, in the churches, had the Pope allowed them. Father *Couplet* presented the translation and the request at Rome; but his Holiness had no faith in any but *Latin* prayers.—*Le Compte*, p. 391.)

"These were the reasons which led to the resolution of getting the New Testament cut in 12mo. A printer was accordingly engaged, who undertook to cut the blocks for 500 Spanish dollars, and to cast off each copy for half a dollar. But there are always a great many incidental expenses, which cannot at first be brought into any calculation. From the despotic nature of the Chinese Government, and the covetousness of the people, such expenses exceedingly multiply. Strangers are so completely in their power, that any remonstrance is entirely vain.

"The Mission had hitherto laboured to diffuse knowledge; and it was hoped that salutary impressions were made on the minds of some of those who attended on the Sabbaths, and of others who read the Scriptures and tracts at home; but until 1814, no individual had resolution to seek to be admitted into the Church of Christ by baptism. The Chinese Government, it is true, had not then, and never yet has officially noticed the proceedings of the Protestant Mission; for it was always an object with those engaged in it, to proceed quietly, and attract as little notice as possible; still it was feared that an open profession of Christianity might excite their attention; and it was possible that they would not be at the trouble to examine and discriminate, between different modes of Christianity; but condemn it *in tôto, as a foreign religion.* This, it was believed, tended to hinder two or three persons from declaring themselves on the side of the Gospel. However, a native Chinese, named Tsae-a-ko, aged twenty-seven, after a considerable time of previous instruction and examination, came forward and confessed his faith in Jesus, in the following terms:—

"'Tsae-a-ko desires baptism. His written confession respecting himself is as follows:

"'Jesus making atonement for us, is the blessed sound. Language and thought are both inadequate to exhaust the gracious and admirable goodness of the intention of Jesus. I now believe in Jesus, and rely on his merits to obtain the remission of sin. I have sins and defects, and without faith in Jesus for the remission of sins, should be eternally miserable. Now that we have heard of the forgiveness of sins through Jesus, we ought with all our hearts to rely on his merits. He who does not do so is not a good man. I by no means rely on my own goodness. When I reflect and question myself, I perceive that from childhood till now I have had no strength—no merit—no learning. Till this my twenty-seventh year I have done nothing to answer to the goodness of God, in giving me existence in this world as a human being. I have not recompensed the kindness of my parents, my relations, my friends. Shall I repine? Shall I hope in my own good deeds? I entirely call upon God the Father, and rely upon God for the remission of sin. I also always pray to God to confer upon me the Holy Spirit.'

"Tsae-a-ko is the son of a second concubine. His father's wife died without children, when he was sixteen years of age. When he was 21, he came to my house, and heard me talk of Jesus, but says he did not well understand what I meant. That was my first year in China. Three years after, when I could speak better, and could write, he understood better; and being employed by his brother in superintending the New Testament for the press, he says, that he began to see that the merits of Jesus were able to save all men, in all ages and nations, and hence he listened to and believed in him.

"His natural temper is not good. He often disagreed with his brother and other domestics; and I thought it better that he should retire from my service. He however continued, whenever he was within a few miles, to come to worship on the Sabbath day.

"He prayed earnestly morning and evening, and read the decalogue as contained in the Catechism. He says that from the decalogue and instruction of friends, he saw his great and manifold errors—that his nature was wrong—that he had been unjust, and that he had not fulfilled his duty to his friends, or brother, or other men.

"His knowledge of course is very limited, and his views perhaps obscure, but I hope that his faith in Jesus is sincere. I took for my guide what Philip said to the Eunuch, 'If thou believest with all thine heart, thou mayest be baptized.' O that at the great day he may prove to have been a brand plucked out of the burning. May God be glorified in his eternal salvation!

"He writes a tolerably good hand. His father was a man of some property, which he lost by the wreck of a junk in the China seas, returning from Batavia. Tsae-a-ko, when at school, was often unwell, and did not make so much progress as his brother Tsae-a-heen, who is with me. Tsae-a-heen is mild and judicious, but is, I fear, in his heart, opposed to the gospel. His attendance to preaching on the Lord's day is also constant—but insincerity and want of truth are vices which cling to the Chinese character.

"At a spring of water, issuing from the foot of a lofty hill by the sea side, away from human observation, I baptized, in the name of the Father, Son, and Holy Spirit, Tsae-a-ko, whose character and confession have been given above. O that the Lord may cleanse him from all sin in the blood of Jesus, and purify his heart by the influences of the Holy Spirit! May he be the first fruits of a great harvest: one of millions who shall believe and be saved from the wrath to come.

"From this confession, the writer would remark, that if great imperfections attend the most enlightened Christians who have, from their very infancy, been trained up in the ways of God; how much more may this be expected to be the case with the first converts from paganism, who cannot be supposed in a short time, to divest themselves entirely of the influence of native prejudices, or completely to break the force of former habits!—To object to first converts, because they are less perfect than Christians who have enjoyed greater privileges, discovers great ignorance of human nature, and great inattention to the history of past ages. None but narrow-minded bigots, who take up subjects by halves; insipid moralists, swelled with pharisaical pride; and skeptics, in whose eyes religion and vice are mere relative terms, which may be changed and rechanged, according to the tempers and circumstances of mankind;—none but such will sneeringly object to them. Tsae-a-ko adhered to his profession of the Gospel until his death, which took place in 1818. He died of a consumption; but being removed to a distance from his instructer, there was no means of ascertaining the state of his mind in view of eternity." (If these pleadings for candour towards the first Chinese converts be only fair, what rampant folly it is to treat as FATHERS of the Church, the first converts from the *Gnostic* Schools of the second and third century? Tsae-a-ko's views of Christianity could hardly be more crude than those of Chrysostom or the two Gregories, Nyssen and Nazienzen. Do the Oxford Tract School imagine that no one can read the Fathers but themselves? The author of "Natural Enthusiasm" has read too much for them! His own enthusiasm, however, is *unnatural*, when he claims a monopoly of this knowledge. Not a few contemporary Dissenters had read the Fathers before he knew their names.)

"Nearly about the same time, two other persons, the one a teacher of the Chinese language, and the other a writer, who had both attended Dr. Morrison's instructions, gave such an account of their views of Christianity, as would in the eyes of most Christians have justified their being baptized; but it was thought better to be backward, and err on the side of caution, rather than on that of haste, in dispensing baptism. These two persons were not baptized; and circumstances in which they were not to blame, have since concurred to remove them from connexion with the Mission. They still manifest a friendly disposition, and peruse *Christian* books, and it is hoped, may at some future time, declare themselves ' *on the Lord's side.*'

"On July 28th, 1814, a native Chinese whom Dr. Morrison had employed as a writer in transcribing the New Testament from his MSS. was seized by the police, for a debt owing to his father who had been dead eleven or twelve years. He was put in irons, and apprehended much ill usage. Dr. M. being acquainted with the magistrate, obtained his liberation on bail. It was the object of the prosecutor, by intimidation, to force the man's employer to pay the money. This mode of attack occurred more than once to the Mission.

"On the 2d September, the same year, there was issued a very violent edict against the Tien-choo-keaou, that is, the Roman Catholic Christians. Harsher language was employed than had ever before been used; they were said to be worse than the Pihleen-keaou, that is, white *water-lily* sect, a certain fraternity which had rebelled several times during the former and present reigns. This was no doubt overstrained; for though there might be here and there, perhaps, found an individual Catholic or two in the different provinces, who, acting contrary to his profession and instructions, behaved ill, it is not to be believed that any such charge applied to them generally. They ought perhaps rather to be viewed as a *peaceable* people. Indeed were they otherwise disposed, their number and means are so very small, that it is not to be supposed they would attempt any thing against the Government. What can a mere handful of persecuted people, whose numbers are not as one to ten thousand of their oppressors, effect? When we look back on the history of the Christian Church, we can hardly be at a loss for the motives of Government in such a charge: 'they are ill-affected to the priesthood and to the state,' are charges which have often proved convenient to the enemies of Christians, both in Pagan and Christian countries.

"From his first arrival in China, Dr. Morrison had been preparing materials for a Dictionary of the Chinese language; and it became now a subject of serious consideration how it could be printed. The New Testament was finished—another member was added to the Mission; and others were expected to join it at no very distant period. In mere manuscript form, had it been completed, the dictionary could not be very extensively useful. The labour and expense of transcribing it would have been too discouraging, few could have afforded the expense of getting a copy made, and still fewer would have had fortitude and patience to transcribe it themselves. The 8,000 character Dictionary, composed by the Romish Missionaries, cost about 200 Spanish dollars to transcribe, and it does not contain more than one sixth of what Dr. M.'s plan embraced. He had gone to considerable expense for books necessary in the compilation, and bestowed considerable labour on the materials. If the work could not be printed, not only the public in general, but also the Mission, for the use of which it was primarily and chiefly (though not exclusively) intended, would in a great measure lose that assistance in acquiring the Chinese language, which, it was presumed, the book would furnish. It was a work, the execution of which would necessarily be protracted through a course of several years. The expense would have been far too heavy for any individual not in affluent circumstances; and few societies for religious purposes were adequate to it. However, the work was undertaken by the H. E. I. COMPANY, on that scale of liberality which generally characterizes the operations of that opulent and distinguished body. It had been previously brought to their notice, by individual gentlemen of the Factory in China, who thought the work likely to facilitate their commercial intercourse with the Chinese, as well as to promote the interests of general literature. The views of the H. E. I. Company in taking up the Dictionary, were no doubt chiefly, if not solely, for commercial and literary purposes; but that will in no way lessen the usefulness of the work, to those who wish to promote the knowledge of the Gospel in China. The members and friends of the Chinese Mission could not but feel grateful, and rejoice, that it had been undertaken on so full and liberal a plan, by a body of men who would not feel the expense. In conformity with a previous resolution of the Court of Directors, Mr. P. P. Thoms was sent out with a press, types, and other requisites for printing. He arrived at Macao, 2nd September, 1814, and applied himself with great assiduity to the fabrication of moveable metal types, in which, after conquering great difficulties, he was finally successful to a degree far beyond expectation. The printing proceeded very slowly the first year, owing to the many obstacles which attended the casting and cutting the characters. The first number of the Dictionary was finished and sent home in January, 1816. The second number, and a volume of Dialogues, have since made their appearance.

"After the establishment of the Mission at Malacca, Mr. Thoms often rendered it considerable service by his advice in what regarded the printing, and in every other way in his power, for which the writer of these pages takes this opportunity of expressing his gratitude.

"During the greater part of the following winter, Mr. Milne resided at Canton, studying the language, and enjoying the occasional assistance of Mr. Morrison. By the kindness of A. P., Esq., of the H. C.'s Factory, he obtained the use of several rooms gratis, which saved a considerable sum of money to the Mission. For this favour, as well as for many subsequent civilities, he considers himself much indebted to that gentleman.

"On the 16th December, 1814, the sum of 1,000 Spanish dollars was paid to Dr. Morrison, to whom it was bequeathed by the late William Parry, Esq., one of the English East India Company's Factory at Canton, to be employed as Dr. M. should deem most calculated '*to diffuse the knowledge of our blessed religion.*' The principal part of this sum was appropriated to the printing of the 12mo edition of the Chinese New Testament."

(The Chinese Dictionary, as one of the achievements of the Mission, deserves more notice than Dr. Milne has bestowed on it. In 1810, even the *Quarterly* Review despaired of England, as incapable of giving to the world such a work. "That honour," they say, "we greatly fear is reserved for *Bonaparte*. We have heard that Langlés and Le Guignes are to execute it." In 1809, they mocked "the festive board" of the East India Directors, as consuming annually *thrice* as much as a Dictionary would cost! This is a mean insinuation. *Auber* claims more credit for the Company than it deserves: but still, the Directors deserve much. If they *feasted* as usual, they also devoted Ten Thousand Pounds to the publication of Dr. Morrison's Dictionary. Thus Bonaparte did less, and the Directors more, than the Quarterly predicted; and a Nonconformist Missionary did what the Quarterly would *not* have predicted, had an angel told the editor. When will the Universities do for Chinese literature what the Company did? When will their Oriental Chairs attempt to vie with Canton and Serampore? Both Popery and Dissent throw the Church into the *shade* by translations. This should not be the case! It would not, if the Church Missionary Society could help it.)

CHAPTER IX.

THE MALACCA MISSION.

"In the course of the year 1814, Dr. Morrison had translated the book of Genesis. It was revised, and printed in the beginning of 1815, in a 12mo size, to correspond with the late edition of the New Testament.

"For a considerable time, Mrs. Morrison had suffered great indisposition; and a sea voyage and change of climate were pointed out as the most likely means for the restoration of health. In countries where friends of a congenial mind and edifying conversation, are but few, it is no easy matter for the members of a Christian family to separate; and especially where urgent and important duties of a local nature prevent those that are in health from accompanying, and rendering the needful attentions to the afflicted party. But it is a trial which duty often calls upon them to bear. The members of the Chinese Mission have had it to encounter more than once. It was severely felt by them all in the present instance, especially by Dr. and Mrs. Morrison themselves. Yet they considered that his labours were at that time of so important and urgent a nature, as that the suspension of them even for a few months, would have been a great loss to the cause in which he was engaged; and hoped that, as they were separating at the call of duty, God would support their minds and afford his gracious protection. Mrs. M. accordingly embarked with their two children on the 21st January, 1815, for England, where, by the good providence of God, she arrived in safety. The change of climate and the society of friends, proved at first very beneficial to her health and spirits." (I owe much of my intimate knowledge of my friends in China, to this visit of Mrs. Morrison's. She came prepared to tell me all their history from the time they joined her at Macao. Mr. John Morrison, although very young then, has not forgotten, I am sure, the rapture with which his sweet mother was wont to speak of the Milnes at my fire-side in Liverpool. She was introduced to me by a letter from Mrs. Milne, thus: "I refer you to her for information concerning us. I have raised her expectations of finding a *friend* in you. You see, Robert, I have not lost my good opinion of you, although I am peevish because the fleet has brought me no letters from any of my friends. You will find Mrs. Morrison a clever, well-educated woman, and pious. I do love her! She has been very kind to me." Macao, 20th January, 1815.)

"Religious people seem often to feel such separations more keenly than others do; the reason of this may perhaps be, that they view the relations of life, and the obligations of relative duty, in a more *serious* light; as formed by the wise appointment of God, binding by his express authority, and having an influence upon their own present and eternal state. And this, by the way, may account for the great measure of grief which some eminently pious persons often manifest at the death of relatives and particular friends. Those who think that because a man is a Missionary, therefore he should feel less interest in his family, and less concern for afflicted or poor relatives, than others do, should read their New Testament *again*, and learn more carefully the nature and obligation of relative duties. Such a supposition, if it ever exist, is very dishonourable to those that entertain it; and will never be suffered to remain in the heart of one who lives under habitual impressions of what the Scripture teaches concerning the human relations. Who, that fully knows the Gospel of Jesus, as a system of doctrine and duty, would ever deem that Missionary worthy of patronage, who, whatever his zeal, talents, and self-denial may be, overlooks his aged parents, his afflicted relatives, and his own family? How can he be considered fit to inculcate on the Heathen the morals of the Gospel, who himself attends not to the most obvious dictates of the law of nature! and what judgment shall we form of the consistency of those supporters of Missions, who seem desirous of inculcating principles, which, if followed, would inevitably tend to lead those whom they send forth, to trifle with the duties of relative life!" (Who those "supporters" were, to whom Dr. Milne refers, I cannot tell: but, during no short nor slight knowledge of the Board, have I ever seen any such directors, or heard of such principles. The *leanings* are all the other way now.)

"During the time Mr. Milne remained in Canton, he composed a Treatise on the Life of Christ, in Chinese, which was printed at Canton in February, 1815. It was divided into twenty sections, and a preface; and the style of the greater part corrected by Dr. Morrison, without whose sanction he could not, at that early period of his Chinese studies, have ventured to publish it. He derived considerable advantage, in composing it, from the New Testament already translated, as well as from the other Christian publications formerly noticed. For, although the *style* of these was nearly as difficult as that of native Chinese books; yet, from previously knowing the *subject*, he could read them with more facility, and perceive more clearly the proper arrangement of characters in a sentence, and the peculiarities of the Chinese idiom. For this advantage, among others, subsequent labourers are indebted to those who went before them. In the earlier part of a man's application to foreign languages, such helps should be diligently used; as he advances to higher degrees of attainment, the most proper models of style will be found in the writings of learned natives.

"The blocks cut for printing the life of Christ were carried to Malacca, where the work has undergone many corrections and improvements in the language; but still the author thinks the style of an inferior kind. It was gratifying, however, to find that the book was generally understood by the lower classes of Chinese; and often read with some degree of interest. This was as much as could reasonably be expected from a *first* attempt; and it encouraged him to persevere. Many copies of it have been printed and widely dispersed. May it prove the means of leading many sinners to the 'knowledge of the true God and of Jesus Christ whom he hath sent.'

"As Mr. Milne could not remain for any length of time in Macao, it was necessary to determine on the place to which he should, at the close of the season, remove. While absent in the islands the preceding year, every possible inquiry relative to the most proper place for the chief seat of the Mission was made. Java appeared to possess very great advantages for a Missionary station. The Chinese population was great; the intercourse with China, by junks, frequent; and the constituted authorities disposed to afford facilities. The Honourable T. S. Raffles, the Governor, expressed a readiness to forward the establishment of the Mission, should Mr. Milne determine to settle in Java, during the time of his administration; and the Rev. Professor Ross, and several other Dutch gentlemen engaged to use their influence with the Netherlands' Government, in favour of the Mission, at the time of the expected restoration of the island.

"At *Malacca* the Chinese population was small; but the place was near to China itself; commanded a readier intercourse with all parts of the Archipelago where Chinese have settled—lay in the direct way between Cochin China, Siam, and Penang—and possessed a frequent and ready intercourse with India and Canton. Though the number of Chinese at Malacca was vastly smaller than in Java, yet it was supposed that a Mission established at the former place would, in consequence of its more favourable locality, afford an opportunity of communicating with a much greater number than one established at the latter place could. Besides, it was considered a more healthy place than Batavia, and consequently more fit for a Mission which, it was wished, might grow into a kind of central station for Missions in different countries; and ultimately become the seat of a Seminary where the Chinese, Malay, and other Ultra-Ganges languages should be cultivated. Should the Missions extend, ill health would sometimes oblige those engaged in them to remove—old age, death, and other causes would render some peaceful asylum to widows, orphans, and survivors, necessary. The children belonging to the members of the several Missions, would require education. Malacca seemed well adapted to these several purposes. It was a quiet place; the existing authorities were favourably disposed; and should a change of Government take place, no obstacle, it was supposed, would be thrown in the way by the Dutch.

These reasons determined Dr. Morrison and his colleague to fix on Malacca in preference to Batavia or Penang, where the Mission might have also been established. The station, it was possible, might not answer all the purposes which they had in view; but they were guided by what seemed, for the time, most probable. Mr. Morrison had long thought it exceedingly desirable to have, in some *quiet* place, near to China, a station which would be a centre of union and communication, and which should be furnished with such means as give to Missions the most rational pledges of permanency and utility. Though he and his fellow-labourer might not have the happiness of living to see the new station furnished with all necessary means; yet that did not seem a sufficient reason why a commencement should not be made, or why their plan should not, from the first, embrace them as its ultimatum. They were aware that the progress of human institutions is in general slow; and especially so where there is neither influence nor wealth at command. They resolved to begin on a small and unassuming scale; but constantly to keep their eye upon, and direct their efforts towards, great ends. They looked forward to the attainment of the object, as the traveller does to some very distant, but highly important eminence, which he longs to gain; but between him and which there lies a rugged, winding, and fatiguing road, which must be trodden always with cautious, often with trembling, steps; and under the painful suspense of uncertainty, whether he can ever reach the desired point, or not. It appeared clearly to be their duty to make an attempt; should it prove abortive, the experience of the failure would be useful to those whose good fortune it should be to prove more successful. The substance of their views, is contained in the following resolutions;"—(which I preserve here, although they exist in Dr. Morrison's life, because that valuable work is too expensive to find many readers in Dr. Milne's old circle. Besides, they are taken from his Retrospect.)

" 'I. That the present state of China is such as renders printing, and several other labours connected with our Mission, very difficult; and even personal residence uncertain. It is desirable, therefore, to try to obtain a station under some European Protestant

Government, near to China, where the chief seat of our Chinese Mission may be fixed with more rational prospects of perpetuity and utility; and where preparations may be made for entering China with more effect, as soon as it shall please God to open a door for us. Malacca, we consider as a place adapted for this purpose—and it is accordingly resolved, that Mr. Milne proceed to that place with a view to commence the Mission.

" 'II. That on Mr. M.'s arrival at Malacca, an attempt be made to obtain, by grant or by purchase, a spot of ground, which shall be the property of the Mission; and on which, such buildings as are requisite for our purposes, shall be erected.

" ' III. That the establishment of a Chinese Free School be attempted as early as possible, in hope that it may prepare the way for a Seminary, in which pious natives shall finally be instructed with a view to the Christian Ministry in China, and in the adjacent countries.

" 'IV. That a small Chinese work in the form of a Magazine, be published at Malacca monthly, or as often as it can with propriety be done; in order to combine the diffusion of general knowledge with that of Christianity.

" 'V. That the station shall be regulated chiefly with a view to the CHINESE; but not exclusively so. As soon as instruments and means are obtained, Missions in the Malay and other adjacent countries, may be connected therewith. This is the more important, as it is highly probable the Missionary Society will shortly send out Missionaries to the Malays, &c.

" 'VI. That the station, being intended for the

combination of various objects relative to Chinese, Malay, and other Missions on this side of India, it shall assume some general denomination fit to include all, which shall be afterwards fixed upon. "The Ultra-Ganges' Missions," has since been chosen; not with any wish to insinuate that there are no other Missions on this side of India, but as a fixed term, under which those sent out to these parts by the Missionary Society could be included. It is to be viewed rather as pointing to the scene of our labours, than intimating that we consider ourselves as sole possessors of the field.

"'VII. That printing in Chinese, Malay, and English, be attempted as soon as proper persons and means can be obtained; and that the remaining parts of the Chinese version of the sacred Scriptures, other Christian publications in Chinese and Malay, and such English books as may tend to illustrate the native languages, customs, and opinions, or otherwise to facilitate the progress of the Missions, be printed.

"'VIII. That a small periodical publication in the English language, with a view of promoting union and co-operation among the Missionary Society's Missions in different parts of India, and of promoting the love and practice of Christian virtue generally, is very desirable; and that it be attempted at Malacca with all convenient speed; and our fellow-labourers in the Gospel invited to assist us therein.

"'IX. That there be stated and occasional religious services conducted in the Chinese language, for the instruction of the Heathen; and a place of Christian worship built or procured as soon as the circumstances of the Mission may admit.

"'X. That as Mr. Morrison's engagements with his Chinese Dictionary, &c., do not now admit of his undivided attention to translation, the second member of the Mission shall engage in translating some parts of the Old Testament—thus uniting their labours till the whole version be completed.'

"These particulars contain the substance of the resolutions which were then formed; and, (as will appear afterwards) the several objects which they point out were, by the help of a gracious Providence, some of them obtained, and most of them begun within three years after the commencement of the Mission at Malacca. It is to be understood that these resolutions were formed with all due deference to the Directors of the MISSIONARY SOCIETY, who had the power to confirm or annul any or all of them. They were drawn up as a sort of guide to the members of the Chinese Mission, to enable them to manage, to the best advantage, that discretionary power which the Directors had reposed in them. These objects were to be constantly kept in eye, and all the proceedings of the Mission at Malacca, managed with a view to their final accomplishment. It is, no doubt, important to have fixed and defined objects in view. Where this is not the case, the mind hesitates; and the time which should be employed in vigorous action is too often spent in reasoning between various objects, which appear of nearly equal importance.

"The season being nearly over, Mr. Milne and family began to prepare for their departure from China—Chinese books, printing paper, a teacher of the language, and workmen were procured. Mr. and Mrs. M. experienced much kindness from the

Members of the English, and other foreign Factories in China. The benevolent attentions of J. B. U., Esq., and J. L., Esq., and of their families, were such as deserve a lasting place in their most grateful recollections. While in Canton, Mr. Milne received many kindnesses from several American gentlemen, and was laid under particular obligations to B. C., Esq., American Consul, for a letter granted to him, under the seal of the UNITED STATES, requesting that, if by the war (which then existed between Great Britain and America) Mr. M. should on his passage fall into the hands of any American vessel of war, cruizing in these seas, he might be treated with *kindness*, and landed at some port, as near as practicable to his destination. The Consul thought, that as Christianity was no national thing, the war, which unfortunately existed, ought not to throw obstacles in the way of those whose sole object was to promote the Gospel, and who devote their lives for the instruction and benefit of mankind.

"To part with their friends, under whose roof they had experienced from their first arrival in China a continued display of Christian attentions of no ordinary kind, was very painful to Mr. and Mrs. Milne. But the call of duty was imperious. They accordingly, after great difficulty in reaching the ship, embarked on the 17th of April. The fifth day they were at sea Mrs. Milne was delivered of twin boys, under circumstances *peculiarly distressing;* but, by the care of Providence, her life and their lives were mercifully preserved." (It was, perhaps, right to state the matter thus generally in his own public narrative: but the fact is, that to save expense to the Society, he had gone to sea without any female servant or companion for Mrs. Milne; having no reason to suspect that she would need help so soon. I have seen his private account of the *crisis;* and it is more than *touching*—it is overwhelming—and yet both bore up nobly, and, between them, nursed the twins thirty-three days on board!) "After thirty-five days' passage they safely reached Malacca, and were most kindly received by Major Farquhar, the resident, who has on every occasion manifested his friendly regards to their family and objects.

"In China, during the summer of 1815, the indiscretion of a native, who was engaged to prepare metal types for the Dictionary, induced him to collect a *great many* workmen, in a situation adjoining one of the public offices, in consequence of which some alarm was occasioned, and an attack from the local government on the press was dreaded. This circumstance, though totally unconnected with the Mission, yet occasioned the loss of 500 Spanish dollars to it. The person in whose possession the blocks of the 12mo New Testament were, hearing of the impending danger to the press, and fearing that it might reach him, in a fit of apprehension destroyed the chief part of them. They have been since recut.

"On the 24th August, Dr. Morrison finished a revisal of the large edition of the New Testament, and was gratified to be able, upon the whole, to judge of it favourably, as he gradually advanced in the knowledge of the language. Various verbal and typographical errors and omissions were discovered, to correct which, measures were taken. None of them were of great importance, and to be without any was a thing rather desired than expected.

"In the autumn of this year, that noble institution, the British and Foreign Bible Society, to which almost every modern version of the Scriptures into Heathen languages is indebted, gave a donation of £1000, to assist us in the Chinese translation. A considerable part of this grant went to defray the expense of the first edition of the New Testament, which was this time nearly circulated. Thus Providence furnished the means of paying the expense already incurred; and we were encouraged to proceed with a second edition." (It must not be supposed, from the *triumph* with which Dr. Milne so often refers to Dr. Morrison's Version of the New Testament, that he confined himself to the circulation of it, or of general tracts. He translated and circulated many striking ANECDOTES, to awaken curiosity and interest about the word of God. He was fond of anecdotes and apothegms, which spoke *volumes*. He enriched both his letters and sermons with them: and having seen their effect upon his hearers and correspondents at home, he tried their *point* upon the Chinese mind. It is very likely, therefore, that future Missionaries may find Chinese versions of some of our familiar anecdotes and emphatic maxims, where they little expect either: for *"winged words"* live long! Missionaries should remember this fact, and try to give *currency* in all languages to our best English proverbs and watch-words. They are *leaven* which will work in any lump. Could the *history* of some of our maxims be written, it would rival any influential example.)

"The favourable reception which those who were appointed to the Mission at Malacca, met with from the constituted authorities, greatly encouraged them; and they were led to cherish a hope that, by the favour of Providence, a foundation might in course of a few years be laid, for the accomplishment of the objects specified in the last section. While in China, comparatively little exercise of the judgment was necessary. The Mission there being established, it was only requisite to fall in with plans already in existence. At Malacca, it was otherwise; that friendly personal counsel which lays the giver under a a sort of responsibility for the consequences, if his counsel be followed, was at a distance; and the only alternative left, was, to adhere as closely as possible to the resolutions formed in China, and to the spirit of those advices which were frequently received by letter from thence. It was wished that the Mission should become important, and a centre of exertion. Hence Mr. Milne felt it a great satisfaction to his mind, that the idea of his settling at Malacca did not proceed from himself, but from one better acquainted with Missionary affairs, and in whose judgment and affection he had perfect confidence. To man, who knows but little of what is past, and less of what is future, it should always be deemed a privilege, to have the counsels of the wise and good. And those who know themselves, and who have not *sworn* consistency with rash assertions made in a moment of irritation or warmth, will readily acknowledge that the mind often fluctuates and hesitates, in determining on measures which have originated with themselves; which stand on the basis of their own individual judgment; and, in case of the failure of which, both the consequences to others, and the reproaches of their own mind for presumption or temerity, must fall with full weight on their shoulders alone. In extraordinary cases, extraordinary wisdom, confidence, and courage, may be expected. In the pursuit of objects which, though not extraordinary, are yet highly important for the benefit of mankind, we generally feel that the concurrent testimony of those whom we esteem, and the approbation of good men, give fresh energy to our heart, and impart new strength to our arm. At any rate, it was so in the present case: while Mr. Milne felt himself charged with the responsibility of whatever steps might be taken, nearly as much as if the proposal had been entirely his own, he also felt no small satisfaction in knowing that he was pursuing a plan, which had been revolved for years, in the mind of his fellow-labourer in the Chinese Mission.

"As the Dutch Protestant Christians in Malacca, had some time before lost their Minister by death, and were entirely destitute of religious instruction, it was proposed by the Resident and the Deacons of the Church, to Mr. Milne, that he should take charge of the Church, and perform the duties of a Christian pastor among the people. But, considering himself as a Missionary sent to labour among those who had never made a profession of the Gospel, he did not feel himself at liberty to undertake the duties of a fixed charge among Christian people. He therefore declined the PASTORAL CARE of that Church, but promised to afford them all the assistance which an almost exclusive attention to Missionary concerns would admit of; at the same time, admonishing them to take the earliest opportunity of providing themselves with a Minister who should have due leisure to attend to their spiritual interests. This offer was accepted. He preached a short discourse once every week among them; but from their very partial knowledge of the English language, it is not to be supposed that much good could be done. The influence of the truth upon an individual or two, in reforming their lives, and in producing a hearty regard for the things of God, was visible, and afforded high satisfaction. This stated service on the Sabbaths has been continued to the present time; and, notwithstanding earnest and repeated solicitations to seek a minister of their own, the people are still without one. A small salary was granted, with the sanction of the Penang Government, for these occasional labours. It was continued during the time the English held possession of the colony, and has been so also since the Dutch reassumed the Government. Deeming it a duty to lessen as much as possible the burden of the Missionary Society, Mr. Milne was enabled by this means to support his family for *two* years, without putting the Directors to *any* expense. But after that, an indifferent state of personal health, and the wants of an increasing family, rendered it necessary for him to draw on the Society as formerly." (Dr. Milne omitted here the fact, that he offered what services he could to the Dutch *gratuitously.* So sincere was he in this offer, that when they sent him the first quarter's salary, he wrote back to them, that they had mistaken him entirely. They were, however, as generous as he was disinterested.)

"How great a pity is it, that those who bear the Christian name, should be ever left destitute of the preaching of the Gospel, in a language which they can understand. Were a Malay congregation formed among the nominal Christians in Malacca, and a pious and devoted servant of Christ, set over it, the most important results might be expected. Multitudes would attend, and many who, though Christians in name, live in gross ignorance, and, it is to be feared, die in their sins,—would be made wise unto salvation. The writer would earnestly recommend the spiritual state of this people, to the consideration of their rulers, and of the clergy of the Reformed Church.

"In conformity to the third resolution passed in China, (vide sect. 3, page 176,) an attempt was soon made to establish a *free-school* among the Chinese, for the instruction of the children of the poor. Good order required that the constituted authorities should be previously informed, which was accordingly done; and the measure was favoured with the sanction and hearty approbation of the Resident and Commandant. But there was no school-house, or money to build, or hire one, or to support the school; and a sufficient acquaintance with the Christians in the place, had not been acquired, to justify an application to their liberality. It was therefore, both from principle and from necessity, judged best to begin on a very small scale.—To build a school without having first obtained scholars, or a high degree of probability of obtaining them, might have proved a waste of property, and exposed the Mission to ridicule. Mr. Milne resolved to begin with two or three scholars, if they could be procured: hoping that the number would increase, and that necessary means would be procured. A Chinese teacher, who had formerly acted as a school-master, and since been reduced to poverty, was engaged at a very small salary, but with a promise that it should be increased in proportion as the number of the scholars should increase. This method was followed with all the teachers that were subsequently employed. A regard to their own interest makes them seek out scholars; and they are much better fitted for this work than a newly-arrived Missionary can be. It tends also to make them kind to the children; for if they are not, the parents take them away; and the teacher's salary diminishes. When a Missionary cannot meet with men who will discharge such duties well from better principles than those of interest, he must take them as they are, deal with them according to the motives which they possess, and daily endeavour to impart to them others of a higher character." (This is a very questionable principle! It may have been a plausible plan then, but the results of *such* schools are beginning now to open the eyes of the public. Mr. Malcom's work on this subject deserves serious attention.)

"A small house in the compound, which had been formerly occupied as a stable, was fitted up, at a very trifling expense, for a school; a few seats were prepared, and a notice written in Chinese pasted up in different parts of the town, intimating that a school for the children of the poor was about to be established. This was something entirely new to the Chinese. They had never heard of such a thing in the place before; and it need not be matter of wonder to the reader to learn that a people, in whose breast scarcely any motives but those of *interest* bear sway, could not at first, or indeed for twelve months, believe that the children were to be taught and furnished with books gratuitously. They suspected that some presents would be looked for; and that, however fair and liberal the proposal appeared to be, there were still motives of interest at bottom. This kept many back for the first year. But the necessities of the teacher made him active. The poverty of some parents who had a wish to see their children able to read and write disposed them to embrace the offer; and, perhaps, the curiosity of others, who wished to prove whether the professions of the Missionary were any thing more than a pretence to get gain, inclined them to make a trial for a few months. Thus, from one motive or other, *two* names were given in—a short time after, three more came forward—and again, three—and, finally, about fifteen names were on the list. I think it of some importance to my fellow-servants in the Gospel, who may be about to commence their work among the Heathen, to trace, as we go along, the genuine motives which, I believe, influenced those of whom I write; and which they may expect will in a measure, at first, influence those among whom it may be their lot to labour. For why should we hide the naked truth from ourselves; or vainly imagine that there is any charm in *our* presence, which will speedily bring the people in our station to a better mind than they have been found to possess elsewhere? When the character of a Mission is once established, and time, sufficient to prove that professions of disinterestedness are founded in truth, has elapsed; then, indeed, parents will send their children without suspicion and from a real desire for their improvement.

".The Chinese, as above noticed, are greatly addicted to judicial astrology. The principles of this preposterous science, influence them in all their undertakings. Hence they will not begin any important work but on a *lucky day*. This is strictly adhered to in opening a school. The teacher would not think himself happy, or the parents expect their children to make progress, if the day on which the school begins, be not marked in the Imperial Calendar, as a Kieh-jih, that is, fortunate day. The teacher employed at Malacca, said, 'We Chinese, never begin any important work like this, but on a lucky day; and, moreover, it is customary to give to each of the children, a Kae-sinping, (that is, a *heart-opening* cake,) to expand their minds, and secure their progress in learning!' Being but very imperfectly acquainted with the character and sentiments of the Chinese people, I was astonished to find even their teachers led away by such gross absurdities, and I objected to the practice. It was, however of no use, to enter the lists at so early a period, with their deeply rooted errors and absurdities. It occurred that it would be better to suffer them to take their own way, and embrace some future occasion of pointing out its folly, than by coming into an immediate contact with their reigning prejudices, to run the hazard of losing those opportunities of subsequent usefulness, which the school seemed to promise." (This was sailing very *near* the wind; and it proves that better men than the Jesuits need to pray, "Lead us not into temptation.")

. "It is also the practice of the Chinese to place the image of Confucius and of Wan-chang, (that is, God of letters) in their schools, before which the children bow and burn incense-matches in the morning, before they begin. They wished to introduce these into the Free School; and the only way in which their wish could be evaded, was, the circumstance that the school house did not stand on the ground of a Chinese—but on that of foreigners. They likewise, often paste up *charms* over the doors of their schools, or hang them up within, to ward off the malignant influence of evil stars, the attacks of disease, and the assaults of wicked spirits. The utmost vigilance could not, in every instance, prevent them from having recourse to this folly.

"The school was opened on the 5th August, 1815, with only five scholars—but they increased, and throughout the remaining months of that year, from ten to fourteen daily attended. They were instructed in reading, writing, and casting accounts,—all in their native tongue.

"How to introduce *Christian books* into the school, without displeasing the children's parents, who might have been induced to take them away, was a difficulty not easily got over. To teach heathen children the bare elements of their own language, is indeed a useful labour, and will contribute indirectly to the spread of the Gospel, by imparting to them an ability to read, and forming habits of mental application; but when we consider the value of the soul, and that its salvation is the chief object of Missionary labours, it is natural to wish for some more direct method of imparting a knowledge of divine truth. By not pressing the matter on them, and by allowing them the use of their own elementary books, the school-master was prevailed on to teach them a Christian catechism at first on Sabbaths, and afterwards occasionally on other days. Chinese youths are accustomed to commit to memory every thing that they read in the schools, hence they committed the catechism also to memory as a matter of course. An attempt to explain it to them was first made by causing them to write and analyze particular characters—then the meaning of important words, such as 'God—Creation—Soul—Death—Heaven—Hell,'

&c., was explained to them—this by and by grew into a kind of catechetical exercise, to which the Sabbath afternoons were devoted. But in order to prevent giving offence to the parents, it was necessary to combine something else with it. The forms of salutation common among their countrymen, were accordingly taught the children, by their teacher; they were instructed how to *bow* to their superiors, parents, and teachers, and to each other. This pleased the parents much, as nothing of the kind was taught in their own schools, of which there were three in Malacca. The children themselves were also amused by some little evolutions which they were taught to go through, as, passing round all at once—lifting their hands and bowing all together—and going from school two and two in a measured pace. The elder boys sometimes learned from six to ten questions of Dr. Morrison's catechism in a week; but their knowledge of the principles therein contained, was, without doubt, very imperfect, notwithstanding the attempts to explain them.

"An effort was made to bring them to attend Christian worship, which was finally successful. It was before practised with some domestics brought from China, and the school-master seeing them attend, was also induced to come, and the children followed him. Thus, two objects of considerable importance were gained almost at once, namely, the introduction of Christian books into the school, and the attendance of the teacher and scholars once a day on the worship of God. It was not expected that great and immediate good would follow; but, as these means have in every age been attended with the Divine blessing for the conversion of sinners, there was every reason to hope that they would be useful in the present instance, however distant the time of actual success might be. It was particularly requisite not to give *much* Christian instruction to the children in the beginning; and there was one instance in which a father took away his children, because they were taught the catechism: he was afterwards prevailed upon to send them back; but the fact of his taking them away, was a signal to Mr. Milne not to urge the truths of the Gospel too strenuously on their attention, till mutual confidence should be more firmly established." (Here, again, Dr. Milne was tempted to the very verge of Jesuitism. He meant, indeed, nothing wrong. But he ought to have considered, that a *full* school was no compensation for an *empty creed*. Getting or keeping scholars, at the expense of keeping back any essential truth of the Gospel is wretchedly bad policy, and worse theology. For, what can a Heathen parent think, but that if *one* part of Christianity may be given up for the sake of his children, why not *any* part for his own accommodation?)

"Gratitude requires the writer to mention here, the encouragement he received from two English gentlemen, who contributed of their money to the support of the school—namely, Captain Latter, of the H. C.'s army in Bengal, who gave *fifty Spanish dollars*, and promised to use his influence with his friends in India for the same purpose. The addition of another and larger school in the following year, was in a great measure owing to this worthy gentleman's advice and liberality. The schools at Malacca, the support of which may be said to owe its origin to him, have since been twice laid under additional obligations to his kindness, by a second donation of *fifty dollars*—and a third of *one hundred dollars.* Missionaries, to whose lot wealth rarely falls, meeting with such a friend, feel greatly encouraged in their work; and useful plans, which would perhaps otherwise never have been adopted, or have failed for want of means, are pursued till they bring forth good to mankind. Wealthy Europeans, or persons in comfortable circumstances, in India, may do much good by their liberality. It may feed the poor, clothe the naked; and teach multitudes of ignorant Heathen children, whom they never saw in the flesh, to peruse the records of eternal life. The other gentleman was Lieut. Col. G. Macgregor, who gave a donation of *thirty Spanish dollars* to the same object. In hope of enlarging the school in the ensuing year, intimation of the same was given to J. H. Harrington, Esq., Bengal, who, in addition to a liberal donation from himself, employed his influence with a number of his friends, and to the great astonishment of Mr. Milne, a letter covering a bill for *nine hundred and thirty-two Sicca Rupees,* to assist in the support of the schools at Malacca, was sent him in 1816. Thus furnished, by the abundant liberality of pious and well-disposed persons at a distance, with the needful supplies, the Mission had enough to support its school for two years. It will be observed, that the writer does not here exactly follow the order of time, but rather puts things of one kind together, as they come to hand.

"In every cultivated language, the advantage of the press for the diffusion of knowledge, both human and divine, is evident to all. In the Chinese language, the importance of *books*, as a means of improvement, is perhaps greater than in any other living medium of communication. The Chinese written language is read by a much larger proportion of mankind, than that of any other people. Its oral dialects are very numerous, and so widely different from each other, that persons of neighbouring provinces, (as the writer has often witnessed,) are frequently unable to carry on a conversation of any length, without having recourse to writing. The written language possesses a uniform identity unknown to some others. The dialects of the Greek tongue, required not only to be distinguished in its pronunciation, but also to be marked by variations in the orthography of its nouns: in the formation of the tenses and moods of its verbs, in its adverbs, aorists, &c. In Chinese scarcely any thing like this takes place. Throughout the whole of that empire, as well as in most of its tributary, and several of its neighbouring countries, the written character and idiom are, with a very few trifling exceptions, the same. Again, China being now *shut*, by persecuting edicts and an almost unconquerable jealousy of strangers, the Minister of Jesus Christ is not permitted to walk 'through the breadth and length of the land,' preaching the Gospel by the living voice; —yea, he dare scarcely open his mouth on the borders thereof, to call its idolatrous myriads to repentance. *Books* are universally understood—they travel every where—with proper agents and due caution, they may be poured into China itself." (Dr. Cotton Mather's example had great influence on Mr. Milne in this matter. The various languages he taught himself, and the 382 books or pamphlets he published, although he begun late in life, led Mr. Milne to study his example for himself, and to hold it up to Missionaries as both a stimulant and an encouragement. See *Gleaner*, p. 4.) "The united force of these views led to the resolution above mentioned, relative to a '*Periodical Publication in the Chinese language.*'—Preparations were accordingly made for it. After Mr. Milne's arrival at Malacca, its form was fixed upon, and the first number brought from the press on the 5th of August, 1815, the same day on which the school was commenced. The first specimens were very imperfect, both as to the composition and printing; but they were understood by persons who were in the habit of reading; and the Editor hoped, that a fuller acquaintance with the language, would enable him to improve the style. It was originally intended that this little publication should combine the diffusion of general knowledge, with that of religion and morals; and include such notices of the public events of the day, as should appear suited to awaken reflection and excite inquiry. To promote *Christianity* was to be its *primary* object; other things, though they were to be treated in subordination to this, were not to be overlooked. Knowledge and science are the handmaids of religion, and may become the auxiliaries of virtue. To rouse the dormant powers of a people whose mental energies are bound up by that dull and insipid monotony which has drawn out its uniform line over them, to the length of more than twenty hundred years, will be no easy task. Means of all justifiable kinds, labourers of every variety of talent, resources sufficient for the most expensive moral enterprises, and a space of several ages, will all be necessary to do this effectually. But a beginning must be made by some people, and in some age of the world. After-generations will improve on what the present race of men begin. It is better, therefore, to commence a good work with very feeble means and imperfect agents, than to 'sigh to the wind,' and not attempt it at all. Thus, though that variety of subject intended to be published in the Chinese Monthly Magazine, could not be all brought in at first, or indeed to the present moment; yet that was not considered an argument of sufficient weight to postpone the work. Mr. Milne therefore composed such papers for it as his time, talents, and other circumstances admitted of. The essays and papers published in the Chinese Magazine to the present time have been chiefly of a religious and moral kind. A few essays on the most simple and obvious principles of astronomy, instructive anecdotes, historical extracts, occasional notices of great political events, &c., have at times given a little variety to its pages; but there has been less of these than could have been wished. Among other reasons of this want of variety, it may be noticed that for the first four years, every thing published, with the exception of a few pages, by the first proposer of the work, proceeded from the pen of a single individual, (himself,) who was also engaged in a variety of other labours. To render this work generally interesting, it would require a full half of the time and labour of a Missionary—time and labour well bestowed too,—and should unite the productions of various pens. The editor hopes that he may in future have more leisure to attend to this branch of his work, and that the growing acquaintance of his brethren with the Chinese language, will soon enable them to furnish useful papers on a variety of subjects;—especially on those which have hitherto been but sparingly introduced. The size of the Chinese Magazine has never yet exceeded that of a small tract, and it has been given away gratis. For about three years, five hundred copies were printed monthly, and circulated, by means of friends, correspondents, travellers, ships, &c., through all the Chinese settlements of the eastern Archipelago; also in Siam, Cochin-China, and part of China itself. At present, (1819,) a thousand copies are printed monthly. The demands and opportunities for circulation greatly increase, and it is likely that in three or four years more, 2,000 will be an inadequate supply. Besides the regular monthly numbers, complete sets for each year have been printed as they were required. The labour of preparing the materials has been amply compensated by the extensive range of countries in which the work is read; and by opportunities which the publishing of it monthly has afforded of gradually unfolding many parts of divine truth. To sit down and write a complete treatise on one subject; to compile a series of history through a period of any length; and to enter fully into the discussion of any important topic,—are what the time and strength of a person, who is otherwise variously employed, do not admit of his effecting at once, or without many interruptions. By taking monthly in order, the several parts of an intended treatise—the lesser divisions of a series of history—or the different branches of a discourse,—the labour may go on; the plan fill up gradually; and the close of the year present the writer with a dozen of essays or discourses on different departments of his subject. The addition furnished in one month may appear too insignificant to deserve much notice; but twelve or twenty such additions will form a complete volume; and the author will be pleased with his plodding perseverance, and will also be able, by reviewing the whole in its complete form, to correct, expunge, or add, as errors or defects may require. On this plan, several pieces, published as monthly numbers in the Magazine, have been completed, and others are now carrying on. There is indeed some want of uniformity in the style of these, the latter parts being better Chinese than the former: an imperfect acquaintance with the language in the first stages of the work, may account for this. Mr. Milne found that, while the writing on divine subjects tended to refresh the mind, the regular monthly demands of matter for the press, proved a useful stimulus to labour.

ORAL INSTRUCTION should, in every Christian Mission, hold a prominent place. The preaching of the Gospel is an ordinance of divine appointment. In its own nature, it is remarkably calculated to arrest the attention and diffuse knowledge; and it has been attended in every age of the church, with the peculiar blessing of Heaven for the salvation of men. I record it with deep regret, that even to the present hour, the circumstances of the Mission at Malacca have never been such as to admit of devoting that portion of time and attention to oral instruction and preaching, which the extreme ignorance of the Heathen require. For more than two years all the concerns of the Chinese Mission devolved entirely upon an individual. He had a translation of part of the

Old Testament in hand—the papers for the magazine to prepare monthly; the schools to oversee; and his knowledge of the language being imperfect, a good deal of time was necessarily taken up daily in study; so that very little time or strength remained for stated preaching, or for going from house to house. The third year he was absent from the station for more than six months, through ill health; and the time of his fellow-labourer, who had been sent out to assist in the Mission, was from necessity devoted to the study of the language. These important means were not, however, entirely neglected. In the first year of the Mission, regular services were begun on the week days, and on the Sabbaths, which have ever since been continued. Every morning the Chinese domestics, workmen, and scholars, met for Christian worship. A portion of the New Testament, or of such other books as had then been printed, was read, and short practical remarks made on it; after which prayer was offered up. On Sabbaths, this morning exercise was postponed till midday, in consequence of having to preach in the Dutch church at ten o'clock. At one o'clock, the Chinese Scriptures were read, and something in form of an exhortation, longer than that usual on week days, was delivered. At half-past three, the scholars were examined and heard repeat their catechism. About five Mr. Milne frequently spent an hour in town distributing tracts, or conversing with the Heathen. At eight o'clock, the Scriptures were again read, remarks made on them, and a short prayer concluded the service. The number of hearers was always small—sometimes one—two—four, &c., from the neighbouring streets, joined the regular attendants, and twenty grown persons was the largest number that attended. Three, five, or eight, were the ordinary number of adult hearers. The others came occasionally; some from curiosity, some perhaps from a wish to be employed. When the curiosity of the former was satisfied, and the latter perceived that there was no worldly gain proposed to their view, they came but seldom. But from whatever motive they came, the preacher was always glad to see them, knowing that the Heathen never attend to the Gospel at first from sincere attachment to the truth. It is under the Gospel alone that we can expect this attachment to be formed. It is, indeed, lamentable to see how completely the benighted inhabitants of Asia are under the dominion of mere *secular* principles; but we must by no means conceal or disguise their real character. The plain matter-of-fact may excite the sneer of semi-infidels, at the folly of those who attempt a reformation; it may shut up the channels of benevolence in those who expected immediate conversions; it may even discourage the hearts of some of the best friends of mankind. But the judicious and enlightened Christian will see in it a practical confirmation of those sentiments, which the Gospel teaches concerning the ignorance, depravity, and misery of mankind in general, and of the Heathen in particular; it will show him how little the best Pagan systems (for such I consider those of China) can do to bring their adherents to real virtue; and consequently, will strengthen his conviction of the necessity of redoubled exertion in the cause of the Gospel. For, with a firm believer in Divine Revelation, the utter impossibility of the eternal salvation of those who live and die with the love of this world predominant in the heart, can be no matter of doubt. That the Gospel shall finally triumph over the idolatry and wickedness of the nations, notwithstanding its apparently slow progress, is to him equally certain. Let every fresh display of the native depravity of the Pagan mind, (a depravity indeed common to man) give ardour to our prayers, wing our zeal with velocity, enlarge our benevolence, and teach us to join laborious perseverance in active service, with unshaken confidence in the divine promises. In dispensing oral instruction to the few Heathen that attended, Mr. Milne found the catechism and tracts, composed by his colleague, of great assistance. Written in a plain style, and free from the stiffness which generally adheres to translations, these tracts were easily understood by the Heathen: and a page or two often furnished the ground of the exhortations addressed to them. He placed a copy before each individual, and went over the portion selected for the occasion, amplifying and enlarging where either his own small stock of Chinese words would admit, or where the subject required most illustration. The same method was observed in reading the New Testament. The people, having the books before them, could more easily understand the explanation. He had seen in Scotland, his native country, the beneficial effects of this practice on the people, who generally keep their Bibles open in church, at the chapter which the minister is explaining; and follow him, by turning to the passages which he quotes; thus, their minds are fixed on the word of God *itself*, and they are enabled to peruse the same passages again in private with more advantage. He wished, of course, to introduce this useful practice among the people to whom he was sent; and it has been continued in Malacca to the present time; not, it is hoped, without some benefit to the Chinese." (Happily, Dr. Milne's son, and Mr. Legge, know the worth of that *Scotch* habit too well, not to promote it in China. Their ears have been accustomed from childhood to the *rustle* of "the leaves of the Tree of Life;" and it will gladden their hearts to hear it again.)

"Occasional opportunities of conversing with the heathen and explaining the radical principles of Christianity to them, offered.—Sailors and passengers from Chinese junks, from Siam, Java, &c., called to get tracts; they were also visited on board their own vessels; and something said with a view of awakening their minds to inquiry after the true God and the Saviour. Mr. Milne likewise visited the heathen in their own houses and shops from time to time; and tried to impart to them the knowledge of salvation. On these occasions, a tract or part of it, or a verse of the Testament, was read to three, six, or more persons as they chanced to attend; and a little explanation added. When this was ended in one shop or house, he went on to another; and here, as in the stated services at home, he experienced great assistance from the labours of his predecessor in the work. To have something in an intelligible form drawn up and printed, to put into the hands of the people, assists both the speaker and hearers, and will be understood by the latter, when much that is spoken through a foreign accent, will not be comprehended. A remark naturally arises from this, namely, that a Missionary who has the labours of a senior fellow-servant, in print, to assist him, may be able to be useful much *earlier* among the people, than if he had to depend solely on his own resources; and he should gladly avail himself of such aid, thankful to the great Head of the Church for the gifts which he has been pleased to bestow on his servants of former ages, or on contemporary labourers. An indolent man's making himself dependent on the labours of others, that he may enjoy the repose of sloth; and a diligent, persevering man's seizing on every facility furnished him, that his progress to usefulness may be accelerated,—are quite different things: in a Missionary, the former would be unpardonable; while the latter is evidently his duty." (So much did Dr. Milne avail himself of such *helps*, that, notwithstanding his inveterate hatred of popery, he culled freely from the "*sleeve-gems*," or devotional writings of the Romish Missionaries. He wanted "suitable words," and therefore sought them out and seized upon them any where.) "After the establishment of the Mission at Malacca, many opportunities of circulating *the Holy Scriptures and religious tracts*, presented themselves; not only in the settlement itself, but also, by means of native trading vessels, passengers, &c. to China, Cochin-China, Siam, and almost every Chinese colony on the Malayan Archipelago. These books and tracts were indeed as 'bread cast on the waters,' and may not be 'received again till after *many* days;' yet, when a Missionary cannot travel personally to a neighbouring country, and declare with the living voice, the great doctrines of Revelation, it is his duty to send the readiest substitute; and who can tell that these little Ministers of peace, which neither eat nor drink, are neither affected by climate, nor afraid of persecution,

—may not 'prepare the way of the Lord, and make ready a people for him.'

"In every Mission established among the heathen, *difficulties* are to be looked for. At Malacca, some were soon experienced, but of a different kind from those felt in many other parts of the heathen world. Here, there were no particular difficulties in regard to food, clothing, habitation, and personal safety. There was no persecution or opposition from the government; but on the contrary, the utmost freedom to promote Christian truth by every approved means. The difficulties arose chiefly from three sources. The *variety of dialect* that was found to prevail among the Chinese, constituted a great difficulty in the communication of knowledge. The Fokien dialect was spoken by the greater part; that of Canton, by a considerable number; and the Mandarin or Court dialect, though understood by a few, was not generally spoken. The first, Mr. Milne had had no opportunity of learning; the second, he could speak but imperfectly,—to the third, he had paid most attention. Thus, when going among the people, in one house the chief part of what was said, was understood; in the next, perhaps a half; and in a third, not more than a few sentences. In addressing a small company of fifteen or twenty persons, a knowledge of two dialects, is in many instances necessary, in order to impart instruction with effect to all. This difficulty will be generally met with in the Chinese colonies, settled on the Archipelago, as persons from various provinces are collected together in the same place: therefore, instead of a knowledge of one dialect answering the end, a Missionary would require some knowledge of *three*, in order to be extensively useful as a *preacher*. In China itself the case is different; the knowledge of one dialect will enable a man to preach the Gospel intelligibly to hundreds of thousands of persons. Among those Chinese who are settled in what is called K'ow-wae-kwŏ, that is, the *outside* nations, the *Fokien* dialect seems to prevail most extensively, and hence for a missionary, whose time is to be chiefly devoted to preaching and oral instruction, it is of the utmost importance. To acquire a knowledge of several spoken dialects, and a facility therein, requires a *talent* for languages, a set of good *teeth*, a peculiar flexibility in the organs of enunciation, a nice discrimination in the ear, much attention to the modulation of the voice, and frequent intercourse with the people. It is also a rare thing to see a man, after the age of twenty-five, acquire a good pronunciation of a foreign tongue. Hence, by the way, we see the necessity of *native* Missionaries, or of some Institution in which foreigners can, from an early age, be initiated into the languages. Where the concerns of a Mission devolve chiefly on one person; where there is much literary labour; and where the attention is often diverted by various duties,—the learning of several dialects to such a degree as to render them really serviceable to the interests of truth, is impracticable. Very little, therefore, was done at the Fokien dialect in Malacca, till the year 1818, when the attention of another labourer was directed to it, who made very considerable progress therein.

"The difficulty arising from a variety in the language, was found to be greatly increased from the inter-marriages of the Chinese with Malay women. No *females* ever leave China: the prejudices of the people against this are exceedingly strong. The consequence is, that most Chinamen, when they settle in a colony abroad, marry women of the place, and the children produced from such connexions, learn the language of their mothers first. In Java, Malacca, &c., many Chinese, from their earliest infancy, being accustomed to speak Malay, scarcely understand the language of their fathers at all. They speak Malay almost entirely; but never learn to read it. Their reading is always in Chinese; yet with many reading is carried to so small an extent, as to leave them without the ability of perusing even the plainest book. The task of communicating knowledge to persons of such various spoken dialects, is much greater than any one, who has not repeatedly made the experiment, can conceive. If it were allowable for Missionaries to *shift* difficulties, there are perhaps few that they would more readily turn aside from than this.

"Again, it was *found impracticable to collect any number of hearers.* In other parts of India, we read of hundreds and thousands listening to a Missionary. Here, *ten persons* could scarcely be brought together, either in the streets, or in a place appointed for worship. The heathen are allowed to buy and sell, and carry on their ordinary labours on the Sabbath, just as on other days; it was, therefore, in vain to expect any reverence for that day among them, or any more readiness to attend on divine things. The writer of these pages is very far from supposing that true religion derives much advantage from mere acts of *civil* authority, or that any people should be compelled to observe the institutions of the Gospel; at the same time, he thinks there are very strong reasons to question the propriety of *allowing* the Sabbath to be thus openly profaned, in Christian colonies. Christian rulers would do well to consider what the Scriptures say on this subject. But if it be wrong to permit idolaters to carry on open trade and every kind of labour on the Sabbath, it must surely be a greater crime to *employ* them to do work on that day, and to wink at the gross breaches of the Sabbath, of which professing Christians are guilty.

"The same difficulty of collecting a congregation has all along been felt; and it will not be easily or speedily overcome. The Chinese spend the whole day in hard labour; and their evenings are very commonly devoted to *gambling*, where that ruinous practice is permitted. When a few persons came to hear, it was no easy matter to fix their attention. Some would be talking; others, laughing at the newness of the things spoken; others, smoking their pipes; others, on coming in and going out, would pass through the usual routine of their ceremony, just as they act in the temples of their own gods, before which nothing like reverence is ever seen. They did these things, it was believed, more from habit and ignorance, than from intentional disrespect to the word of God; but the difficulty to the speaker was nearly the same. The few, indeed, who attended regularly, became, after a short time, remarkably decorous and attentive. But this can never be expected at first.

The prevalence of the *skeptical philosophy of the school of Confucius,* constituted another difficulty in the way of the Mission; but as there will be occasion to notice this afterwards, we shall pass it over for the time.

The establishment of *a Malay Mission* in these

countries, was a thing exceedingly to be desired.' The chief part of the inhabitants of the numerous islands of the eastern Archipelago, as well as of the Peninsula of Malacca, are enveloped in the delusions of Islamism; not indeed of pure Islamism, but of a species of it, mixed with the superstitions and even idolatries of the aborigines of the countries into which it has been introduced. This heterogeneous mass of error and superstition, renders the moral and spiritual state of the Malays very wretched, their conversion very difficult; and the planting of the Gospel among them, an object worthy of more attention from Christian Societies, than it has yet received. They are but a partially civilized people; a very small proportion of them can read, and their reading is much confined to the Arabic—the language of the Koran, and, as they suppose, of paradise too! The improvement of mankind has suffered greatly in many countries, from the notion of one language being exclusively proper for religion—from their self-devised *lingua eclesiæ*, as if Deity were to be charmed by strange sounds, or his creatures instructed through the medium of a language which they do not understand!" (The French Missionaries felt this, and translated the *Missal* into Chinese, and presented it to the Pope. This was a broad *hint* to infallibility, but his holiness would not take it; and neither Couplet nor Le Compte dared to speak out. The translators thought him a *fool*, and he thought them *rogues*, in the church; but each party kept its own secret. He called them his "dear sons," and they called him their "holy Father;" and thus the Chinese Missal was *shelved* in the Vatican!) " Of all the *insults* offered to common sense and the human understanding, from the day that sin first entered our world to this hour, there is none greater than this; and its extensive prevalence, is but an additional confirmation of our belief, that mental 'blindness has happened' to our species. This partial preference for the Arabic, has led the Malays to think lightly of their own language, which they call *baha' sa dunya*, that is, the language of this world; and hence, though perhaps the most harmonious of all the languages of the East, it has been less cultivated than the greater part of them. This prejudice forms an obstacle to their religious improvement, in two ways: it has led to a very general neglect of Malay education, so that but one here and there is found capable of reading books written in Malay. Again, having been taught to consider the *Arabic* as the only language acceptable to God, and fit to be employed in his worship, it has weakened their veneration for every kind of religious instruction which does not pass through that medium. And yet were a Missionary to preach to them in Arabic, there is not perhaps one in a hundred that would understand him. They are found to possess much of the bigotry and prejudice which are inseparable from Islamism, without one half of the knowledge of the system which is possessed by their fellow believers on the west of India. A knowledge of the unity and perfection of the divine nature, of the doctrines of divine providence, the resurrection, and future judgment, &c., they indeed possess; but it is obscure and feeble, and moreover, mixed with such a mass of error, as almost entirely to hinder its operation on the mind, and prevent its tendency to produce a virtuous conduct; so that they may still be said to be almost 'Atheists, and without hope in the world;' for there is in reality very little difference as to virtuous effects on the heart and life, between not believing that there is a God at all (were such a pitch of atheism possible,) and believing him to be something totally different from what he is. The meager specimens of Christianity which the Malays and Javanese have commonly seen displayed by those who call themselves the followers of Christ, have not tended to produce reverence for the system. The abominable idolatries of the Church of Rome, the idle and ostentatious trumpery of ceremony that attends her masses, processions, funerals, &c., excite in Mahometans the deepest disgust; and lead them to think with abhorrence of that noble system, of which those absurdities are but the unhallowed appendages. Nor has the conduct of Protestants had a better effect upon them. Though the Protestant religion be free from the absurdities which attach themselves to the Catholic, yet the practice of its adherents has been equally *injurious* to the cause of truth, and equally tended to *harden* the hearts of Mahometans against the Gospel. The total neglect of all religion which prevails too generally among the Protestants of these colonies; and the public and bare-faced profanation of the Sabbath by both Catholics and Protestants; the avarice, lying, and cozening which appear in carrying on commerce; the drunkenness, loose morals, and hardness of heart towards slaves, which have at times been manifested by the professors of the Gospel, have steeled the Mussulman's soul against Christianity. He has scarcely ever seen its excellencies displayed; hence he conceives that it has none. He cannot think well of a system, the adherents of which pay so little regard to God, to truth, and to duty. These remarks show both the necessity of attempting the conversion of the Malays and the difficulty of the task. But as Christian duty ought not to vary with human opinions, so neither ought Christian zeal to be impeded by difficulties. The ardour and liberality of Christians in the present age seem to acquire strength and expansion from impediments; hence there is no fear, that the former will subside or the latter contract, by a full statement of the real condition, the strong prejudices, and the deep depravity of people to whom the Gospel is sent.

"It was above stated, that Missionaries to settle among the Malays, were expected. Accordingly, on 27th September, 1815, the same year in which the Chinese Mission was begun, the Rev. C. H. Thomsen, (originally from Holstein in Lower Saxony,) with Mrs. T., landed at Malacca, to begin the good work among the Malays. Mr. T.'s time during the remaining part of the year was spent in assiduous application to the study of the language, and in making preparations for a school, which he began the year following. As his acquaintance with the language, and intercourse with the people, increased, he conceived that a version of the scriptures in a plainer style, and more purely Malay, than that which was re-printing at Bengal, would greatly facilitate the communication of Christian truth to the people. That highly respectable version, originally executed by Dutch Clergymen, abounds with numerous Arabic words; Portuguese words are also found in it; and it is generally written in what is called by the Dutch, '*the high Malay;*' hence it is not so easily understood by common readers. These considerations induced Mr. T. to form the resolution of attempting a translation of at least part of the New Testament, in a simpler style, as soon as his attainments in the language should enable him to undertake it.

"In the close of the year, *Ultra-Ganges' Mission Library* was begun. The advantages of public libraries are sufficiently known to be appreciated. In foreign countries, where European books are not easily procurable, a good library is an invaluable treasure. Where a few Missionaries labour together in the same place, they cannot be badly off for such works as lie most in their own way. When their labour calls them to separate, each one requires his own library with him; hence the necessity of a public general one, to which all may have access when near, but over which no individual can have control. In a station at which there is a view to establish a public Seminary, a large collection of books in all languages, and on all subjects, is necessary. There, the best works on all the different departments of theology, literature, science, and history ought to be collected. Native books, or those written in the vernacular tongues, are of peculiar importance. They should be principally sought after, and no means left untried to procure a full supply; because Missionary objects cannot be accomplished without a knowledge of the languages, and that knowledge cannot be fully attained without books, written by the learned men of the country.

"In regard to useful objects, it does not seem necessary to wait till a large collection of materials be made before they be begun. The conviction of their utility being once firmly fixed in the mind, let them be attempted in dependence on Divine Providence, and on the co-operation of those men to whom they approve themselves. If they be essentially connected with the improvement and happiness of but a small portion of mankind, they will ultimately prosper, however unpromising in their first stages. The Ultra-Ganges' Mission Library was begun with only about ten small volumes of European books, and a very few of Chinese. It was hoped the number would increase;—which hope has not been disappointed." (I must add, however, that the catalogue, although respectable now, would sadly disappoint any scholar, who knows what the libraries of Europe contain on the subject of the *ancient* Syriac Missions to Asia. In that department, it is even poorer than some private libraries: a fact, which will, I hope, draw out some contributions for the College.)

CHAPTER X.

MISCELLANEOUS LABOURS.

"The Mission at Malacca was, for the first year, without any land of its own, on which to erect such buildings as were necessary for the accommodation of the Missionaries, and for the execution of the various labours in which they were engaged. It was therefore considered advisable, that an application should be made to the Government of Penang, requesting a grant of land. In January, 1816, Mr. Milne went to that island, and by the advice of some friends, presented a memorial to the Honourable the Governor in Council, soliciting a grant of land to the Mission at Malacca; permission to establish a printing press; and the privilege of free passages in cruizing vessels under the orders of Government, for the Members of the Ultra-Ganges' Missions, to such parts of the Archipelago as the cruizers should be visiting, and the labours of the Missionaries require them to go. The following is an extract from the answer of the Government:—

"'I have the honour to acknowledge the receipt of your letter to the address of the Honourable the Governor in Council, which having been submitted to his consideration, he is pleased to express his warm and cordial approbation of the benevolent objects in view, and disposed to afford the countenance and support of Government thereto.

"'The Governor in Council has therefore pleasure in complying, as far as he is enabled to do, with the several applications conveyed in your letter, and although the expected restoration of the settlement of Malacca to the Sovereign of the Netherlands, puts it out of his power now to make any alienation of any part of the lands, he has instructed the Resident at Malacca to allot to the Mission a piece of waste ground, under a conditional grant, the confirmation of which, or otherwise, must, of course, depend upon the Dutch government. The Governor in Council at the same time indulges a hope, that the laudable and pious objects of the Mission will appear to the future Government of Malacca, not less than they do to himself, deserving of every liberal encouragement; and he will not fail, in the event of the restoration of that settlement, to bring under the particular notice of the new authorities this conditional grant, and the objects for which it has been granted.

"'The Governor in Council accedes to the other requests preferred by you, and will give directions that the cruizers under the orders of this Government shall afford every accommodation to yourself and the brethren of the Mission, that the service on which they may be employed may admit.

"'The request to establish a printing press at Malacca, for printing in the native languages, is also acceded to, and the Governor in Council, in conclusion, desires to express his wishes for the success of the objects of the Mission.'

"Here it is proper to acknowledge the obligations under which these Missions have been laid, by the late Honourable W. Petrie, Governor of Penang, and his successor, the Honourable Colonel Bannerman, together with the Honourable the Members of Council, for the kindness manifested in the instance under consideration, and in various subsequent instances: a cordial readiness has ever been shown by that Government to promote our objects both at Penang and Malacca, which, while it demands our grateful thanks, ought to stimulate us to pursue our work with increasing ardour and prudence.

"While at this presidency, Mr. Milne had many opportunities of circulating the Scriptures and tracts among the Chinese; and experienced much politeness from Major M'Innes, the Rev. Mr. Hutchings, the Clergyman, W. Scott, Esq., and other English gentlemen, to whom his acknowledgments are justly due.

"After returning from Penang, it was found, on inquiry, that the Government possessed no land in the immediate vicinity of Malacca. A spot at St. John's Hill was accordingly granted; but, being at a considerable distance from town, it was suggested by Dr. Chalmers and John Macalister, Esq., that an attempt to exchange it with one of smaller dimensions, and more convenient for our purposes, should be made. By the assistance and counsel of those gentlemen, an exchange was made with *Tambe Amat Saib*, for the premises at the western gate of the town of Malacca, on which the Mission now stands. *Seven hundred Spanish dollars* (£200,) together with the ground at St. John's Hill, were given him in lieu of his property; and in order fully to secure his premises to the Mission, on the one hand, and to prevent him from being a loser by future uncertainties on the other, it was farther stipulated that, in case of the Dutch Government's refusing, at the expected transfer of the settlement, to confirm the grant of land conditionally made to the Mission by the Penang Government (a thing which was not, however, anticipated)—in this case it was stipulated, that the Mission should pay to him the sum at which the ground at St. John's Hill was valued in the agreement.

"This year Mr. Thomsen began a *Malay and English School*, which promised very favourably. But, in consequence of the protracted and complicated illness of Mrs. Thomsen, a sea voyage was rendered necessary; and the school, with the other departments of the Malay branch of the Mission at

Malacca, were necessarily put a stop to, and suffered a long intermission of more than fifteen months. Mr. and Mrs. T. left Malacca 12th September, and went to Java; but as she derived no advantage in regard to health in that place, they proceeded on to England. But it pleased the Sovereign disposer of all things to cut short the sufferings of this pious and spiritual-minded woman on the passage. On the 4th February, 1817, she died at sea, in the triumphs of Christian faith and hope, exclaiming, 'I am happy! I am happy! come, thou blessed Spirit! Oh! come.' Mrs. T. was a woman of a very tender and delicate constitution, eminently devoted to God, and 'of a meek and quiet spirit.' Mr. T. proceeded to England, and returned to Malacca again in December, 1817.

"From the very commencement of the Mission at Malacca, an English school had been proposed for the children of the Christians, which met the cordial approbation of the local Government. A house for the purpose was accordingly erected at the expense of the Consistory of the Reformed Church, and means taken to procure a teacher from Madras. But in the interim, news arrived that a speedy transfer of Malacca to the Dutch Government might be expected, which made the people more indifferent about the English language. Hence the school-house, which had been erected for the children and youth of the Christians, was, for a time, employed as a Chinese school.

"During the preceding year, there was only one Chinese school. It was taught in the Fokien dialect, and the number of scholars, as above noticed, was but small, not exceeding sixteen. At the commencement of this year, the number increased to forty; and in the course of several months, to about fifty-seven. The use of the new school was obligingly granted for these Fokien children. A second school, to be taught in the Canton dialect, began with this year. The number of Canton people in Malacca is comparatively small: hence twenty-three is the highest number of boys that has yet appeared on the list of this school—it has often been much below that number. There were twenty-three on the list the first year, so that in both schools there were eighty boys—about fifty-five formed the average of the daily attendants.

"In trying to impart religious instruction to the scholars, the want of a catechism, written purposely for *young* persons, was felt. The catechism which they had been learning, was better suited to grown persons, and those who had some previous knowledge of the Christian system. In the close of 1815, Mr. Milne had begun a translation of Watts' 'Second Catechism,' with this view; but in reviewing it the following year, there appeared something wanting to render the instruction exactly suited to the state of a *Pagan* mind. Most books written for Christian youth, suppose more knowledge and fewer prejudices than we find existing among Heathens of the same age. There is also a certain stiffness almost inseparable from a mere translation, which prevents the reader from perusing it with that ease and pleasure which the perusal of an original composition might be expected to afford. In books for children, the difficulty of attaining sufficient plainness and simplicity of ideas and of words is very great; particularly in a foreign and Pagan language, where many theological terms, however simplified, will be new, not to children only, but also to men of years and understanding. These considerations induced Mr. Milne to give up the idea of a mere translation of Watts, and to make it rather a kind of foundation to go upon—using the ideas where they seemed to be suitable, and adding, or paring off, as appeared most for edification. He composed and finished this little work, which was called 'The Youth's Catechism,' in the spring and summer of 1816. A considerable part of it was written in affliction, and under an impression that it might probably be the *last* service he should be permitted to attempt for the instruction of the Chinese. This impression, which should never be long absent from any Missionary's mind, led to a greater fulness of matter than was at first intended: so that it contains a summary of the whole Christian faith. It was printed shortly after, and used in the schools; and also widely circulated along with the other tracts of the Mission.

"Two new tracts were written and printed in Chinese this year: one called 'The Strait Gate,' the other, 'The Sin of Lying.'

"A translation of the book of *Deuteronomy*, undertaken at Mr. Morrison's suggestion, was completed at Malacca, in the month of July. It was subsequently revised by Mr. Morrison and the translator, and printed." (Thus modestly did Mr. Milne record his first achievement in the translation of the Scriptures into the Chinese!)

"Till now, no individual of the Chinese, connected with the Mission at Malacca, had manifested any serious wish to make a public profession of Christianity. Some appeared to be at times impressed with what they heard and read; but none had courage or decision to declare themselves on the Lord's side.

"In course of the summer of 1816, a more than usual attention to the truth was observed in a Chinese employed as a printer to the Mission. He professed his determination to take up his cross and follow Christ. Means were used to inform him more fully on the nature and qualifications of a true Christian profession. Frequent seasons of private conversation and prayer with him were fixed on. The following extract from Mr. Milne's journal for that year, relates to this person:—

"'*Nov.* 3.—*Sabbath.*—At twelve o'clock this day I baptized, in the name of the adorable Trinity, Leang-kung-fah, whose name has been already mentioned. The service was performed privately, in a room of the Mission-house. Care had been taken, by private conversation, instruction, and prayer, to prepare him for this sacred ordinance: this had been continued for a considerable time. Finding him still steadfast in his wish to become a Christian, I baptized him. The change produced in his sentiments and conduct is, I hope, the effect of Christian truth, and of that alone,—yet, who of mortals can know the heart? Several searching questions were proposed to him in private; and an exercise suited to the case of a heathen candidate for baptism, composed and given to him to read and meditate upon.

"'He belongs to the province of Canton, is a single man, about 33 years of age, and has no relatives living, except a father and brother. He can read a plain book with ease, but has had only a common education; is of a steady character, and frugal habits. His temper is not so sociable and engaging as that of many other Chinese. He was formerly stiff and obstinate, and occasionally troublesome. Of late, there has been scarcely any thing of this kind to complain of. He came with me from Canton, in April, 1815, to Malacca. He told me the other day, that he was employed in printing my 'Treatise on the Life of Christ.' Whether he had been seriously impressed with the contents of that book, I am not able to say.

"With respect to his former life, he observed: 'I was never much given to idolatry, and seldom went to the temples. I sometimes prayed towards heaven, but lived in careless indifference. Although I rarely went to excess in sin, yet I have been occasionally guilty of drunkenness and other kindred vices. Before I came hither, I knew not God; now I desire to serve him.' He wished to be baptized *exactly at twelve o'clock*, 'when' to use his own words, 'the shadow inclines neither the one way nor the other.' What his view in fixing on that precise time was, I cannot tell; but, I suppose, it arose from the remains of that superstitious regard to 'times,' which prevails so generally among the Chinese. I told him that God had not distinguished one hour from another; and that he, as a disciple of Christ, must in future regard every day and hour alike, except the Sabbath, which is to be devoted specially to the service of God. Aware that some superstitious attachments may, for a considerable time, hang about the first converts from Paganism, and that it *is in the Church, and under the ordinances thereof*, that these attachments are to be entirely destroyed, I did not think it advisable to delay administering the initiatory ordinance.

"'At baptism, the following questions were proposed to him, to which he answered as below:—

"'*Question* 1. Have you truly turned from idols, to worship and serve the living and true God, the creator of heaven and earth and all things?—*Answer.* This is my heart's desire.

"'*Q.* 2. Do you know and feel that you are a sinful creature, totally unable to save yourself?—*A.* I know it.

"'*Q.* 3. Do you really, from your heart, believe that Jesus Christ is the Son of God, and Saviour of the world; and do you trust in him alone for salvation?—*A.* This is my heart's desire.

"'*Q.* 4. Do you expect any worldly advantage, profit, or gain whatever, by your becoming a Christian?—*A.* None: I receive baptism because it is my duty.

"'*Q.* 5. Do you resolve from this day till the day of your death, to live in obedience to all the commandments and ordinances of God; and in justice and righteousness of life before men?—*A.* This is my determination; but I fear my strength is not equal to it.

"'On my part, the ordinance was dispensed with mingled affection, joy, hope, and fear. May he be made faithful unto death; and as he is the first fruits of this branch of the Mission, may an abundant harvest follow, to the joy of the chuich, and the honour of Christ.

"'Since his baptism, some private means have been used to increase his knowledge; to impress his heart more deeply, and to strengthen his faith.'

"He and his instructer met once a week for reading the Scriptures, conversation, and prayer together. On those occasions Leang-kung-fah used to bring such passages of Scripture, as in his private reading he could not easily understand, to get them explained. Many important paragraphs were gone over in this way, as Mr. Milne considered that to fix his mind on the word of God itself, was of vastly more importance to vital and practical Christianity, than to employ the time in conversation about the mere feelings and exercises of the mind, although these were not neglected in their proper place and measure. To make men well acquainted with the word of God, is the only way to fill their minds with the materials by which alone the regeneration and sanctification of their own souls can be effected; and by which alone they can be really useful in turning other sinners to God and holiness." (Here Dr. Milne's account of Leang-A-Fa stops. Mr. Bridgeman, the American Missionary, adds,—

"After continuing in Malacca four years, A-Fa returned to China to visit his family and friends; and when he saw them wholly given to idolatry, his heart was moved to pity. He earnestly desired their conversion and their salvation; and with a view to effect this purpose, he prepared a little tract, in which he imbodied a few of the clearest and most important portions of Scripture respecting idolatry, the need of repentance and faith in Christ, &c.; and having submitted the manuscript to Dr. Morrison, he engraved the blocks and printed two hundred copies, intending to circulate them among his acquaintance. But, unexpectedly, the policemen, having been informed of what he was doing, seized him, and his books and blocks, and carried them all away to the public courts; the books and blocks they destroyed, and A-Fa they shut up in prison. In that situation he began to review his past conduct, and the course he was attempting to pursue, in order to promulgate the doctrine of Christ among his countrymen. Though he was conscious of having done right in preparing his 'little book,' yet, at the same time, he was thoroughly convinced that it was on account of his sins that he was called to suffer persecution, and he viewed his imprisonment as a just chastisement inflicted by his heavenly Father, to whom he earnestly prayed for the pardon of his sins.

"He had been only a few days in prison, when Dr. Morrison heard of it, and immediately interceded with influential native merchants, that they would endeavour to arrange with the officers of Government and procure his release. This, however, was not done, until, by the order of the magistrate, he had received thirty blows with the large bamboo. This instrument of punishment is five and a half feet long, about two inches broad, and one inch and a quarter thick; and so severely applied in the case of A-Fa, as to cause the blood to flow down from both of his legs. After they had thus beaten him and received a considerable sum of money, about seventy dollars, they set him at liberty.

"The effect of this imprisonment and beating, which took place in Canton, was to make him more humble and more devoted to the cause of Christ. Soon after he was released from prison, he went to visit his family in the country, where he spent forty days. He then returned to Malacca, continued there for a year, and then came again to China to visit his family. He was especially interested in the spiritual welfare of his wife, and was exceedingly anxious for her conversion; he read to her the Scriptures; prayed with and for her; and at length, by his instrumentality she was brought to believe in Jesus, and was baptized by her husband. 'From that time,' says A-Fa, 'we have been of one heart and one mind in worshipping and serving the one only living and true God, the Ruler and Governor of the universe, and in endeavouring to turn those around us from the service of dumb idols.'

"He became anxious also for the conversion of his countrymen, and desired to make them acquainted with that Gospel which he had found so precious to his own soul. To prepare himself in some measure to effect that object, he went again, with the consent of his wife, to Malacca, where he was received and cherished as a brother by that man of God who had brought him into the fold of Christ. He resolved now to apply himself with new assiduity to his work, and especially to the study of the Bible, under the direction of Dr. Milne. But alas, before one year had passed away, he was bereaved of that endeared friend and brother. Dr. Milne died in 1822.

"Having no one at Malacca on whom he could depend, A-Fa returned once more to his family, all the members of which he found in health; their number had been increased by the birth of a son; the heart of the father was greatly rejoiced at this happy event, and 'he bowed down and gave God thanks for his great favour.' When the lad was about two years old, he carried him to the house of Dr. Morrison, where, in the ordinance of Christian baptism, he consecrated him to the Lord, with the hope that 'he might grow up and become a virtuous man, thoroughly acquainted with the holy Scriptures, and able to preach the Gospel to his countrymen.' Leang Tsintih, for that is the name of the lad, is now twelve years old; he reads the Scriptures, both in his own and in the English language, and has made some proficiency in the study of Hebrew. The father's interest in the boy has always been very great; and it is his earnest and daily prayer, and he intercedes with others that they would pray for him also, that the child may live and become a preacher of righteousness, and turn the hearts of many unto the Lord.

"Still farther to qualify himself to preach the Gospel, A-Fa continued his studies with Dr. Morrison for about two or three years, who then, having sufficient evidence of his qualification for an evangelist, 'laid hands on me, and ordained me,' he says, 'to publish to men every where the true Gospel.' From that to the present time, about ten years, he has continued steadfast in the faith and in the labours of the Gospel; and has employed his whole time in making and circulating Christian books, and in proclaiming the word in other ways as he has found opportunity. His aged father still lives, but loves not the truth. He has a little daughter, six years of age, who has been given to the Lord in baptism. His friend Lee, who went with him to Malacca, and continued there till Dr. Milne's death, lives to this day without hope and without God in the world. Among his kindred and friends, for a long time, none but his wife believed; but recently more than ten souls have professed their faith in Jesus; and there are others, who inquire what they shall do to be saved. His labours, his faith, and his zeal, increase as he goes forward with his work. During the last five months he has distributed in the city and suburbs of Canton, more than 15,000 Tracts. And now, like holy Paul, his heart's desire is that the good seed may bring forth fruit unto eternal life." (Mr. Malcom has visited him since. Ackerman published a print of him.)

"The establishment of a *printing press* had been before contemplated, as an object of much importance, and resolved upon, as soon as circumstances would allow. Accordingly, in the spring of this year, after permission to establish a press had been obtained from Government, the kind offices of a gentleman in Bengal, whose name has already been mentioned, were engaged to procure founts of English and Malay types, a printing press, with the necessary apparatus, and workmen. In the month of November, these all arrived from Bengal; but a great difficulty arose about the way of employing them to the best advantage. Through some mistake, six workmen were sent instead of two, and their wages amounted to a considerable sum. When the press was sent for, there were two Missionaries labouring at Malacca, and preparations were making for beginning to print in Malay, as soon as it should arrive. But one of them, and the one engaged in the Malay department, was by Divine Providence removed from the station for a time, and the period of his return was uncertain. The whole work devolved on an individual who had for the time nothing important to employ the press upon, and who had no knowledge of the way of managing a printing establishment to advantage. The workmen had left their homes on the faith of being employed for a considerable time; and justice required that they should not be dismissed. It occurred to Mr. Milne that, as *the Missionary Society* had printed an edition of 'Bogue's Essay on the New Testament'—and 'Doddridge's Rise and Progress of Religion in the Soul,' in French, for sale, or gratuitous circulation in France, and on the Continent of Europe,—an edition of the same inestimable books might be printed in English, and either sold or given away gratis, among our fellow-countrymen in the East. Though the expense would, doubtless, considerably surpass the proceeds of the sale, yet it appeared the only way of employing the men for the time. It was also considered that though there might be some pecuniary loss, yet the circulation of the great mass of important truth, contained in these publications, might do good to the souls of men, in which case their eternal gain would infinitely counterbalance a pecuniary loss. Many young men come from England to these countries, both in the land and sea service, either before their minds are established in the truth, or after they are corrupted by infidelity and vice. Parental and pastoral instructions, administered perhaps with a careful hand, weeping eyes, and a bleeding heart, are often lost, or apparently so, in the contagion of vice which reigns around the young man when he comes to the East. Every well-wisher to his soul must be desirous of having some useful book to put into his hand, which may, through the Divine blessing, cherish the principles of piety planted in his heart in early life, which may be his 'vade mecum,' while he 'ploughs the trackless waves,' or his companion in the camp; or his consolation in solitude, sickness, and death—and, perhaps, also the means of awakening in his breast, a train of reflections which may ultimately issue in repentance, faith, holiness, and eternal life. When a young military man, or a young man engaged in the sea-faring line, passes a seaport, it never fails to afford a religious pleasure to a good man, to be able to put some highly and generally-esteemed Christian book into his hands. Considerations of this nature led to the printing of 'Bogue's Essay,' and 'Doddridge's Rise,' at Malacca; some copies were subscribed for, some purchased by a benevolent gentleman, who wished to give them to his young friends; some placed for sale in different parts of India, and a greater part put into the hands of Missionaries in various stations, for gratuitous distribution to proper persons. There are, perhaps, few modern books of human composition read with more universal and deserved acceptance, or better calculated to do good to mankind, than the two here noticed.

"Another grant of £1,000 was this year received from *the British and Foreign Bible Society*, to assist in printing the 12mo edition of the New Testament which had been before determined on.

"It ought to have been noticed in a preceding section, that in consequence of an application to *The Religious Tract Society*,' a sum of £300 was voted for the purpose of assisting the Chinese Mission in printing and circulating religious tracts in the Chinese language. A second grant of £400 was subsequently received from the same Society, and for the same purposes. Great are our obligations to that most useful institution; and great is the necessity that exists, in these Pagan lands, for the exercise of its beneficence. Tracts are soon read through, and easily carried about with one. Several hundreds, of different sorts and on different subjects, may with facility be packed up in a very small compass. They admit of greater familiarity of diction and a more diffuse style, than is befitting the majestic sublimity of the sacred oracles themselves. They may be circulated more widely than the sacred Scriptures can. If we calculate either the price, or the persons capable of deriving profit from religious books among the Chinese, we shall find that *fifty* tracts may be given away for *one* New Testament. Thus *fifty persons* may be made acquainted with at least *one* important truth, for the expense of one Testament. A Missionary, in his itinerant labours among the Heathen, can carry a hundred tracts in his hand; and he will ever find great satisfaction in leaving an appropriate one in the house where he has been visiting; or by putting one into the hands of those with whom he has been conversing; or by dropping one on the high-way, where it is likely to be taken up by some passing stranger; or by reading and explaining one to those that are inclined to hear. A tract may be enclosed in a letter, and sent into a persecuting country without much risk of discovery. Several have been actually sent into China in this way. These things show the high importance of the Tract Society, and how powerful an auxiliary it may become, in the conversion of the Heathen to Christ. Indeed, it holds the *third* rank in point of utility among those societies which constitute the glory of Christendom. *Missionary Societies* must ever be considered as entitled to the *first* place, at least in as far as the Heathen are concerned; in as much as without their agents, translations of the

Scriptures are not likely to be extensively made, nor tracts written. Next in order comes the *Bible Society*, that mighty agent of Divine Providence for uniting the energies of the Christian public, and to which almost every Protestant Mission in the known world is indebted. The *Tract Society* is the last of this sacred triad; and though in some respects it holds a lower place than the other two, in others its utility is more immediate, extensive, and apparent, than that of theirs. Nothing is farther from the writer's mind than a wish to excite a dishonourable rivalship among those noble institutions, which will doubtless, by their united efforts, in course of time, make true religion to surround the globe on which we dwell, and extend the boundaries of the Christian church as widely as the habitations of men. But it is right that each institution should have its due honour; and we ought to know in what particular each excels, and how they all unite to promote the great cause of truth and righteousness in the earth. May Heaven continue to smile on them all—and may 'the joy of the Holy Ghost,' dwell abundantly in the hearts of those who direct their concerns.

"On the 7th July, (1816,) Dr. Morrison left Macao in the suite of Lord Amherst, British Embassador to the Court of Peking. They went up the Yellow Sea, arrived at the Palace of *Yuenming-yuen* on the 29th August, and the Embassy having failed, they returned by land to Canton, at which place they arrived on the 1st January, 1817. This journey afforded a little relaxation to him, which was very necessary after nine years' close and incessant study. His health was much improved, considerable historical information of a local kind was obtained; and many opportunities of becoming acquainted with the various spoken dialects which prevail through the country, presented themselves in course of the trip. He wrote a short Memoir of the Embassy, which it is hoped, he will yet publish, accompanied with copious notes, literary and historical. Besides tracing the failure of that important political Mission to its real causes, (which may be supposed to have been done, at least in part, by those who have already written on the subject,) his personal knowledge of Chinese Literature would enable him to add many interesting illustrations of manners, customs, and opinions, both ancient and modern, which cannot be expected from those who have no knowledge of the language, however well they may write in other respects. This may be farther urged on his attention, from the consideration that, by entering pretty fully into the more important illustrations, and accompanying the notes with copious and appropriate quotations, in the Chinese character, (a translation of which, however, for the sake of the general reader, would be required)—much benefit to his fellow-labourers in the Chinese Mission, and to foreign students of Chinese, would be likely to accrue. The theory, and especially the modern practice of the Chinese Government, not being detailed in the books which the student reads, he must remain ignorant of the same, and be content to learn what China was several hundred years back. Something to illustrate *modern* China, is quite a *desideratum*, and it could be very well appended to, or blended with, this Memoir. The writer trusts, that the author may be induced to re-consider the subject, and gratify the wishes of a large circle of friends by bringing the Memoir forth to light."

(Dr. Morrison's widow has felt the weight of Dr. Milne's appeal, and in her life of her illustrious husband, just published, has given his own account of this visit to Peking. *Vol. 2, p.* 444. It is interesting, although not extensive. The fact is, he laid it down as a maxim, that "the political discussions and transactions of the Embassy were irrelevant to his pursuits;" and as the results were not pleasant, it was not a *favourite* subject with him. Many, in common with myself, found it impossible to draw him *out* on this subject, even when he was enriching his conversation with *allusions* to what he had seen. It was, however, evidently a *school* to himself, although he did not admit others far into it.)

CHAPTER XI.

MILNE'S ESTIMATES OF CHINESE CHARACTER.

It will give weight to the following estimates, when I say that they had Dr. Morrison's *imprimatur*. Even this is not saying enough: he selected many of them from Dr. Milne's manuscripts, and sanctioned the whole. I mention this fact, that they may be known as the joint judgment of competent authorities.

"The character of nations, like that of individuals, often changes. This remark applies to China as well as to other countries, though perhaps not to the same extent. The Chinese national character is not now what it was in the commencement of the present dynasty; nor was it then what it had been in the days of Confucius. From the time of Yaou and Shun, down to the time of that philosopher, it had also undergone those changes which commonly attend a state of progressive civilization. In the reign of these excellent chieftains, China was yet a small country, and but just emerging from barbarism. A little before their days, the people lived in the savage state. They resided in woods, in caves, and in huts, dug in the ground. They covered themselves with the skins of beasts: they also made garments of the leaves of trees, of reeds, and of grass. They ate the flesh of animals, with the blood, and the skin, and the hair; all unboiled, unroasted and undressed. They could neither read, nor write, nor cipher.

"Their dead often lay unburied. Sometimes they were thrown into ditches, and sometimes cast without shroud, coffin, or ceremony, into a hole dug in the ground with the end of a stick.

"They were in a state equally barbarous and savage to that in which the Britons lived during the reign of Druidism, before the conquest by Julius Cæsar.

"From the time of Yaou and Shun, the Chinese territory extended, its population increased, and its character improved. While it remained in the feudal state, neither arts nor sciences flourished. Necessity was the mother of invention in China as well as in other nations. Increasing numbers taught them the necessity of labour; labour of instruments; and instruments of skill; this produced some improvement in the practical arts, the progress of which was secured for a time by the impulse of the principle which gave them birth.

"In literature, nature itself became their instructer. By the impression of the feet of birds on the sand, and the marks on the bodies of shell-fish, they caught the first idea of writing. Their written character continued for a considerable time purely hieroglyphic; but after passing through various changes, suggested partly by convenience, and partly by genius, it gradually lost its original form, and approximated to one better adapted for the purposes of government and of literature.

"In the earlier ages of China, before its inhabitants were collected into towns, and cities, and large associations, along with their rusticity of ideas, manners, and virtues, they also preserved the ruder vices of uncivilized life; but were not yet contaminated with the intrigue, the falsehood, and the hypocrisy, which too often attend a more advanced stage of society. Hence many of their sages of subsequent times, affected with the evils which passed under their more immediate review, and forgetting those which existed of old, pass the highest encomiums on the ages of antiquity. Even things which were really the consequences of ignorance and barbarity, they sometimes mistake for virtues of high character. They erroneously conceived, that the vices of their own times were rather the necessary consequences of high civilization, than the native corruption of the human heart, displaying itself in another form. In the days of Confucius, and for some time after, China continued divided into a great many small kingdoms, which all united in acknowledging the supremacy of the emperors, while each possessed within itself all the arbitrary power of a feudal state.

In the dynasty Tsin, the power of states was abolished, the whole amalgamated into one, and the government erected into that gigantic despotism the great lines of which it preserves to this hour.

"The wisdom of the ancient rulers and sages of China formed a code of laws which, with many defects, possessed also many great excellencies. Through the numerous ages in which these laws have existed, they have been executed with various degrees of moderation and humanity; and sometimes without the oppressive exertion of arbitrary power. The huge machine of their government has been often battered both from without and from within, and still its essential parts hang together.

"For ages, the arts and sciences in China have been stationary; and from the accounts of the last English embassy, seem, at present, rather in a retrograde state. The obstinate refusal of the Chinese to improve, is rather to be viewed as the effect of principle than the want of genius. They consider the ancient sages, kings, and governments, as the prototypes of excellence; and a near approximation to the times in which they lived, the highest display of national wisdom and virtue. They are still the blind slaves of antiquity, and possess not that greatness of character which sees its own defects, and sighs after improvement.

"Tartars now govern China. The milder sons of Han* could not withstand the arms of the conquering Khan. The wild Scythian, who ate the

---

* Han is a term often used by the Chinese themselves to distinguish them from the Tartars. They call themselves Hantsze, that is, "Sons of Han."—*Dr. Morrison.*

flesh of horses, and drank the milk of cows, was fit for every enterprise. His restless ambition, nothing but universal empire could satiate; and scarce any obstacle could resist his savage prowess. At length, after the reverses attendant on a state of warfare, continued with various interruptions for several centuries, he seated himself securely on the throne of China, where he now holds the most permanent place among earthly princes; and assumes to be 'THE HEAD OF ALL—THE SON OF HEAVEN—THE EMPEROR OF ALL THAT IS UNDER THE STARRY FIRMAMENT—AND THE VICE-GERENT OF THE MOST HIGH.'

"It is now nearly one hundred and eighty years since the Tartars obtained the government of the whole Chinese dominions. They united China to their own territory, and thus formed one of the most extensive empires that ever existed. They adopted many of the customs of their newly acquired subjects; but did not give up with those which formed their own national peculiarities. They continued to preserve the essential parts of that code of laws which they found existing in China; while they, at the same time, imposed certain regulations which were viewed by the conquered either as highly disgraceful or oppressive; and the non-compliance with which, cost some of them their lives. The executive government was soon filled by Tartars; who at times affected, and still affect, to treat the Chinese with contempt. To contend is of no avail: the Chinese must submit, and (as they sometimes express themselves) 'QUIETLY EAT DOWN THE INSULTS THEY MEET WITH.'

"Since the union of China to Manchow Tartary, there have been TWO NATIONAL CHARACTERS in the empire, reciprocally affecting each. The high and exclusive tone which had ever been assumed by the emperors of China, was highly gratifying to the mind of the victorious Tartar; while the power of his arms secured the honour of superiority to himself. The ruder qualities of the Scythian character have been softened down by the more mild and polished ones of the Chinese; and the cowardly imbecility of the Chinese has been in part removed by the warlike spirit of the Scythian. The intrigue and defeat of the Chinese, and the rude courage of the Tartar, seem to unite in what may be considered the present national character of China; and in as far as that her union exists, it will render her formidable to their enemies. What cannot be effected by force, may be by fraud, and *vice versa;* and what any one of these qualities singly may not be able to accomplish, the union of both may. But this mixture of qualities is heterogeneous and unnatural; and there is reason to suppose that the seeds of national evil are in it, like those liquid compounds, for example, water and oil, the parts of which are made to adhere for a time by mechanical agitation; but, when allowed to settle, resolve themselves without any external cause to their simples; so it may perhaps be with China.

"The tempers of her own legitimate children, and those of the strangers who rule over her, are discordant, and refuse to coalesce; and if they do not by their own operation work her complete ruin, they may either make the country an easier prey to its foes, or prevent the emperors from sitting easy for any length of time on their thrones.

"In point of territory, RICHES, and population, China is the greatest of the nations; and has perhaps, to a degree beyond any other, the art of turning all her intercourse with foreign countries to her own advantage. But here she shows but little honourable principle. Idle displays of majesty and authority must satisfy those nations that seek her alliance; for in vain will they look for truth and respectful treatment from her. If they be contented to knock under, and acknowledge that their bread—their water—their vegetables—and their breath, are the effects of her bounty; then she will not deal unkindly with them—she will not oppress them—she will even help them. Proud of an imaginary benevolence, which is high as the heavens and broad as the ocean, she will throw the boon to them; but withal is sure to remind them, with the tone of authority, to cherish feelings of respect and submission towards those by whose beneficence they subsist. But wo to that nation that dares presume, even in the secret corners of its heart; to consider itself equal —or within a thousand degrees of equality—that country is rude, barbarous, obstinate, and unfilial; and not to tear it up, root and branch, is considered a display of forbearance worthy of the celestial sovereign alone!

"If, in the intercourse of China with foreign nations, she cannot with truth and justice make all things appear honourable to herself, she makes no difficulties about using other means. She discolours narrative—she misquotes statements—she drags forth to the light whatever appears for her advantage—and seals up in oblivion whatever bears against her. She lies by system—and, right or wrong, must have all things to look well on the paper. This view of her POLITICAL character is not less true than it is lamentable.

"Let us turn to her MORAL character; and here we shall, as in other countries, see much that is good, with great preponderance of that which is evil. The morals of China, as a nation, commence in filial duty, and in political government. The learned reduce every good thing to one principle, namely, that of paternal and FILIAL piety; every other is but a modification of this. In this they think they discover the seed of all virtues, and the motives to all duties. They apply it in every case, and to every class of men. They trace its origin high up to those operations which at first separated the chaos, and see its importance illustrated in every operation of nature. IMMEDIATE PARENTS are considered the father and mother of the FAMILY. The RULERS OF PROVINCES, the father and mother of the PROVINCE. The EMPEROR and EMPRESS, the father and mother of the EMPIRE. HEAVEN and EARTH, the father and mother of the emperor and of all this inferior world. YIN and YANG, the father and mother of the post-chaotic universe. The principle now under consideration is supposed to teach the good emperor to treat the people with the tenderness of a father; and the people to obey the emperor with the veneration of children. Under its influence, the good parent stretches his views forward to thousands of future generations, and lays up good for his unborn posterity; and the good child turns his thoughts backward to thousands of past ages, and remunerates the favour of his deceased ancestors. China considers herself as much a PARENT when she punishes as when she rewards—when she cuts off the heads of her obstinate children, as when she crowns the obedient with riches and honour; and the minister of state, but yesterday raised from the rank of a plebeian, is not more obliged to render thanks for the paternal grace that has elevated him, than the criminal just about to be cut in a thousand pieces, is to bow down and to return thanks for the paternal discipline which will in an instant exterminate his terrestrial being.

"The criminal laws of China operate very powerfully against the exercise of benevolence in cases where it is most needed. Whatever crimes are committed in a neighbourhood, the whole neighbours around are involved; and, contrary to what is the case in most other civilized countries, the law considers them guilty until they can prove themselves innocent. Hence the terror of being implicated in any evil that takes place, sometimes prevents the people from quenching fire until the superior authorities be first informed—and from relieving the distressed, until it is often too late. Hence it not unfrequently happens, that a man who has had the ill fortune to be stabbed to death in the street near to his neighbour's door, or who having fallen down through fatigue or disease, dies, is often allowed to remain on the spot until the stench of the putrid corpse obliges them, for their own safety, to get it by some means or other buried out of the way. It is easy to see how powerfully this operates as a national check to benevolence." (The whole of these opinions were selected by Dr. Morrison himself from the papers of his coadjutor, and marked by him as "Extracts from Dr. Milne's MSS." Those which follow were submitted to his revision, by Dr. Milne.)

CHAPTER XII.

CHINESE OPINIONS.

We have already seen not a few of Mr. Milne's opinions of Chinese character. He prepared himself for studying it, during his voyage, and only ceased to study it when he lay down to die. The following results of his close observation and deliberate judgment speak for themselves.

"In a former section we took notice, briefly, of the state of the Chinese as to religion and morals. With regard to their sentiments and prepossessions against the Gospel, they are very numerous. We can only name a few. Among others, the following claim the attention of Missionaries and Missionary Societies.

"1. Their views of the Supreme Being are obscure in the highest degree. The confusion that pervades their sacred books on this fundamental subject, is extreme. He is generally confounded with visible nature. Now and then a sentiment relative to divine justice and goodness occurs; but where, or in whom, these attributes are lodged, the reader cannot possibly discover. On meeting with a just idea of God (for there are some such in the most blinded nations,) he will feel pleased to see that the great Governor of the Universe 'has not left himself without a witness;' yet the very next page will most probably present him with some sentiment utterly inconsistent with all our notions of Supreme Power and excellence, and highly derogatory to the natural and moral attributes of Deity. To impart the knowledge of the true God,—the Triune Jehovah,—to this people, will be no easy task. We have to combat many of their popular notions, and most revered opinions; and to discriminate clearly between those opinions that are radically and entirely wrong, and those partly founded in our natural notions of God, but partially mixed with error,—is difficult.

"2. They do not understand, or fully recognise, the doctrine of Divine Providence. The government of the world is sometimes divided by them between heaven and the gods, or between heaven, earth, and man, or between the SAN PAOU, (that is, three precious ones of the Buddhists,) each of which rules in his turn. Instead of acknowledging the condescension of God in employing his creatures as instruments in the execution of his purposes, they teach and believe, that the sages are essentially necessary to him, and that without them he could not govern the world!

"3. Their notions of a future state form another obstacle to the Gospel. Some profess to expect no rewards after death, and to dread no punishment; nay, such do not even believe that they shall exist after their breath departs. To these persons, the doctrine of the soul's immortality, and of the resurrection of the body, are as 'idle tales.' This is not, however, the general belief of the Chinese. The far greater part of them believe the doctrine of the transmigration of souls; and they are apt to confound the Christian doctrine of future retributions with their own preposterous dogmas. With these, the difficulty is not in convincing them that there are rewards and punishments after death; but in explaining to them the nature, causes, and extent thereof. In dealing with the mass of the Chinese, their popular belief in the existence of future retributions must be considered and improved as an auxiliary; to attempt to shake this would be to undermine a part of the foundation of our own system. What is to be done, therefore, is to show the difference between that gross felicity and misery which a bewildered imagination, a guilty conscience, and an interested priesthood have painted, and placed before the credulous people; and that pure and rational happiness, and that terrible and endless wo, which the mercy and justice of God have prepared for mankind—to point out the true causes which bring men to everlasting ruin, and shut them for ever out of heaven—to show the heaven-devised method by which the soul can be saved, in contradistinction from the multifarious causes of future misery, and means of future happiness, which their own gloomy and unfruitful system points out—to prove the endless and unchanging duration of future retributions, in opposition to their views of innumerable revolutions and temporary sufferings after death;—and to direct to the practical uses of such a faith, in deterring men from sin, and in stimulating them to a life of holy obedience. Now, this will be found a task of uncommon difficulty; so confused are their views and books on these points, that it is no easy matter to discover what it is which we ought to combat; and having discovered this, to maintain and cherish their general belief in future retributions, while at the same time we show the futility of the arguments by which their particular definitions thereof are supported—and prove the insufficiency of the means by which they hope to escape misery and attain felicity—and demonstrate the injury of their system to virtue and to happiness; to do this will be a labour of peculiar delicacy and difficulty. The representations of future glory and misery, in the sacred Scriptures, are too exalted, too chaste, and too deeply marked with the holiness and justice of God, to be acceptable to those Pagans who are deeply studied in the doctrine of Metempsychosis. The Christian view of eternal realities is neither minute nor gross enough for those who profess to have measured, with geometrical precision, the height and depth, the breadth and length, of the prison of darkness; to be capable to describe the furious evolutions of the flames of Tophet; and to exhibit to ocular inspection the modes of torture by which the various classes of the miserable are punished. The pleasing and sanctifying glories of eternal life are too distant and spiritual for those who think they can hold forth to open view the mansions, the dress, the equipage, the employment, and the grandeur, of happy men in the life to come.

"4. Their notions of the nature of virtue and vice are indefinite and obscure. Those flagrant sins against which natural conscience lifts its voice in every country, are condemned, it is true—and those virtues of which it approves are commonly considered honourable, and men exhorted to practise them. But Chinese philosophers and metaphysicians have explained and refined, till they have refined away virtue and vice to mere relative terms—made man his own end—his prince and parents, his god—the laws of his country, the standard of his actions—and interest, in some shape or another, his only motive in doing good, and in avoiding evil. Moralists and priests have erred in a rather different manner. Overlooking the grand foundations and essentials of virtue in general, they drive on some particular one to such extravagant lengths, as that it no longer appears to be a virtue, but an oppressive, burdensome, impracticable condition of some present good. The essence of vice is supposed to consist chiefly in opposing, or dissenting from, the ancients, and its malignity, in the injury it does to individuals and societies." (Le Compte has given many illustrations of this fact; and of another on this subject, which Dr. Milne has not mentioned;—the light in which the Divine law appears to the intelligent Chinese. The Emperor said to Adam Schaal one day, "How can any one practise your laws? Take away two or three of the hardest of them, and we will think of the rest." This was said playfully. But he said to Verhiest, on another occasion, "Your law is hard: but if I believed it, I would obey at once. And were I to become a Christian, all would follow me.")

"5. Their high and unlimited veneration for their sacred sages, whom (as above noticed) they consider necessary to God; yea, sometimes equal with him,— constitutes a great obstacle to the Gospel; as they consider the circumstances of our blessed Lord's life and death as not only unworthy of a wise and good man, but rather as the proper awards of Divine justice for personal or relative crimes. This, at first sight of the Gospels, or at first hearing the history of Christ's Life, is, I believe, not an uncommon impression among them. Thus, while 'he was wounded for our transgressions, and bruised for our iniquities, we sinful mortals, in the height of our ignorance, esteem him to have been judicially smitten of God and afflicted.' How strikingly is this fulfilled among the Chinese! They praise Confucius in language and terms similar to those with which we sing the praises of the eternal God, the Creator of the ends of the earth! To set forth Christ, the only begotten of the Father, among such a people, as crucified, and yet the hope of a lost world—as Lord of life, death, and eternity, to whom even their sages must bow down and be indebted for their salvation, is a most grating and unwelcome subject. 'It is foolishness to them.' It is therefore absolutely necessary, before this nation can be truly virtuous and happy, that its veneration for ancient names be destroyed, or at least greatly weakened; for the names, examples, and writings of the wise men of former days, are considered the only sanctions of virtue, and the infallible standards by which opinions and vices are to be tried.' (What Dr. Milne says of the influence of the Chinese sages, has a fearful parallel at present in the influence of the Greek and Latin Fathers upon the theology of high churchmen. Foe and Confucius abet nothing, in China, more opposed to the spirit of the New Testament, than the Fathers are now made to abet by the Anglian School. Thus there is just as much need for an exposure of the Fathers in England, as for the refutation of Confucius in China. Dr. Milne's remarks are equally applicable to both.) "But this will be a most delicate, difficult, and tedious operation. It will require a very full understanding of the real state of the question, of what is to be condemned, and what to be commended in them—and the reasons for and against them. To reject these in the lump, would be to condemn much of what our own system acknowledges, commends, and enjoins; to shrink entirely from the task of showing wherein they have been the means, or occasions, of keeping the people in ignorance, idolatry, and vice, would be unworthy of those who have a revelation from God, and an eternity laid open before them. Still, the work will be difficult —none ought to attempt it without a competent acquaintance with theological science, and with the Chinese classical books. And if any thing should ever be written with this view it ought to be in the first style of language. A failure would be, for a time, very prejudicial to the cause of truth—while a successful effort would prove of the greatest possible service.

"6. The Chinese are taught to think themselves superior to all other people. A certain contemptuous feeling towards foreigners runs through the books of Confucius and Mencius; it seems to have actuated their minds, and influenced their language. 'Foreigner' seldom occurs in either ancient or modern Chinese writings without being joined by some disrespectful epithet, implying or expressing something about the ignorance, brutality, barbarism, obstinacy, and meanness of other nations; and their obligations to, or dependance upon, China. This feeling is studiously cherished by the Government, and manifested in all its transactions with strangers. Now, for a people thus elevated, in their own conceptions, by nature, and civilization, and wealth, to receive such a religion as the Gospel of Jesus from strangers whom they despise and look down upon, strikes directly at the root of their national pride. Against this the Gospel has to work its way into China." (Schaal and Verhiest say, that nothing was so offensive to the Chinese literati as that their country should not have been the *first* one visited by the Gospel. Their indignant question was, "Is China so insignificant as not to be thought of until now?" I have endeavoured to prove that God did not leave China " without a witness." Still, this is an embarrassing question! Some one, I hope, will enable our Missionaries to give a better answer to it than the Jesuits did.)

"7. The Chinese have generally a high idea of the character of a TEACHER. They think he should be grave, reserved, dignified, perfect; and held in honour by the Government and people. This may, it is true, ultimately turn to the advantage of the Gospel; but at first there is reason to fear its operation will be hurtful; for the 'humility with which the messengers of Christ should be clothed'—their 'condescending to men of low estate,'—their 'preaching the gospel to the POOR,'—their 'teaching in the market-places, and from house to house,'—in short, their being without secular dignity and eclat,—are considered ill-befitting the rank of teachers. While this shows the necessity of a circumspect and dignified behaviour in those who preach the Gospel to the Chinese, it likewise points out the propriety of not employing very *young* men in that work, unless they be under the direction of some elder labourers. The Chinese are, perhaps, more accustomed to order and subordination in the different ranks of society, than any other people: the idea of a community in which all the members have *equal* authority, does not so much as exist among them. How far this deserves the consideration of Missionary Societies, and bodies of men labouring for the conversion of China may, indeed, be a question with many. But that it deserves very serious attention, at first, is with the writer beyond a doubt. Some well organized system of order and ecclesiastical polity should be fixed upon by those societies that attempt the work; otherwise, there is danger that a community without laws, or where each one's will is the law, will fall into disrespect, and the dignity of character that should attach to the teacher of religion, be lost." (Whatever may be thought of this, both Milne and Morrison acted upon it. It is the secret of what seemed *consequential* in their spirit. They both loved deference, although not for its own sake, nor from vanity. And who can wonder? They saw nothing around them but the influence of office, for many years. Their notions on this point, however, did neither of them any good. Their official dignity would have defeated itself, but for their moral greatness. It was their " weak side.")

"When the truths of Christianity are proposed to this people, they attempt to find in their own system something similar. I have seen a man for many successive months, spend a considerable portion of time, in trying to find in their classical books something like the doctrine of redemption, the immortality of the soul, and the resurrection. The ingenuity of the learned in forcing resemblances of this sort on one before he is aware, is such as to require him to be constantly on his guard, that he may not make concessions derogatory to the Gospel. It is very true, that we should avail ourselves of the aid of every good sentiment which we find existing among the heathen—not to do so would be dishonourable to the goodness of God, who has for wise purposes maintained them in the most depraved heathen nations, from the beginning; but it is equally true that great caution is necessary in admitting in full, the explanations even of moral duty, given in Pagan writings—how much more in bringing in their philosophical opinions to the aid of the Gospel. The example of Origen of Alexandria, and of Tertullian in Africa, stands to this day as our beacon in such cases. These eminent fathers, indeed, differed widely in what they took from the Heathen; Origen borrowing endless speculations from them, which led to allegorize away the genuine sense of Scripture; while Tertullian stood forth as the champion of Monasticism, and pleaded for the introduction into the Church of Christ, of mortifications practised by Pagans for ages before.

"So unwilling are the Chinese to allow themselves to be surpassed, or that any other people possess that of which they cannot boast, that they fancy resemblances where there are none, and, after striving in vain to find them, they still hope that such there are, and that if there should happen to be none, they are of no importance, or surely they would have been there. Even those among them who love the Gospel, need to be carefully watched over, lest their former opinions should warp their judgment, and lead them to mix the truth of God with the mere dictates of Pagan wisdom.

"These hints are offered, not with a view to discourage attempts for the conversion of the Chinese, but rather to show the nature of the work to be done, with the obstacles to be removed; and to produce in all who are actually engaged in the work, a just conviction of the importance of seeking competent qualifications for the arduous service; and of impressing on the venerable body of men with whom the writer is connected, the necessity of furnishing their Chinese Missions with an adequate number of labourers, endowed with various talents; so that no part of the Pagan system may remain unshaken, and none of the means enjoined by our Lord and Saviour left unemployed. It is obvious that division of labour, and concentrated exertion, are essential to the accomplishment of any thing that will be of real and permanent service to the best interests of mankind. Hurried efforts, and works executed without due leisure and ability, will not abide the test of future ages." (The London Missionary Society, to whom this appeal was made, have not been unmindful of Dr. Milne's hints, so far as the "qualifications" of his successors are concerned. The varied erudition and versatility of talents in both the medical and ministerial Missionaries, who have just gone to China, are not unknown to the schools of science, literature, or theology. Were not these gentlemen my personal friends, and one of them related to me, it would be my duty in this work, to describe their high standing both as scholars and Christians. It would, however, be a dereliction of what is my duty, were I not to say, that they are just the kind of men which Drs. Morrison and Milne would have wished to see "baptized for the dead." The prospect of having such successors would have made them sing their "*Nunc Dimittis*" louder than even they did. The Churches expect much, and the spirits of Morrison and Milne expect more, from these young men. I congratulate my young friends on the fact, that great things are thus expected from them, in both heaven and earth! With so many eyes, from both worlds, upon them, they must almost *see* the eye of Omniscience in the very sun, from day to day.)

CHAPTER XIII.

MISSIONARY EVENTS.

"In January, 1817, a row of buildings on the right side of the garden, in which were a printing office, paper store, and various rooms for the accommodation of the people employed in the service of the Mission, was completed. The building, which was begun in 1816, is strong, and having many doors and windows, is well adapted for useful purposes; it is well ventilated, and capable of being divided into many small but commodious apartments, in each of which an individual, on the plan of the natives, could live in a very comfortable manner. Should the objects so far prosper as to bring a few native students under the superintendence of the Mission, they will be comfortably accommodated in such parts of these as can be spared from the printing. This was in eye when the plan was formed.

"The proximity of our premises to the sea, and the daily inroads which that potent element makes on the east side of the straits of Malacca, made it necessary to construct a strong fence in front of the Mission House. A stone wall, running across all the breadth of the premises, was erected on the beach in the summer of 1816, under the superintendence of Mr. Thomsen, previously to his departure to England.

"The difficulty of printing Christian books in China, had great influence in determining the minds of the Missionaries to seek a quiet retreat at some little distance, where the Scriptures and other books could be printed without subjecting them to the constant fear of interruption. That quiet retreat was now obtained; and in order to take an early advantage thereof, a large supply of paper, workmen, &c., was sent to Malacca in course of the spring of 1817, to print the duodecimo edition of the New Testament. The translation had been revised by the translator himself, and the blocks prepared in China. An unfortunate occurrence occasioned the principal part of the blocks to be destroyed; and there was no resource but to go to the expense of having a new set prepared. When the paper, blocks, and workmen came the new range of houses was found insufficient, being already pretty well filled with the press, printers, and Chinese teachers. A second range was accordingly built on the opposite side, fronting the other; and as soon as ready, the paper, &c., placed therein. This range was built much on the same plan with the former, and may be appropriated either to the purposes of business, or for the habitation of natives employed on the establishment. But more than a half of these houses was built on a slighter scale, than those first erected. Those were all of good, strong, brick walls, and tiled; but more than half of these were built of the bark of a tree, and covered with reed. The reason of this, was, partly from narrow funds, and partly from an idea, that after the New and Old Testament should be printed so many houses would not be necessary. The bark houses, were also made wider than the others, that they might answer for schools. At the present time, (July, 1819,) both ranges are quite full, and more will very likely be required. The same year a wall of brick was raised along part of one side of the premises; and the back part of the ground, behind where the garden now is, was partly cleared of brush-wood and useless trees, which obstructed the current of air and made the situation less healthy; but not sufficiently cleared to render the place either useful or comfortable;—that was an after work which Mr. Thomsen superintended on his return from Europe, the following year, when a wall round the back of the premises was built; the ground drained; the roots of trees taken out; a road made; a garden formed; and the soil dug up.—This was a most troublesome labour, and very expensive; but absolutely necessary to render the Mission property safe from depradations, and the situation comfortable. What added to the difficulty of the work was, that the wall having to pass through a marsh, behooved to be built on piles of wood, driven into the ground, which were covered with durable plank, after which the brick work was put on.

"The size and expense of these houses, walls, &c. are as follows:

"The range on the right side of the garden, 114 feet by 16—expense dolls. 530.

"The range on the left side, brick part, 49 feet by 16—bark part, 54 by 18—expense dolls. 260.

"Stone wall on the beach, high 10 feet, long 250, dolls. 260.

"—— Subsequent repairs rendered necessary by breaches made in it by the sea, about dolls. 100.

"Wall on part of the right side of the garden, high four and a half feet, long 250, dolls. 40.

"Wall round the back of the premises, high nine and a half feet, long 735, dolls. 763.

"Railing (wood,) in front, 220 feet long, dolls. 40.

"The first expense only is here calculated. It is indeed great, when we consider the limited nature of the Society's funds; but it was laid out with much economy, and in a way that will prove of permanent utility to the establishment.

"A small Periodical Publication, in English, had been contemplated for years, and it was embraced in the 8th resolution, relative to the Ultra-Ganges Missions. The first number was published at Malacca, in May, 1817; and under great disadvantages, as the materials were very scanty, not very interesting, and moreover, put together by the Editor in a time of great family affliction. It was called the 'Indo-Chinese Gleaner,' and has been continued quarterly; but has not yet been able to pay itself. The original projectors afterwards agreed that a trial should be made for at least two or three years; that they should themselves bear whatever loss might for that time attend it; and that if any profits should accrue, they should be devoted to some benevolent object. The following extract of a prospectus, published in the spring of 1818, will show the design and objects of this little work.

"'Published at Malacca, every quarter, namely, in January, April, July, and October, 'THE INDO-CHINESE GLEANER,' containing various intelligence from China, and the neighbouring countries; miscellaneous notices relative to the History, Philosophy, and Literature of the Indo-Chinese nations; translations from Chinese, Malay, &c.; essays on religious subjects; accounts of the progress of Christian Missions in India; and of the state of Christianity in general.

"'Should any profits, after clearing the expense of paper, printing, and postages, result from this publication, they are to be divided equally between the following objects:'

"'1.—THE FUND FOR WIDOWS AND ORPHANS OF MISSIONARIES BELONGING TO THE ULTRA-GANGES' MISSIONS, and for such of their brethren on this side the Cape of Good Hope, as shall subscribe to that fund, and contribute papers to this Publication.

"'2.—CHARITIES AMONG THE HEATHEN.—That is, to feed, clothe, and educate such Heathen orphans and poor children, as may be placed under the care of the ULTRA-GANGES' MISSIONS; and to assist widows, the aged, deaf, dumb, blind, and lame; and such other Heathens, or converts from among the Heathen, as have no relatives, or strength to labour, or are persecuted, or otherwise deprived of the means of support."

"Like most other of our labours, the 'Indo-Chinese Gleaner,' is yet but in its infancy. Correspondents and contributors have hitherto been few. Usefulness is more its aim than excellence. To those who wish to collect authentic information on its principal topics, it will not be found unworthy of their attention. Those who are either desirous, or qualified, to blame and criticise, may find abundance of room. Little comparatively, is yet known of the subjects which fill the most of its pages. Such materials are selected, as are likely to be interesting to the philosopher, to the historian, and especially to the Missionary. Common Christian edification, though not over-looked, does not so properly belong to its province, as to that of some other Periodical works. It rather aims to unfold the Indo-Chinese nations to those who have little opportunity of knowing them, than to circulate European intelligence.

"As the number of correspondents in various parts of India is increasing, it is not perhaps presuming too far to expect that the work will become interesting. Whether it will ever, in a pecuniary point of view, be of service to the benevolent objects which are to share its profits, is a problem. The number of English readers on this side of India is small, and the sending of the work to other parts, especially to Europe, is attended with some expense and uncertainty. But should it never be able to do more than pay its own expense, it may nevertheless be serviceable to Missionaries, and to the cause of knowledge in general, to continue the publication thereof. Important questions may be discussed. Useful essays will now and then appear, Hints of Asiatic and European intelligence, will be animating and instructive to those who are much shut out from foreign communications. To a body of men whose views are united in what regards the truth and its propagation among mankind, some common medium to the public is desirable. Our distance from Europe renders our intercourse with it seldom and precarious. Periodical publications are calculated to excite the mind to profitable reflection. In the intellectual *wastes* which Missionaries generally inhabit, thought rusts; mental energy languishes; and sentiment, destitute of the necessary support, degenerates. When a periodical publication combines (as it is hoped this will) religion and philosophy, literature and history, there is something for minds of various moulds; something to inform the understanding; something to rouse the dormant feelings; something to awaken caution; something to encourage languishing hope; something to excite benevolent sympathies; something to draw out fervent prayer to God, cordial thanks for his blessings, active zeal in his cause, and ardent love to all his children. Missionaries have but little time for letter writing, and yet they cannot do well without it. When they write to their brethren around, they must of necessity write the same things over and over again; now, by uniting in the support of a periodical publication, the most interesting things (fit for the public eye) which occur to them, in their families, station, and labours, would, by once writing, find an easy and expeditious communication through its medium. Thus, while edification would be promoted, time would also be saved. While fraternal intercourse would be maintained, the peculiar sentiments of the Heathen would be also unfolded. While each would read with interest and profit his brother's communication, the labour and research, the study of native books and manners, necessary to prepare his own quota for the general good, would be of the greatest possible service to himself. Taking all these things into consideration, a small pecuniary loss (should that be inevitable) may be undergone for the sake of continuing a work which may, by increased communications, be made so directly useful to all concerned, and perhaps rendered interesting to the public. Should the loss be too heavy for an individual or two, if equally shared by ten or twenty, it would not be felt; and perhaps, if necessary, the Missionary Society would assist them.

"In the month of April, this year, Mrs. Milne was visited with a most serious illness. On the 7th she was delivered of a daughter, whom it pleased the Sovereign disposer of all things to remove by death, after a few days' residence on earth. She was baptized on the morning of the 10th, named Sarah, and died about noon the same day. This event bore hard on her mother. Fever almost instantaneously ensued, and reduced her so low, that for a whole month there was scarcely any hope of life. But it pleased God so far to restore her, as that she was able on the 1st of July to undertake a sea voyage. She arrived with the children at Macao, on the 29th. Having no assistant in the Mission, her husband could not at that time accompany her, notwithstanding her extreme weakness and need of the aids of affection and friendship. How desirable is it that there should be in every Mission at least *two* resident labourers! In case of heavy affliction, one could for a time take charge of the whole; and the other, if the case urgently required, attend his afflicted family. Those who speak and write as if they thought Missionaries should make no efforts for the health, comfort, and respectability of their families, or to protract their own lives, have learnt their notions of relative life from the *cant* of monastic days, not from the Epistles of St. Paul.

"In course of this summer, two evening services in Chinese were begun in town, and continued about two months; after which they were, in consequence of Mr. Milne's departure, given up till the summer of 1819, when they were recommenced by his colleague. Some efforts were made, after the month of January this year, to keep up the Malay Mission. Two small tracts, composed by Mr. Thomsen, were printed, and some distributed. Occasional opportunities were embraced of conversing, though in a very imperfect manner, with children, slaves, and other Mahometans. No *stress*, however, can be laid on these feeble attempts. They proceeded from a wish to continue something in the shape of Malay instruction, till the return of him who laid the foundation of the Mission among this people. They were from the same cause as the other services, interrupted, and at the same time.

"Never was the weight of the establishment at Malacca so sensibly felt as at this time. Quite alone, without any helper in the work; and obliged to part with his family, and struggling with a load of labours and cares, far too heavy for an enfeebled constitution, Mr. Milne hailed with unspeakable pleasure the arrival of a colleague, the Rev. Walter Henry Medhurst, who landed with his family at Malacca, on the 12th of June. Mr. Medhurst, who received his classical education at St. Paul's School, founded by the celebrated Dean Colet, came out from England by way of Madras, at which place he was detained for several months. He began his Chinese studies with that teachableness of spirit which never fails to secure respect and affection for a young man's character, and to produce a cheerful readiness in others to assist him wherever they can; and he pursued them with a persevering ardour which excited in the mind of his fellow-servant the pleasing expectation of his making good progress as a Chinese student, and becoming at no very distant period, a useful coadjutor in the Mission; an expectation which has by no means been disappointed. His more immediate object was to superintend the printing." (Mr. Medhurst is now well known by his volume on China, and by the publicity which the Times has given to his opinions on the Opium question.)

"In about a month after Mr. Medhurst's arrival, Mr. Milne departed for a season to China, partly for his own health, and partly on account of his afflicted partner, who had gone thither a little before. He left Malacca on the 9th of August, and landed in China on the 3d September, and did not return till the month of February following. During this time, some of the labours of the Mission at Malacca were necessarily interrupted; while other things were carried on as well as the circumstances of the case would admit. The printing, the schools, and the general superintendency of the whole devolved on Mr. Medhurst, who, with his Chinese studies, had a heavy burden on his shoulders. The regular morning worship was conducted for part of the time, (that is, till Mr. M. had committed a form of prayer in Chinese to memory) by a sober heathen, of good moral character, who read a portion of Scripture and a form of prayer which had been composed some time before. The same person also read, on Sabbath and Thursday evenings, passages out of the books and tracts already printed, to about the usual number of hearers. This he did, it may be supposed, rather as a matter of *obligation*, considering it a duty to his employers, than from *real love to the truth;* for though he has ever been friendly, he has not yet shown any decided attachment to the Gospel of Christ. He is a devoted follower of *Confucius*, whom he considers the prototype of all excellence, and the immaculate teacher of myriads of ages! However, as the efficacy of God's word is not derived from him who delivers it, and is not suspended even on the faith of the teacher, cases may occur when the services of such men as this may, I conceive, be employed in some parts of the Missionary work, though it is by no means desirable, if persons more radically qualified could be obtained—a thing often impossible in Missions of only a few years' standing. If there be any case in which *written forms of devotion* prove useful, (and I have no doubt but there are many,) it is at the first planting of the Gospel among the Heathen. Their minds are a perfect void as it regards Divine truth; to both the spirit and mode of expression proper for the duty of prayer, they are equally strangers, and must be taught either by book, or by imitation of others. To confine them to forms of prayer, or to suffer them to satisfy themselves with these, would, in my opinion, be doing them a serious injury: but yet, as in such cases as the above, what sober-minded man would not rather see a *form* of prayer read in the hearing of a few sinful and dependent creatures, than that they should be for weeks and months left without any acts of public worship addressed to the Deity?

"Previously to his departure for China, Mr. Milne had finished a translation of the book of *Joshua;* and while there, he translated the book of *Judges.* An exposition of the Lord's prayer, begun by weekly lectures in a small temple at Malacca, was filled up and finished there; and a tract, on the 'Folly of Idolatry,' written, both of which have been since printed. Various opportunities offered for the distribution of tracts, and of the Holy Scriptures on the borders of that country, for whose numerous inhabitants they are chiefly intended; but in doing any thing there, the utmost caution and reserve were necessary. Very little else of a Missionary nature was done, the object of the visit being *health* and not labour.

"As Dr. Morrison and his colleague were thus, in the providence of God, brought together again for a few months, it appeared desirable to make some arrangements for their future proceedings. They had always considered a principle of *order* as of the very first importance; and in as far as their own labours were concerned, had ever observed it. Indeed, without fixed objects and some general rules of pursuing them, the most ardent zeal, united to the greatest diligence, can effect very little. They considered that, while regulations of a very minute 'kind, or over-strained explanations of the most liberal rules, prove vexatious and burdensome impediments; a general plan, formed of a *few* important and leading particulars, while it keeps the mind bent on one or two prominent objects, secures, at the same time, a liberty for every person concerned, to pursue his own department of the work in his own way—on the contrary, greatly promotes a good cause. Being, for the time, the only Missionaries, Mr. Medhurst excepted, then known to them to be in the country, and of consequence the majority, they, in the month of Sept. 1817, drew out a few resolutions which related principally to themselves; and to their brethren only, in as far as the latter should not consider their '*wishes and convenience thwarted*' by adopting the same. These resolutions were signed on the 2d of November, the same year, by the two Missionaries in question, who denominated themselves, '*The Provisional Committee of the Ultra-Ganges' Missions,*' intending, as soon as convenient, that a third or fourth person should be added to their number.

"The friends of religion in America had all along taken an interest in the Chinese Mission; of which they gave substantial proof by contributing liberally to aid the progress of the Sacred Scriptures; Divie Bethune, Esq., New York, and Robert Ralston, Esq., Philadelphia, were the authorized mediums of remitting to the Mission, the sum of *three thousand six hundred and sixteen Spanish dollars,* made up from the contributions of several Christian communities in their highly favoured country. Our most cordial thanks are, on behalf of the Chinese nation, due to these friends of the Redeemer, for their liberal assistance to the hitherto expensive labours in which we have been engaged. May these proofs of their ardent and well founded zeal for the advancement of truth and righteousness in the earth, be abundantly rewarded, by the rich effusion of the Holy Spirit on their respective churches and families. The day may come, yea, it doubtless will come, when the Protestant Mission to China will not merely have to make appeals to Christian liberality, but also have reports to make equally calculated to excite pious gratitude to God for what he has actually wrought, and to strengthen the faith of those who are waiting for the time when 'all flesh shall see his salvation.' At present, the church is called to the exercise of *patience,* prayer, and active zeal, with regard to China; and it is highly probable that the slow progress of the Gospel among that people, will, for a *very long period,* call for the continued exercise of these in a prominent degree, before the joyful shout be heard—that 'this vast kingdom also, has reverted to our Lord, and to his Christ!'

"In 1817, Mr. Morrison finished his translation of the *Psalms,* and of the book of *Ruth.* Some progress was made with other portions of the Scriptures; but as they were not finished, we shall notice them by-and-by. This year he wrote and printed 'A View of China for Philological Purposes,' which contains a sketch of Chinese chronology, geography, government, religion, and customs; designed for the use of persons who study the Chinese language. In this work the author has made a very copious use of the Chinese character; and, in my opinion, rendered a most important service to the foreign study of Chinese. In a subsequent edition of the work, besides correcting typographical errors, it may be useful to add the *pronunciation,* in cases where that has not been done, for the benefit of readers in Europe, who may not have the means of ascertaining the sounds of the written character. In the years 1817–18, he translated 'The Morning and Evening Prayers' of the English Church, just as they stand in the 'Common Prayer Book,' without bringing in the Collects. These forms of prayer he printed, together with the 'Psalter,' divided for the thirty days of the month. He considered it better to give a translation than to modify them, deeming their richness of devotional phraseology and generally-acknowledged excellence, amply sufficient to compensate for any want of suitableness to the state of a partially-informed people. He found it necessary to alter a little the prayers for the *rulers* of the land, so as to render them applicable and suitable to the Chinese Imperial Family and Government. The sentence respecting '*enemies*,' he left out;* for he thought it often a very difficult matter to determine whether kings and rulers do not frequently *make to themselves enemies,* by acts of injustice and oppression. And here we may remark, that in exercises of devotion, in which an immediate appeal is made to the Supreme Being, who judges not according to the human partialities, there should not only be an absence of all acrimony and enmity of feeling from the heart, but also an entire absence of all phraseology which may tend to excite contempt of other men; to fire the mind with the desire of revenge; and to strengthen the often ill-founded prejudices and antipathies of one nation against another Under the Gospel, we have not such direct light to point out our national enemies, as the Jews had, who lived under the immediate government of God, as their political ruler;-and had either express precepts, or the guidance of inspired prophets, to regulate their conduct towards their public enemies. While it is doubtless the duty of nations to pray and be thankful for deliverance from the designs of their enemies; yet it is surely the most delicate part of public worship—and one from which it is most difficult to exclude the worst passions of the human heart. It is worthy of the attention of the many pious and eminent ministers and dignitaries in churches of our native land, whether or not some alterations, in *this*

---

* The sentence referred to is, 'strengthen him that he may vanquish and overcome all his enemies.'

particular, would not be a great improvement to the otherwise useful formularies of devotion used in one part of the kingdom; and whether or not public prayers and sermons, on national feasts and days of thanksgiving in all parts of the United Kingdom, be not susceptible of, and do not greatly need, improvement. It is truly lamentable to perceive how directly some prayers and forms of thanksgiving, composed on purpose for such days, and sermons delivered on such occasions, tend to cherish a spirit of hatred, revenge, and love of false glory. Not to speak of some particular precepts of the Gospel, which inculcate a spirit and conduct the very reverse, surely the insufferable presumption and ignorance of the Divine nature, which seem to lie at the foundation, ought to awaken in every serious mind the deepest disgust at such an outraging of the principles of our common faith, and animate all to the most strenuous efforts for improvement. We justly abominate the conduct of that bloody church, which, after ravishing virgins; ripping up women with child; plucking off the hair and beard; roasting men over the coals; boiling them in caldrons; cutting out the entrails of the yet living mortal;—of that church, which, after butchering her thousands and slaying her ten thousands, could send her priest and friars in solemn procession through the streets, with flying banners and elevated crosses, singing '*Te Deum Laudamus!!*' and surely we ought to dread every approach to a similar spirit.

"At all events, if the evil cannot be speedily cured at home, it becomes the more important for the Missionary abroad to keep every such unscriptural and unhallowed sentiment at the utmost distance from every thing he publishes to the Heathen. He will find among them but too much of the spirit and practice of that wicked Prince, who said, concerning his public enemies: '*curse me them from hence*'—and if, either from a fondness for the remains of that Paganism which once overspread Europe, and which has unhappily so blended itself with Christianity, as in some places nearly to have altered the very nature and complexion of the latter; or if from a mistaken notion that his object will be sooner gained by partly falling in with the reigning sentiment and spirit of the people, he allow himself to deviate from New Testament principles,—he will encumber the sacred system of truth and duty with a rubbish which the labour of twenty ages may not be able to remove!" (It appears, from Dr. Morrison's Life, that Dr. Milne wished to "modify" such of the prayers as were not adapted to the circumstances of the Mission or the Heathen. They were, however, both of one mind in regard to the general excellence of the Liturgy. "We are of no party," was their maxim. *Life*, Vol. 1, p. 478.)

"To return from this digression. During the stay of Mr. Milne in China, the translation he had made of Deuteronomy and Joshua (already noticed) was examined by Dr. Morrison, and, after some corrections, approved and resolved to be printed. They also divided between them the remaining books of the Old Testament, wishing, if possible, to complete the translation of the whole within the year 1818. Dr. Morrison yielded the *first* choice to his fellow labourer, who fixed on the remaining part of the historical books, from Ruth forward to the book of Psalms; judging these to be the easier, and better suited to his less extensive knowledge of the language. The books, from Genesis to Deuteronomy, and from the Psalms forward to Malachi, inclusive, fell to Dr. Morrison's share. They resolved that, if they lived to complete this work, some subsequent arrangement should be made for their meeting together, in order to revise the whole Scriptures, and publish them in what should then appear to be the most convenient form. But it was, as we shall afterwards notice, found impossible for them to accomplish this work within the time limited.

"Mr. and Mrs. Milne's health having been considerably improved by the change of climate and the many attentions of kind friends, they returned to their work at Malacca, where they landed on the 17th of Feb., 1818." (This was a great relief to Dr. Morrison. His colleague was so "emaciated," as to alarm him at first. "Milne is very poorly! What will become of this Mission, if he should die now!" he wrote to Dr. Waugh.—*Ibid.*) "They found, on their arrival, that fresh assistance was sent from England to the Missions on this side of India. Rev. C. H. Thomsen, after an absence of fifteen months from Malacca, had returned on 29th December, 1817, accompanied by the Rev. John Slater and Mrs. Slater. They came out by way of Java, at which place they were detained through Mr. Slater's illness (the Batavia fever) for a considerable time.

"Mr. Thomsen resumed his labours in the Malay department of the Mission; after a little time reopened the Malay and English school; and began one in the Malabar language, which was shortly filled. Though no person then connected with the Mission knew the Malabar, yet it was hoped there would soon be an opportunity for some one to study it; and as the teacher and children all understood Malay, the operations of the school could be directed through the medium of that language. The total want of Christian books in the Malabar, at Malacca, proved a great difficulty, which has not yet (October, 1819,) been overcome. Several applications to Bengal and Madras for Malabar books have been made, but hitherto without effect.

"During this year, Mr. Thomsen wrote and printed *A Malay Spelling Book*, with lessons appended. This is the first Malay work of the kind we have heard of, in the *native character*, either by foreigners or Malays, and will doubtless prove a great facility in the education of youth. He also reprinted, with corrections, his translation of Dr. Watts' First Chatechism, and the Tract on the Ten Commandments.

"Mr. Slater came out to assist in the Chinese Mission; and employed himself in the study of the language. His ardour and application were highly creditable to him; but his state of health was such as to oblige him frequently to cease from study, and, indeed, to leave very little hope of his life. He left Malacca on the 9th of August following, and went to China, from whence he returned in the month of December, having greatly benefited by the change.

"On the 14th of September, the Rev. Samuel Milton, Thomas Beighton, and John Ince, with the wives of the two latter, arrived safely at Malacca. In the early part of their passage out from England, they sustained the most imminent danger at sea; but were mercifully preserved. They spent some days at Madras, and touched at Penang on their way to Malacca.

"Immediate calls, in different places, for labourers in the Chinese department, and also the importance of having, where practicable, a Chinese and a Malay Missionary settled together in each station, showed at once the propriety of two of these brethren applying themselves to Chinese studies. Mr. Milton was appointed by the Directors of our Society to assist in the Chinese department of the Mission at Malacca; Messrs. Beighton and Ince, who were desirous of labouring together, settled it between themselves, that the former should study Malay, and the latter Chinese. They began and followed out their studies with ardour and diligence, having as much assistance from native teachers, and from their senior brethren, as the other labours of the Mission could admit of.

"Those that studied Chinese, four in number, (including Mr. Slater, who was absent a few months for his health,) read regular public lessons twice a day in that language, with the writer of these pages; and after the month of December, each had, besides, the aid of a native teacher through the chief part of the day. They had opportunity also, once every week, as long as they remained at the station, for making their attainments in the language to bear on practical purposes, by writing exercises and pieces of composition, in Chinese—a most valuable branch of Chinese study, to the man who wishes to be early useful, and an accurate scholar. The student that omits it, while he may have the assistance of those who are able to correct and revise his compositions, does himself a great injury. Several parts of Dr. Morrison's Chinese Dictionary had been sent to the station, which, with the Grammar and Dialogues, proved exceedingly helpful. Greater advantages for learning the language, are commonly enjoyed by those who come out a few years after a Mission has been established; and it is every Missionary's duty and wisdom to improve them to the utmost, that he may be able, as early as possible, to enter on the more pleasing and more important work of teaching the Heathen. Mr. Milton's health was several times so ill as to oblige him to cease, and at other times much to abate, his assiduous and undeviating application.

"In the month of September, this year, a change of Government took place at Malacca. The colony was, according to the treaty of 1814, restored by the British Resident and Commissioner, Major William Farquhar, to the Honourable the Commissioners of his Majesty the King of the Netherlands. Here, the writer feels it a duty publicly to acknowledge the unremitted attention of the British Government, and of the Resident and Commandant, Major W. Farquhar, to the interests of the Mission at Malacca, ever since its commencement. In his public as well as private capacity, Major Farquhar rendered every assistance to the objects carrying on by the Missionaries; and on many occasions greatly promoted their domestic comfort. To Dr. W. Chalmers, of the Bengal Medical Establishment, who was surgeon to the British garrison, *and attended the Missionaries and their families gratis, for upwards of three years and a half; spending often, with some of them, long and tedious nights in their afflictions*, and who, to the exercise of his well known professional talents, joined the attentions of a friend and brother,—to him we are under the greatest obligations, and cannot pass over this part of the history of the Mission without openly acknowledging the same.

"Nor would it be pardonable in this place not to acknowledge how kindly their Honours, the Dutch Commissioners, received an official statement of the objects and views of the Mission, which was laid before them, in the name of the Missionary Society. The Mission was recommended to them by the Penang Government, and by Major Farquhar, and they were pleased to assure the Missionaries, that they should continue to enjoy the same liberty under the Dutch Government which they had under the English. These assurances have hitherto been fully realized, and there is every reason to hope that they will continue to be so. To the Honourable J. S. Timmerman Thyssen, the Governor, our most cordial and public thanks are due, for the unrestrained freedom which we, in all respects, enjoy, to pursue every branch of our work.

"On the 10th of November, the foundation of the *Anglo-Chinese College* was laid, on which occasion the principal Dutch and English authorities were pleased to attend. But as this subject will be more fully noticed hereafter, we shall pass it over for the present, only remarking that, as a free school had been established for upwards of three years, there appeared now a still nearer approximation to an object specified above, namely, '*A Seminary*,' on a larger scale than had been hitherto attained.

"In China, the translation of *Exodus* and *Malachi* was finished this year by Dr. Morrison, and good progress made with other parts of the sacred volume. In the spring of 1819, the following books were received from him, all ready for the press: *Isaiah*,

Hosea, Joel, Amos, Micah, Obadiah, Jonah, Nahum, Haggai, Zephaniah, Habakkuk, and *Zechariah*. Besides these a Chinese pamphlet, containing 'Miscellaneous Essays,' doctrinal, practical, and polemical, written in 1818, was sent down from him, and printed at Malacca. A small volume, containing 'A Voyage round the World,' he composed with a view of combining entertainment with instruction; which was printed in China. To introduce some knowledge of Europe and the western parts of the world among the Chinese, had long been looked upon by him as a most desirable object. He thought it would tend to enlarge their views; and would form an important counterpart of some other efforts of the Mission, which have more immediately in view the transmission of Chinese knowledge to the west.

"This year Mr. Morrison was unanimously and gratuitously created Doctor in Divinity by the Senatus Academicus of the University of Glasgow, in consequence of the philological works he had published, and was publishing, with a view to facilitate the acquisition of the Chinese language. The act of the University, conferring this honour, is indeed dated the 24th of Dec., 1817, but it did not reach China till the summer of 1818.

"During 1818, the progress made at Malacca, in the translation of the historical books of the Old Testament, was much impeded by a variety of other labours. *Both the Books of Samuel, together with the two Books of the Kings,* were translated. Three new Chinese tracts were written and printed in course of the year; one on 'The duty of justice between man and man,' one on 'The evils of Gambling,' and the third, containing 'Twelve short Discourses,' on twelve texts of Scripture, embracing the chief doctrines of the Gospel.

"The Chinese preaching, Magazine, &c., continued as before; a new Chinese school was opened; many more tracts were circulated this year than ever before in an equal space of time. Mr. Medhurst had the schools, the printing office, and the distribution of tracts, more immediately for his department. He often visited the Chinese junks in the roads, and the villages, and plantations in the country; distributing tracts, and speaking the word of life to the people.

"Thus far the Lord helped. For upwards of eleven years from the commencement of the Mission in China, though several children had been removed by death, yet there had been but one grown person called away, namely, Mrs. Thomsen, who died at sea on the 4th of February, 1817. Another bereavement of a similar nature, but much heavier in its consequences, by reason of the motherless children who were left behind, now awaited the Mission, in the death of Mrs. Milne, which took place at Malacca, on the 20th of March, 1819; exactly two years and twenty-four days after the death of Mrs. Thomsen. Her last child, who was named Farquhar, was born on the 6th of February, after which, for some days, she appeared to recover rapidly. But she soon fell back, and a very speedy decay of the constitution followed. An anomalous train of the puerperal affections, with a predominant determination to the stomach and bowels, was the means commissioned by God to remove this excellent woman from the scenes of mortality. She had lived to God from her early youth; and she died in humble hope of eternal

salvation, through the merits of Jesus Christ. She possessed in a very high degree that motherly sense which is beyond all price in domestic life; and was eminently fitted for moving in the family circle. Dignity of mind, honest frankness, and consistent and scriptural piety were displayed in her daily walk. Nor would it perhaps be easy to find one in whom there is such a concentration of that which is amiable from nature, endearing from temper, useful from education, and excellent from divine principles, as there was in her. But what she was, she was 'by the grace of God;' and, as is generally the case with the followers of Christ, while in their proper spirit, she seemed to herself to be 'the chief of sinners.'"
(This is all he said of her in the narrative of the Mission; but not all he wrote. The following account of the life and death of this excellent woman, is chiefly from his own pen. I add nothing to the memoir; but when my own earlier acquaintance with her enables me to illustrate it.)

CHAPTER XIV.

MRS. MILNE'S DEATH.

Mr. Milne began this eventful year of his life, with the following appropriate prayer.

"O blessed God, be near to me in mercy, in all the vicissitudes of this year. Help me to see thee present. Assist my weak and enfeebled faculties, I pray thee, in every duty, temptation, and affliction.

Enable me to derive real good from thy word. Give me a right heart; soften, sweeten, and sanctify my temper. Lord, make my intercourse with my family, with my brethren, with the Heathen, and with the people around, profitable to them and to myself. Enable me to bear all things. Give me more self-control. So direct my plans and labours this year, as that they shall most effectually tend, upon the whole, to promote the interests of thy kingdom in these parts. Give me wisdom and energy to know and seize on all the facilities furnished by thy Providence, for promoting truth and righteousness. May I be humble in myself, and greatly value the talents of others. Let me not labour in vain. O bless my family—my partner in life, my children, my mother, and sisters; and my fellow-labourers. In the expected time of domestic solicitude, be near to help. Bring us safely through it, O Lord; and compass us about with songs of deliverance. Look in mercy on the fruit of our bodies. Bless our little ones with the beginnings of eternal life. Fit me for a useful life, and a happy death. My eyes are this evening lifted up towards thy mercy in Christ. It is my only hope—my sole plea. Look upon me—pardon me—bless me—and mine in time, 'through eternity, for Christ's sake. Amen. I give myself afresh to Thee, my Creator, Redeemer, and Sanctifier. Seal me, and save me. Amen, and amen.

"January 3rd, Sabbath. Mr. M. preached in the Church.—I dispensed the Lord's Supper in our family, and trust the season was profitable to all; more so than ever I remember; every body's heart seemed to obtain something new, and 'to presage something great or painful.

"January, 4th, 5th, and 6th. These three days I have had a dreadful onset from ———, and a great deal of personal abuse and impertinent language poured upon me, and, as I conceive, very unjustly and ungratefully. I have tried to bear it. O that my efforts to bear this load may not be the bare effect of a natural temper, or of calculating discretion; but of a divine principle. O that, like the holy Psalmist, I may, in a special manner, at this time, 'give myself to prayer.' How difficult is it, under such circumstances, to preserve temperate language and equanimity of mind! It has been partly said in words, and partly insinuated, that I am a deceiver—an impostor—a deluder of the public—a Pope—insincere—careless—imprudent: and insinuations of my ignorance of men, imperiousness, want of humility, &c., have been thrown out. But let me learn never to take men at their worst. Help me, Lord! and if any of these charges are just, graciously pardon—for who shall stand if thou, O Lord, shouldst mark iniquity.

"January 31st. Sabbath. Chinese and English services as usual. Walked into town; conversed with the old priest, and with a few persons in a blacksmith's shop, and discoursed from the *lock* which he was making—conversed with several other individuals in the street—am this evening exceedingly fatigued. Lord, let not my feeble efforts be totally in vain!

"February 1st, 2nd, and 3rd. Rode out in the evenings, and here and there talked with the people about their souls, &c.

"February 4th. Explained part of the tract on gambling in the temple.—I imagine there were upwards of fifty persons—a large congregation compared with what is usual.

"February 6th. To-day Mrs. Milne was confined, and delivered of a fine boy at two o'clock, p. m. Lord, make me thankful for thy goodness, and may every fresh instance thereof leave a deeper impression on my heart of my obligation to be thine. Bless, I beseech Thee, this child—make him thine—spare, if agreeable to thy holy will, his life—confer upon him thy grace. Enable me to give him up to Thee. Bless and restore, I pray Thee, my partner in life, and may she also derive real spiritual good by a suitable improvement of this instance of thy goodness to us. May frequent recollections of thy mercy, in this and similar instances, give fresh energy to our zeal in thy good cause.

"February 7th. Sabbath. I engaged in the usual Chinese services of the day. I had given Afah John iii. 16, to write a little on, as a trial; he wrote very good sense, but left out the article of redemption; and, excepting the divinity of Christ, made it exactly a Socinian discourse on the design of Christ's coming into the world.—By this, after hearing the gospel so long, I see two things: 1st. How difficult it is to explain the doctrine of redemption to the Heathen mind, so as to convey, I will not say an adequate, but a just view of the subject.—2nd. The importance of catechising; and, by questions, endeavouring to bring their minds to a distinct and edifying consideration of particular subjects and particular passages of Scripture.—Things delivered in the *general* are apt to lose their effect.

"February 10th. In the Temple—about thirty persons.

"February 14th. Sabbath. I went through all the public work—O that I may not labour in vain!

My —— have again set a quarrelling.—Alas! what is man—what selfishness—what pride—what obstinacy—what envy! Let me never, if possible, foment contentions, but cherish the spirit of peace, and be willing to sacrifice any thing for truth and peace.—I wrote a pacificatory letter, which seemed to have some effect. Matters seem now a little more favourable. Let me be impartial, and try to find out my *own* errors!

"My dear wife is again reduced to extreme weakness, nearly as weak as after her last confinement. Troubles come thick upon me—O for patience, self-command, prayerfulness of spirit, and grace, both to her and myself, to make a right use of this affliction!

"February 5th. Our little babe was this evening baptized at his mother's bed-side, by the Rev. J. Slater, by the name of FARQUHAR, as a mark of regard and gratitude to Major W. Farquhar.—His mother wished to have carried him to the House of God, and made an offering of him to the Lord, as Hannah did of her son—so she expressed herself. She had several times expressed her anxiety about this—and I thought it right not to defer it longer. The ordinance was therefore dispensed at her bed-side, about nine o'clock at night.

"February 17th. We went out to CLAY-BANG, about four miles from Malacca, in hope of Mrs. Milne benefiting by the change.—She was carried out in a chair in the evening, but was exceedingly weak— she never again came down stairs.

"February 18th. Dozed almost all day and night. The diarrhœa and vomiting seemed to stop, and hopes were entertained.

"February 19th. Delirium—several times called me to read hymns to her—afternoon took leave of, and blessed several members of the family who came out to see her—during the following night stupor and fever, and partial wanderings—she recognised me several times.

"February 20th. Clay-bang, about four miles from Malacca, this morning, about nine o'clock, my dear wife was taken from me by the hand of Death. I closed her eyes in death, with my own hands, and assisted in doing the last offices for her. For the last four days of her life she said but little about Divine things; stupor and partial delirium being induced by her complaint—she had previously given charge concerning her affairs, and often said, that though she could not feel as she wished under such circumstances, yet she hoped that the Lord, whom she had chosen in the days of her youth, would be her God: and that her only hope was in Christ Jesus. For several days I had given up every other concern to attend solely to her, with which she was greatly pleased—and it is now to me a source of satisfaction, that I attended her at the *last* with as much tenderness and attention as I then thought I possibly could; but alas! now, what regrets crowd upon me! but they are fruitless. O Lord, if in any thing I have been sinfully negligent; if I ever grieved the heart of her whom thou gavest me; if her passage from time to eternity was attended with pain on my account, in any thing which I neglected to do; or if I did, or said, what I ought not to have done or said—O pardon it! While I weep over my own loss, and that of the children, I feel glad on her account and thankful to the God of all grace for taking her to himself. The words, 'To be with Christ is far better,' have been frequently running in my thoughts since her former illness: especially since her last illness commenced. That so lovely and excellent a woman should be, on her own account, longer detained in this world, under the influence of bodily weakness, which, had she even recovered, must have rendered her life often uncomfortable; she would probably have had to go to Europe, or somewhere else, for health; and it is probable, that in her case, all labour would have been 'travail and sorrow.' Now, to be for ever freed from the pains and dread of seas; storms; separation from me; anxieties about the children; and from the toils and labours of this mortal life; to be set down, as I hope she is, with Christ, saints, and angels, is what I rejoice in! The only thing that damps my joy in this is, a conviction that I have not contributed so fully to her edification and preparation for that happy state as I might and ought to have done. True, I have been almost always engaged in something that seemed either directly or indirectly useful to the Mission; but, alas! while I was busy here and there, she was going! Why did I not read more, converse more, and pray more with her? Ah! surely I have not, in every instance, done what I might. God of all grace, forgive my defects!

"Towards the evening of the day the corpse was brought into town in a boat. How little did I think, when going out to this country retreat, that in *three* days I should be returning with my dearest earthly friend, a cold lump of lifeless clay by my side, in the same couch on which I had taken her out! O, to live more under realizing views of eternity.

"February 21. Mr. Thomsen slept in the room with me, and every one seemed to strive to exceed in kindness. The body was put into the coffin at eight in the morning, at which time all the family attended, and Mrs. Milne's favourite hymn,—

'God moves in a mysterious way'—

was sung with tears by all.

"How expressive is Scripture language on almost every subject. 'The desire of thine eyes,' is a term applied to the wife of a prophet. I now feel the force of this phrase in a touching manner. I contemplate her clay-cold countenance with melancholy pleasure. All the placid sweetness,—the motherly sense,—and the dignity of mind, which used to mark her countenance formerly, seem still to leave their traits there! The face preserves all the appearance it used to have when she was highly pleased—(except the eyes being shut) the face unruffled—the lips about a third open. But alas! there is no more life—and the body now begins to be offensive. I must now bury my dead out of my sight. I hope she is gone before to glory, and that, through mercy, I shall finally follow—she often told me I should not remain long behind. A few days since she said— 'you will not be long behind me—about *five* years only.' O my God, prepare me for joining the happy number of redeemed souls in glory!

"The dear children seem quite insensible of their loss; playing about the dead body, and talking of Mamma's death as if it concerned them not—as if it were a subject of childish play. Amelia, for whom her mother expressed the deepest concern, almost to anguish, poor creature, insensible of her loss, while her mother's ear-rings and finger-rings were taken off yesterday, came to me, with her usual playfulness, and said,—'Papa, when I large, I put.

on that ring—and all Mamma's clothes too—yes, Papa?—I almost feel angry with them; but why should I?—they are but infants.

"O Rachel! Rachel! endeared to me by every possible tie—Oh! what would I not give for but five minutes' converse with thee!—yea, but for one minute!—but the wish is vain—I will try not to grieve for thee, as thou didst often request before thy departure from mortality—I will try to cherish the remembrance of thy virtues and sayings, and teach them to those dear babes thou hast left behind. Were it lawful (but I fear it is not) to wish thy *guardianship* over me and thy babes, especially thy Amelia and thy little 'Benjamin,' I would do it. May thy God keep them—may he answer the many fervent prayers thou didst offer for them.

"A few minutes before Mrs. Milne died she called for me—and, to my now inexpressible sorrow, I was at that moment in another room—before I could come in she could articulate no more. O, why was I absent?—but can I justly blame myself—I had, if I remember right, gone to *pray* for her: I then attended at her couch, from which I had been seldom absent for six days before, till the last—which took place almost immediately by a sound within, resembling that of the chain of a watch, when broke, unfurling itself from the wheel: two long breathings ended the strife; and, but in a few minutes, the countenance, which had for some days been at times partially distorted through pain, fever, and wandering, resumed the meekness, satisfaction, and composure which used to sit thereon. I sorrow not for Rachel as those who have no hope: no, I am not grieved that she has got to the pure land of health and joy by a nearer road than Penang, whither we purposed immediately to go for her health: no, I feel happy in reflecting on the solid evidences of Christian piety which she possessed. But I mourn for myself and for my children: O God, forsake them not. O God, make this painful bereavement really profitable to my soul. I would now try to what account this dispensation can be turned for my own edification; for the benefit of my children; for the good of my brethren in Christ; and for the advancement of my work: so help me to do, gracious God. But alas! how far does my judgment of what is right and proper, in every case, outstrip my feelings and attainments? How soon may I even also forget what I now write!

"On the first Sabbath of this year, while dispensing the Lord's Supper in our family church, I possessed uncommon freedom of speech—unusually impressive views of Divine Truth: the same feeling pervaded every heart; unknown anticipations seemed to fill each heart; tears flowed abundantly from every eye. Mrs. Milne enjoyed the season remarkably. It seemed to me, at the time of the service, that something great, or *afflictive*, might be before some of us. Ah! had I then supposed that I should never more 'eat of the fruit of the vine' with my Rachel in this world, what would my feelings have been? That evening, conversing with Mrs. B. she said, that she thought she should sit no more down at the Lord's table on earth: she talked much of death.

"The fifth morning previously to her death, when I called in, she said, 'O what a sweet moment I have had in thinking of divine things!' She seemed often before her confinement to think that her death was near; and when I would try to wear that impression off her mind, she used to say, 'My dear, you only sought me for a *short* time, and you have had me for more than a year'—meaning, since the time of her former illness. She also, during her illness, often said, with respect to her child, 'I think I have been spared just to bring this child into the world and then go.' She spoke of him as her Benjamin; and seemed to think that he was born for some great and useful purpose.

"March 21st. This afternoon, about six o'clock, the remains of my dear wife were interred in the Dutch burying ground. 'Why do we mourn departed friends?' was sung, and prayer offered, at the grave, by Mr. Ince. But the heavy fall of rain prevented any address, as was intended. A large concourse of people, of all castes, came, and intended to follow to the grave, but the rain prevented a great many: many carriages went. The governor, chief military officers, &c. There her remains lie till the resurrection of the just.

"March 22nd. Went to see the grave this morning with the children; they asked 'where the head and feet were,' and played about, gathering flowers. Every thing seems empty to me; what is life without one of kindred mind to share it with? What melancholy pleasure does the mind take in reviewing the abode, the clothes, the portrait, the seat, &c., of such a friend?

"The family met this evening to pray for the sanctified use of this affliction. O may their prayers be heard!

"For some time previously to her death, and indeed to her confinement, I had been in the habit of reading a little of some theological books at the time of our private prayer; for example, 'Edwards' History of Redemption;' 'Flavel;' 'Brooks;' 'Watts' World to Come,' &c. The last of these we began to read only a few days previously to her death. I read the Sermon on the 'Blessedness of the Watchful Christian at Death,' while she was lying on her couch.

"But I now regret exceedingly that I did not use more means for her edification; pray more frequently with her; read more to her; converse more tenderly and affectionately with her; I indeed thought myself, upon the whole, a good husband, tender, and affectionate; and she often said so to me; but ah! now that I can see her no more, what would I give for lost opportunities? How much more might I have done to please and edify; how much to remove uneasiness—how many things might I have done to promote her comfort and cheerfulness—and how many things might I have omitted to do and say, which perhaps gave her uneasiness? Ah! my God, my hope, wherein I have sinned, or omitted duties, in regard to that excellent woman, whom thou didst lend me for a time—O pardon them!

"For a considerable part of last year and beginning of this, our family enjoyed good health. Mrs. Milne also was so much better than at former seasons, that I sometimes began to fancy ourselves happy:—yet a secret thought often whispered—'Take heed of saying in thine heart, my mountain stands strong'—nor do I think that I did say or suppose so; for a silent sigh often stole from me in looking over these dear treasures—these gifts of Providence—that they must necessarily be short-lived."

(Thus died Mrs. Milne! and were it proper to connect any name, beyond the circle of her family, with the heavy loss, I would link my own with it, although not a few have a better right to the distinction. Her other friends were useful to herself or her family. I was not. She was very useful to me. Indeed, if I have been of any use as a writer on female piety, I owe to her my first perceptions of " the beauty of female holiness." She is not exactly the RACHEL of the "Marys," for she was not sentimental; but my object was, to assimilate that Rachel to her image.)

The following inscription was written on Mrs. Milne's Tombstone.

ERECTED TO THE MEMORY
OF
RACHEL,
WIFE OF THE REV W MILNE,
WHO DIED AT CLAY-BANG, NEAR MALACCA,
MARCH 20TH, 1819, AGED 35 YEARS AND 6 MONTHS,
HAVING BURIED AN INFANT SON AND DAUGHTER,
AND LEAVING BEHIND HER FOUR SMALL CHILDREN AND AN
AFFECTIONATE HUSBAND, IN WHOSE BREAST HER
MEMORY IS EMBALMED.

HER LIFE WAS DISTINGUISHED
AS A CHILD, BY FILIAL REVERENCE;
AS A CHRISTIAN, BY HUMBLE CONFIDENCE;
AS A WIFE, BY MODEST SUBMISSION,
AS A MOTHER, BY AFFECTIONATE TENDERNESS;
AND
AS A MEMBER OF SOCIETY, BY MANY
EXEMPLARY VIRTUES.
SHE DIED IN HOPE OF ETERNAL LIFE, THROUGH JESUS CHRIST.

THE MORTAL REMAINS OF
DAVID MILNE,
WHO DIED 4TH MAY, 1816, AGED TWO DAYS;
AND OF
SARAH MILNE,
WHO DIED 10TH APRIL, 1817, AGED FOUR DAYS,
ARE INTERRED A LITTLE TO THE LEFT OF THIS STONE.

DR. MILNE'S MEMOIR OF HIS WIFE.

"Rachel, the wife of the Rev. W. Milne, Malacca, who died on the 20th March, 1819, was born of respectable parents in the city of Aberdeen, North of Scotland, on the 23rd September, 1783. Her father, Charles Cowie, Esq., was extensively engaged as a stocking manufacturer and hosier, in which line of business he was enabled to support a large family in comfortable circumstances, and give them an education suited to their rank in society. But change of times, and the failure of foreign commerce, threw him ultimately into great difficulties, the pressure of which would have been insupportable but for the filial piety, diligence, and prudence, of his youngest daughter, *Rachel*, the subject of this paper.

"From her earliest infancy Rachel's parents endeavoured to impress religious truth upon her mind. In her diary she gives this honourable testimony to her mother's conduct: 'My mother's instructions were enforced by her prayers and example.'

"Her parents were originally members of the Church of Scotland, but in consequence of the removal of their minister, the family joined the Congregational Church, then under the care of the Rev. John Philip, Aberdeen. When about the eighth year of her age, Rachel was at times seriously impressed with a sense of the omniscience of God; but often felt evil and blasphemous thoughts rising up in her mind, which proved a great source of uneasiand deep self-abasement. She prayed earnestly to God, and was delivered from them; but soon forgot her obligations to divine goodness. In Scotland, the female members of many families in the higher ranks of society, as well as those in middling circumstances, are instructed in some branch of business, suited to the strength and station of the sex. This practice cannot be sufficiently applauded. Much domestic virtue and comfort arise from it. The knowledge of it is easily carried about with them; and should they ever stand in need of having recourse to it for personal support, or for the comfort of aged parents, it may enable them to procure necessaries, comforts, and abundance; and to preserve that *independence* of spirit which should be cherished in every community, and which strongly characterizes the people of Scotland.

"Rachel was early put to learn a branch of the milinery business. The circumstances of the family at that time rendered it unnecessary to attend to that as a means of support; but, in the course of those revolutions which were awaiting her and her parents in the dispensation of Providence, it proved of the greatest service. But while acquiring a knowledge of this, and attending to other ornamental branches of education, she was led into the society of those whose conversation and manners were calculated to weaken the force of parental instruction; and to produce a vitiated taste for the gaiety and pleasures of the world. The reading of novels—dancing, of which she was enthusiastically fond—the ball-room —gay company—and the public amusements—soon engrossed her thoughts, and tended to create a distaste for the nobler enjoyments of religion, and the more rational pursuits of life. These are, I doubt not, their general effects in society, however unwilling persons may be to acknowledge it,

"But God was pleased to water, by the influence of his grace, the seeds of instruction sown by the parental hand. Former impressions were revived and deepened, under the preaching of the gospel. Such had been the influence of public amusements, and of the conversation of ungodly persons on Rachel's mind, that she went one Sabbath afternoon, in company with a few thoughtless companions, to Church, to see what materials for light remark and laughter they could collect from the preacher's sermon and manners. The Rev. Dr. Bennet was to preach. The eloquent address of that popular and useful minister deeply arrested her attention, and those who went to laugh remained to hear. The importance of the truths delivered fell with weight on Rachel's heart." (Dr. Milne forgot to add here, that she was disarmed of her *levity* by the *shrewdness* of the preacher. She soon found that although she might occasionally smile with him, she durst not laugh at him. The alternate piquancy and solemnity of his appeals riveted her attention. She felt that he saw through her, and that she could not see through him; shrewd as she also was, and successful as she had been in "taking off" other preachers. I could not understand her descriptions of Dr. Bennet's preaching at all, until I heard him in England; but then their vivacity was quite intelligible.) "She henceforth attended the ordinances of the Sabbath with increased seriousness and delight; and all the more private means of social worship and Christian edification. She had always indeed attended public worship, and was never so far left as to run into the common vices of youth, or entirely to cast off a sense of religion; but now it became the serious concern of the mind and the business of life. Her own sinfulness and the necessity of a Redeemer were discovered; and she was *enabled to give herself up to God*, and by faith to commit her immortal interests to Jesus Christ as the all-sufficient Saviour. The labours of the Rev. Mr. Stevens she often mentioned with high satisfaction, as having derived great benefit from them. Rachel was by this time grown up, and her fond parents thought it necessary that she should see a little more of life. She accordingly visited London, and spent some time time there. She was introduced into the society of persons of distinction; and visited the chief places of public resort and curiosity. The new scenes of the splendid metropolis she felt had a tendency to dissipate the mind, to unfit it for the duties of the closet and the sober concerns of life. While in London she attended the anniversary of the Missionary Society, the services of which produced so deep an impression of the importance of sending the gospel to the heathen, that she lamented that the circumstance of her *sex* prevented her from taking any part therein. This idea, *romantic* as it may appear to some, was probably the commencement of that train of events which ultimately induced her to prefer the company of one who was destined to labour among the heathen before that of others, in connexion with whom she might have had the prospects of ease and independence, and even wealth, at home; although it was six years afterwards before she had any opportunity of forming a decision on this head. To such apparently *little* circumstances do the events of human life frequently owe their beginning." (This "romantic idea," as Dr. Milne calls it, never left her.

There was, however, nothing romantic in either the manner or the spirit in which she cherished it. She often expressed it *playfully* amongst her friends; and, somehow, it always made me solemn. Not all the *glee* with which she painted Missionary life—on coral shores, and under banyan and bread-fruit trees,—could hide the secret of her heart. She evidently made her vivid pictures extravagant, just that she might conceal her wishes. This was years before Mr. Milne knew her. Then she used to say to me, "If Dr. Bogue, now, wanted a wife, and would marry such a *little wee boddy* as myself, and go abroad, what a *nice* Missionary pair we should make!" Thus she would play with the subject amongst her friends; but she played with it so *often*, that we certainly should have suspected her, had we known any Missionary worthy of her then.)

"She was, shortly after her return from London, received as a member of the church, and sat down at the Lord's table to commemorate the sufferings and death of Jesus. Through the whole of her future life she always attended that ordinance with peculiar delight; generally found it edifying, and wished more frequent returns of the opportunity of celebrating it. The stated dispensation of gospel ordinances after the settlement of the Rev. John Philip, in Aberdeen, through the divine blessing, increased her knowledge of the Scriptures and strengthened her resolution to serve and glorify God, while in the daily morning and evening worship of her father's family she derived the most solid advantages for edification. Happy are the children of those who fear God; and happy are those Christians who live in families where God is statedly and reverently worshipped!

"The time now approached when Rachel's trials were to begin. Her mother, through accumulated infirmities, was frequently unable to leave her chamber. For some time her father's business had been on the decline, and an entire stop being put by the war to all commercial intercourse with Holland, France, and other parts of the continent, on which the success of his business chiefly depended, the house could, of consequence, no longer pay its bills, and became insolvent. To Rachel this was a source of unspeakable anxiety. Her only surviving brother, scarcely out from school, could not well do for himself. Her sister, with a young family, could render no assistance. Her parents, now both infirm, and greatly harassed by inconsiderate and unmerciful requisitions, had no means of supporting their old age. A conscientious wish to discharge the demands of their creditors as far as possible, led them to give up every thing except their wearing apparel and a few books.

"It was in these circumstances that the filial affection of Rachel shone forth conspicuously. It had ever been their aim, in the course of her education, to form in her mind rational and sober views of life, and to fix her attention most on those acquirements which are most useful—which endure the test of affliction, and which wear to the last hour of life; and they were themselves among the first to reap the advantages. Rachel, seeing the declining state of her father's business, thought it her duty, beforehand, to make preparations for future exigencies. She accordingly, with the consent of her parents, began business in the milinery line, partly with a view to provide for them in case of insolvency. She had only a few pounds of money of her own to begin with, but she borrowed a small sum from a friend, and being conscious that her motives were upright and honourable, she earnestly prayed that God would prosper the work of her hands, and preserve her from the snares to which this new situation would expose her. Her efforts were so far crowned with success, that in a few months, she was able to repay what she had borrowed, to furnish a house comfortably, and to leave something over. She now took her destitute parents both to her own house, supported them by her labours, nursed them with the utmost tenderness in their afflictions, attended them in their last moments—saw them die, in hope of the glory of God, and interred their mortal remains with decency and respect.

"She had ever been their favourite child. But who can tell the feelings of aged and dying parents, when nursed and attended, day and night, by such a daughter, in whose countenance the most cheerful satisfaction with her lot, the most anxious wish to serve them, and the most painful solicitude to render the pains of death easier, were ever printed? Ten thousands of blessings from heaven were daily implored to rest upon her head, and the expiring parents both expressed to her a hope that God would make all her bed in her sickness, and raise up kind and tender-hearted friends to her in every extremity; which hope was actually realized in course of her future life: for, in the many personal and domestic afflictions which she had afterwards to pass through, the hand of God, in raising up kind friends, where no obligations existed, and in providing medical attendants, who acted as fathers and brothers to her, was peculiarly visible. It was remarked, both by herself and her husband, and it is worthy of being recorded as an encouragement to filial piety, and as a proof that the prayers of pious parents are available with God, for blessings on dutiful children. Reader, learn, and imitate. In her diary she had taken notice of the gracious providence of God, in providing for her and her parents in their affliction; and concludes by remarking, 'I have enlarged more on this part of my narrative than I at first intended, because it shows the wisdom and goodness of God, and the implicit confidence which his people may place in his promises, that he will supply all their wants, though perhaps not exactly in the way they think or wish.'" (Thus Dr. Milne records the filial piety of his wife. How he acquired the particulars of it, I cannot tell: but I, who *saw* what he has recorded, could hardly have been more minute. I was, not seldom, her companion on Sabbath afternoon, to visit her parents; when we gave them the outline of Dr. Philip's morning sermon, whilst we drank tea with them. Angels would have enjoyed these visits,—the interchange of love between the venerable parents and their devoted daughter, was so full of both nature and grace! I owe much to these interviews; and not least to the regularity of the old lady, in saying always, in good time, "Now, my good *children*, it is quite time to get ready for chapel,"—as if I, too, had been one of the family.)

"While her parents stood in need of her assistance, Rachel could never think it right to listen to any proposals of marriage, though many advantageous ones had been made. About twelve months after her mother's death, an acquaintance was formed between her and the person who ultimately became her husband." (Dr. Milne ascribes this acquaintanceship to Mrs. Conn, his first friend in London.)

"What is commonly called the season of *courtship* was not passed over by Rachel, as it too frequently is, in cherishing extravagant fancies about the pure and unmixed bliss of the conjugal state, or in lavishingly wasting her money on the purchase of finery; no, but in preparing herself for the discharge of the new and important duties of the relation, upon which she was about to enter. She considered the practice of many young persons of both sexes, in the time of their courtship, as a very bad *preface* to domestic life; and indeed as the presage of much misery. The listless, flippant vanity of multitudes of young ladies, she viewed as highly dishonourable to the *sex*. She believed that all the events of life are ordered by Divine Providence, and that the duties of each human relation are binding by a *Divine* sanction. This led her often to her knees to implore the direction of God, and grace to discharge the duties that were awaiting her.

"Thus prepared by education, by piety, by the reverses of fortune, by afflictions, by habits of diligence, and economy, she entered into the conjugal state on the 4th of August, 1812, the duties of which, as a wife and a mother, she discharged for six years and a half in such a manner as to reflect the highest honour on her own principles, to make her partner in life the *happiest* of husbands, to keep her children cleanly in their persons and neat in their dress, to preserve the family expense within its resources, to sweeten the cup of domestic affliction, and lighten the burdens of life, to secure the growing affection of those that knew her best, and to draw forth the esteem of neighbours and strangers.

"In early life Mrs. M. was struck with the description given by Solomon, in the last chapter of the Proverbs, of the woman whose price is above rubies. It was the aim of her parents to make her such, as to answer the description; and it was her own constant study to fall as little short of it as possible. Nor is it affirming too much to say, that it would not be easy to find a person in all respects come so near as she did to the standard of personal, maternal, and domestic worth, fixed by the wise man.

"Mrs. Milne had six children, two of whom were called away at an early period. The bereavement, though borne with cordial submission to the divine will, produced a visible *damp* on her spirits. 'She never afterwards recovered her *natural* vivacity.' (Dr. Milne means much by these words: for her natural vivacity, although entirely free from levity, seemed, like the radiance of her eyes, unquenchable. Indeed, had he not told that this

"Change came o'er her spirit,"

I could not have imagined it possible. Life without liveliness, in her, seemed a contradiction in terms. She was wont at all times, to be all life: and yet, no one ever thought her too lively. Her vivacity created no hurry or bustle in herself, and never pained any one for her. She evidently thought *aloud*, and apparently spoke on the *spur* of the moment; but no one, I ever saw or heard of, remembers any instance of rashness, flippancy, or mistake, in her conversation. She must, therefore, have suffered much and deeply, before her spirits were damped.) "The care of her surviving children engrossed the chief part of her solicitude, time, and strength. She powerfully felt the paramount claims of relative duty, and they occupied the first place in her attention, next to the more serious obligation of creatures to their God. She thought very *meanly* of the religion and understanding of those mothers who neglected their children, their husbands and their household affairs.

"She loved the word of God, and delighted in the ordinances of divine worship, both in the family and in the church. In her last illness she said, 'I cannot think favourably of the personal piety of those who neglect family prayer, nor augur much usefulness from those who do not attend on it regularly when in their power.' The salvation of the souls of her children, was a subject of her most earnest prayers. The short time she was spared with them, afforded scarce an opportunity of *instructing* any of them, except a little girl; the others being too young to fix their attention. In as far as health would allow, to impart some religious instruction to her daughter, was a work of every day. She often said, I have never wished for riches or fame to our children, but that they may truly fear God, and be good and useful members of society. She had a very humbling sense of her own sinfulness, and frequently spoke of herself to her dearest earthly friends in terms expressive of the deepest self-abasement of soul before God.

"Mrs. Milne's heart was much engaged in the good work to which her husband and herself had devoted their lives. But she had a different idea of

the way in which females best subserve the cause of
the Gospel among the heathen, from what is entertained by some. She thought that by managing
the domestic concerns, by endeavouring to make her
husband's mind easy, by a care of his health, by
watching to discover those errors which he might
overlook, and pointing them out, by assisting him
with her counsel, and by such a conduct as would
render the Mission worthy of respect in the eyes of
mankind, in these ways, she conceived, a Missionary's wife might render no small service to the
interests of religion. She was often laying plans for
bringing up and educating a few poor orphan girls;
but lived not to see her plans executed. At the
Cape of Good Hope, the Isle of France, China, and
Malacca, she had many opportunities of witnessing
the deplorable condition of those that know not God.
She felt and prayed for them, and died in faith, that
the labours of Missionaries among the Heathen will
in 'due time' be crowned with the richest success.
About two years before her death, Mrs. M. had a
most serious illness, during part of which her life
was despaired of both by herself and others. She
then made a solemn *surrender* of herself, her husband, and her children, to God her Saviour, and
awaited the call of death. In the very height of
her affliction, the consolations of the Gospel were so
abundantly poured into her heart, and her hopes of
eternal blessedness so clear, that she afterwards said,
'your intimation that my complaint had taken a favourable turn, filled me with sorrow. I felt an unspeakable disappointment to be sent back again, as
it were from the gates of heaven, to spend a little
more time in this sinful and dreary state.' The

sublime and consoling truths delivered by our Lord Jesus previously to his crucifixion, and which are contained in the 14th, 15th, 16th, and 17th chapters of John, afforded unexpressible joy to her soul. She several times said, 'the spirit of divine friendship, in which they were spoken, independently of their own unspeakable importance, gives a peculiar sweetness to those portions of the New Testament.'

"By the blessing of God, a voyage to China, and the kind attention of friends there, (to whom she ever felt grateful,) were the means of restoring her to such a measure of health as that she could attend to the duties of the family; but she never fully recovered her wonted strength. Indeed, she sometimes said that, though her life was spared, she conceived it would be but for a short time. This idea seemed to dwell in her mind. She consequently spent more time in reading the scriptures, and in private devotion, than formerly; but never to the neglect of any relative duty.

"*Dreams and presentiments*, though they have both their uses to mankind, are often sources of unspeakable uneasiness to the credulous and weak-minded. We must judge of them as the Israelites were to judge of prophets;—that if the thing came to *pass*, they might then be assured the prophet was true, and *vice versa*. It has been not unfrequently remarked that, pious persons, shortly before death, have had a kind of presentiment of its approach. This appeared to be the case with Mrs. M. On the first Sabbath of January, about two months and a half previously to her demise, the ordinance of the Lord's Supper was dispensed, and it was a season of peculiar edification to all present; feelings and anticipations of an unusual nature filled every breast, the tears flowed abundantly from every eye, and the whole seemed as if sent to prepare the way to some important though unforeseen event. Mrs. M. experienced more than common edification, but in the evening she told some female friends, with tears, that she thought it was very likely the *last* time she should taste the fruit of the vine with them at the table of the Lord: and so it proved; for circumstances prevented the celebration of that ordinance again while she was in the body; which she deeply regretted, for she considered this, of all Christian ordinances, the most calculated to increase love to the Saviour, and the edification of love to the soul. On the 6th of February, she was delivered of a son. Her recovery, for ten days, went on favourably, and she hoped to be soon able to carry her little one to the house of God, to present him to the Lord in baptism. But she caught cold, which was speedily followed by a fever, vomiting and dysentery, which no means could cure. Often expressing an earnest desire solemnly to give her son to God, he was accordingly baptized at her *bed-side*; after which she felt better satisfied as having performed an important parental duty. The solemn hour of the release from the body drew near. She became daily weaker. Some flattering intervals of the complaint encouraged a momentary hope of recovery, which was as frequently disappointed. She spent the moments of ease in commending her own soul, and those of her family, to God her Saviour. She enjoyed a steady hope of salvation, but had not those *rapturous* feelings of joy which she was favoured with, in a former season of sickness already alluded to. She often said, Christ is my only hope; I seek none else: and I seek not a triumphant death, but a *safe* and peaceful one. One morning, having been for some time left alone, on her husband's entering the room, she said, 'You have interrupted me. Oh, what a *sweet* moment I have had.' She sometimes spoke with the deepest solicitude about her children, especially her little daughter. The idea that she might be left, perhaps, fatherless also, in these countries where there is so much to pollute the infant mind, and so few fitted to watch over its gradual buddings and direct it to God, was quite insupportable; and her mind found relief only by earnest prayer to that God who is the orphan's stay. A change of air was advised, and as there was no opportunity of a sea voyage, a removal to the country was the only alternative left. On the 17th of March, she was conveyed to the country-seat of a gentleman of Malacca. She felt pleased on reaching so retired and peaceful a retreat, where she could enjoy the attentions of her husband without those interruptions which were unavoidable in town. She often called him to read some favourite hymns and pray with her. The disease rapidly increased, though she was not conscious of much pain. She several times called her children, to see them, and bless them. She felt occasional stupor,—was unable to say much;—several times expressed that Christ was her only hope. On the 18th, a letter from a particular friend, who had shown her much kindness, having come to hand, she was able to hear it read; and the news, together with the association of ideas, awakened in the mind thereby, roused her from the stupor induced by disease; and she spent a few minutes in the attitude of prayer, with her eyes directed towards heaven, imploring, no doubt, the blessing of God on him and his family. On the 19th, she took *leave* of several friends who came from town to see her, and blessed them. In course of that night, partial delirium and wandering were observed; but, at intervals, the mind was calm and lucid. She said she felt no pain. Next morning, about an hour before her death, a friend went to prayer at her bed-side. She was pleased, though scarce able to speak. Her children were brought in to see her for the last time in life: but she was no longer able to speak to them. It was now evident that ' the time of her departure was at hand.' She had latterly experienced a frequent sense of suffocation, occasioned by an astonishing accumulation of phlegm in the throat; and supposing that this sensation would be peculiarly felt in her last moments, she had, with great calmness of mind, beforehand, directed her husband to administer some liquids which had often given relief. The constant application of these seemed to ease the final struggles of expiring life. On the 20th of March, 1819, about nine o'clock in the morning, she was released from the afflictions and infirmities of life. Her eyes were closed in death, by the hand of one who had ever beheld them with delight; and whose only consolation was, that, as he could not enjoy her society any longer on earth, he had good reason to hope that she was gone to *be with Christ, which is far better.* Mrs. Milne died, aged thirty-five years, five months, and twenty-seven days. Her mortal remains were committed to the dust, in the Dutch burial-ground, on the following day.

"In the close of these brief memoirs some little circumstances of no consequence to the general reader, have been noticed for the sake of distant relatives. A few particulars relative to the character of the deceased, which could not be so well wrought into the narrative, shall close this paper. Mrs. Milne possessed a peculiar *penetration into the human character*, by a view of the countenance. This is sometimes the case with individuals; and though the decision thus formed ought never to assume the authority of a rule to themselves or others, yet Providence may have some wise end to answer by giving this talent. The general features of the character, the predominant passions, the chief quality of the temper, have all been objects of study with the physiognomist. But in the case before us the discrimination seemed quite natural, without design or effort. She formed a judgment at first sight; and the writer does not recollect a single instance, during upwards of six years, which was not confirmed by facts. Mrs. M.'s *religion* was drawn from the Scriptures. It sought retirement, was free from ostentation, mixed with no singularities, and accompanied with deep humility. It was most conspicuous to those who had access to her closet. It was nourished in the shade, and displayed by the discharge of family duties, by sweetness and mildness of temper, by patience under affliction, by private acts of charity known to few. Though fit to appear in what is called the best society, and fond of social intercourse, *Mrs. M. loved also to be alone or busied with her domestic concerns.* She thought the mother of a family should feel all her attractions at home; that her children should be her amusement; her husband her companion; her needle her employment; and the real good of all within the family circle her constant study. Such were her sentiments, and such was her own conduct. She not unfrequently expressed her astonishment at the conduct of those ladies to whom their own houses are a sort of prison, and her utter abhorrence at the conduct of some who cast aside, as she used to say, their children as soon as born, to *somebody* to care for them, who seldom thinks of them till they be sick or past recovery, through the neglect of servants; or till there be another child to throw aside as the former; and who, rather than deny themselves the pleasure of a dance, a ball, or a card-party, will leave their afflicted infant under the care of an *Indian* nursemaid. It is hoped that the number of such mothers (if they deserve that endearing name) in India is daily diminishing, and that a more serious sense of maternal duty will fill the mind of every Christian female, whatever may be her rank in society.

"Mrs. M. had been often in adversity, and hence she became an excellent *sick nurse*. It often fell to her lot to have sick persons to attend upon, and she possessed a degree of tenderness and skill in treating them which we look for in vain, except from those who possess uncommon kindness of heart, and have been practised in the school of affliction. To the wives of Missionaries who may be placed at a distance from medical advice, a knowledge of the common diseases, at least of children, and the way of treating them, is a very valuable attainment. It may make them useful to their heathen neighbours as well as to their own families.

"After coming to China and Malacca, the duties

of the Mission several times called Mrs. M.'s partner in life to visit other places at a distance. On the occasion of such separations she endeavoured to moderate her feelings, and instead of interposing any hinderance, endeavoured to encourage him and keep up his spirits, hoping that such services would contribute to the promotion of the Saviour's kingdom. She used to say, 'However dearly I love your company, I should be sorry to keep you from your duty. I cannot render you much assistance; but I will try not to *hinder* you. I shall be grieved to think that you spend one hour with me, while I am in health, which should be spent in your studies and labours.' Such sentiments were, without doubt, founded in a deep conviction of the paramount obligations of *duty*, to every claim which ease or gratification could prefer. Mrs. M., in her private papers, particularly took notice of two very important eras in the Chinese Mission: first, the completion of the *New Testament* in Chinese; second, the baptism of the *first* Chinese convert. To have seen these *two* things she thought an ample reward for having left her relatives and country, and come all the way to China. She viewed them as pledges of great future good, and as affording the strongest encouragement to continued diligence and perseverance in the work of the Gospel."

CHAPTER XV.

THE WIDOWER'S CLOSET.

Had not Dr. Morrison *opened* "the door" of his colleague's closet, and introduced into the "Canton Memoirs" the secret sorrows of his friend, and thus thrown open the heart of a widowed Missionary, I am not sure that I should have ventured to do so. Not, however, that there is any thing to conceal, but because it is not easily told, without seeming to sentimentalize. Dr. Milne, however, like Dr. Morrison, was no sentimentalist. Both, "wept much before the Lord," when the desire of their eyes was taken away; but neither sorrowed as they who have no hope, nor allowed weeping to stop working. Each had to say, with Ezekiel, "I spake unto the people in the morning, and at *even* my wife died. And I did (next) morning *as* I was commanded."—*Ezek.* xxiv. 18. This is substantially true of them.

Bereavements of this kind occur now and then on the field of Missions; and therefore, it is desirable to show how they have been borne by wise and devoted Missionaries, that future widowers may have influential examples to study and copy in the day of their calamity. No one need be ashamed to *weep* after hearing Dr. Morrison say, "I will not say, 'Grieve not.' Oh, no! I have shed many tears for Mary! Let us shed many tears of affectionate remembrance; for she was worthy of our love. Oh, what a dismal blank has her demise occasioned."

(*Life*, vol. i., p. 103.) No one need be ashamed to *work*, and ought not to be slow in setting to work, under such circumstances, when he is told that Dr. Morrison, in the very same letter which conveyed the melancholy tidings of this loss to Dr. Milne, submitted to him the design of an elaborate work on the "Systems of Chinese Error." This fact does not appear in his life, in this connexion, if at all. It appears, however, in Dr. Milne's letters. The answer runs thus: "I think decidedly that such a work is wanted, and would be exceedingly useful if well executed. But till that Herculean dictionary be finished, it would require more time for reading the various systems than you can get. Still, however, the outline might be drawn up—materials collected —references made to native works. Tell me what course you purpose to take with it—what subjects you would embrace—to what extent you would carry it? I will most cheerfully give you any idea that may occur to me. I think such a work should be acute and logical in its reasonings, rather embellished in its style, and a strain of scripture *irony* now and then would be required. You must *laugh* them, at times, out of their absurdities, so far as that may not weaken the impression of the truth on your own mind, nor hinder the reception of it by them. The aid of some highly qualified native, rather attached to the Gospel, to give the final polish to the language, would be very necessary. Thus I give you my opinion freely, because you *asked* it."—*October 21st*, 1821.

Thus did these widowers work together. This letter contains also answers to questions concerning the chronology of the Scriptures, and the multiplication of Siamese and Malay MSS., in order to another translation of the Bible. "Oh that we had a faithful man," it adds, "who minded the things that are Christ's, to sit down to this great and good work!" How they could *weep* together will appear from the former part of the letter.

"Dear Robert,

"I wrote you two short notes by Captain Collingwood, who left yesterday. I have carefully read your most afflictive letter on the death of my *dear*, and your still *dearer* friend, Mary. Ah! my brother, may Heaven pity you—effectual help is there, but you have also the tenderest sympathy of my heart—and of all here; each one speaks with sympathy of the bereavement. Our daily prayers in the family are offered for you. Well, dear Robert, after having felt the pungency of a grief which the Scriptures forbid not, think of the many mitigating circumstances of the case. It must be a source of satisfaction to you, that she came out to die in your arms, and to receive the last offices of affection from you. My Rachel's dying under my own care, where I saw the worst, and performed the last duties with my own hands, has been a source of satisfaction to me. Mary's last year's health and employment resembled Rachel's very much: she also had excellent health till her confinement; and as you have observed in Mary's case, so I did in Rachel's—namely, a visible increase of spirituality, and attention to sacred subjects. What a satisfaction, my Brother! May our last year display the same. Mary's last letter to me was truly Christian—it manifested an unusual impression of the value of children's souls—and the weight of maternal duty—and with the openness of heart for which she was always marked by Mrs. Milne and myself,—offered to take and educate Amelia at her own expense. Dear soul! she had better work appointed for her. Mother and child taken to the grave—to heaven at once! Dearest Robert, I weep for you, but I am not at all doubtful of their happiness. Sighing and sorrow have been so much my meat for nearly three years past, that this affliction of yours appears, deep as it is, to produce little more than common effects upon my feelings. It falls in with their general train, and feeds the stream—Providence having so ordered it, that Mary's remains should lie in a spot destined to be enclosed as a cemetery for Protestants, and where you can erect a mournful, but decent, monument to her memory, is just the counterpart of what has been done for Rachel. You therefore say true, that 'as our sentiments are much alike, so have been our afflictions, and the circumstances thereof.' Poor Rebecca and John! they have lost their Mamma, when they began to know her worth, and were able to weep for their loss—so was not the case with mine. Give my love to them—beloved dears! I expect to hear that Rebecca will be sent home to finish her education. I now drop this painful subject to answer your several letters."

Journalizing, in biography, is happily at a discount now, so far as ordinary events, and evanescent feelings, are the staples of a diary. No one is more glad of this than myself; for if it be "a weariness" to both the flesh and the spirit to read mere memoranda, what must it be to copy them out for the press, and revise them in the proofs? Still, it is possible to impoverish biography as well as to overload it. The closet of any thoughtful and devotional man, and especially of a widowed Missionary in a land of strangers, is worth seeing, if it can be entered without impropriety. It is, however, next in sacredness to "holy ground." I would not forget this now. I have not taken my "shoes off my feet" on entering Dr. Milne's closet; but I have only gone as far into that "Bochim" as Dr. Morrison led the way. I feel, too, that I shall be followed in the same spirit, not only by "widowers indeed," but by all husbands who, like myself, can hardly conceive how their spirits could sustain the shock of bereavement so as to rally after it. Biography has been too silent on this subject. Both widows and widowers, and many who live in bondage to the fear of separation, need a better lesson than they have yet read; and it will be found, I think, in the following papers of Dr. Milne, which Dr. Morrison so wisely and carefully preserved: for their extent proves how precious Dr. Morrison felt them to be in the days of his own widowhood.

"I feel how hard it is to keep the mind fixed on spiritual subjects—to give it a relish for and love of them.—I feel a little detached from earth at this time; but I fear am not fitter for heaven. O Sovereign God, the eye-witness of all my past life, and the wise disposer of all events: thou hast taken from me one who seemed almost necessary to my existence in comfort and virtue; thou hast left me alone with four children in the wilderness. I am exposed to temptations and sin—to the gloomy thoughts which rise up in solitude—and to pain and affliction, in which there will be no more my dear and tender-hearted friend to help and advise. Yet thou knowest, I would not murmur—I would not overlook the numerous mitigations which thy providence has graciously afforded me in this affliction, by ordering the time of it when I am surrounded with kind friends. I would learn from it useful lessons; but ah! how weak are my wishes. Blessed Being, have pity on me, diffuse through my soul that spiritual life, health, and vigour, on which the existence and action of holiness depend; I fear I shall soon again forget even those feeble and ineffective desires and resolutions which this dispensation of thine hand for the time excites. O, by thy healthful Spirit, produce lasting good in my soul, temper, and conduct, by it. May this event, which seems to strike so deep at the root of my temporal comfort, be, through thy blessing, the commencement of a new era in the state of my spiritual feelings. May more delight, in prayer, more savour of heavenly things, more relish for the Holy Scriptures, more comfort of mind in view of death and eternity, more care and diligence in the improvement of time, for my own edification and the instruction of others, more constant attention to the state of my heart, more pure regard to God and the Saviour, more feeling regard for the poor distressed, and afflicted, and a more dutiful attention to the state of my children, be the effects of this bereavement: then I shall not have cause, in eternity, to regret it; but rather to bless Thee for it. O let me not indulge even the thoughts of sin in my heart; let me not, in an unguarded moment, fall; fill my mind with a Christian abhorrence and indignation of all sin.

"Help my mind to dwell with more pleasure on what is contained in these words;—'God so loved the world, that he gave his only-begotten Son, that whosoever believeth in him should not perish, but have everlasting life.' Ah! I find the heart needs pulling and dragging to this great and fundamental subject. It ought not to be so: it is not always so with thy chosen. Help, Lord, for I have no strength! May my future labours in the Mission derive a tinge of seriousness, and carry in them deeper impressions of eternity, than before. O that the event may prove that I have not been forsaken of thee, and that my beloved wife was not taken away in thine anger against me; but taken in mercy, to her and to me, from the evils of this world, and that I am only left behind for a little, to be better prepared for meeting thee, my Judge in death, and to be the means of some good in this world. 'Let these words of my lips, and meditations of my heart come up before thee, O my God and my Redeemer.'

"April. Sabbath. Preached morning and evening in Chinese.

"How lonely I feel my situation at times! O for more realizing views of that better world—may I finally attain it.—While here below, may I not be forsaken of God—not suffered to listen to the suggestions of the flesh and of corrupt nature—but to the voice of wisdom and of God. O for more faith, purity, and joy. Oh! what causes of regret I feel when I think of my beloved wife!—What is this? Have I been really guilty of neglecting important duties to her? How death or bereavement changes one's views!—brings the mind more closely in contact with realities.

"A-fah, the Chinese Christian, left us. After giving him some suitable instruction—after prayer and many tears, we parted.—The Lord keep him steady and faithful unto death."

Dr. Morrison added this note.

"*Canton, China*, October 17th, 1823.

"To-day the Chinese Printer, Leang-a-Fa, baptized by the late Dr. Milne, and instructed by him in the principles of the Christian religion, called, and gave the pleasing news of having persuaded his wife to believe in Jesus, and receive baptism. He purposes to bring his son, an infant, to receive, on the same day, baptism and vaccination.

"Leang-a-Fa, after reading 2 Chron. viii. 12—22, knelt down with the Missionary who writes this, and prayed in Chinese, a prayer, dictated by the circumstances and feelings of the moment, with great freedom and fervour.—Blessed be God! O, may the seed sown take root and grow up in China, though man cannot well tell how. Lord of the Harvest! do thou water the seed of the word with showers of the Holy Spirit's influences from heaven.

"During these few past days, Oh! what indescribable feelings of regret and longing have I had!—I seem but just *awakening* to feel the loss of my dear Rachel. Ah! how *empty* is my house! how disconsolate my mornings and evenings! What anxieties about my children! Too big for tears: my grief vents itself in groans and sighs inexpressible. But how good has God been to me—I am not alone—I possess a measure of health—have some kind persons about me—and have, during the past week, been enabled generally to fill up my time and thoughts with things of some importance. Preached in Chinese. Morning—English also—met four.

Chinese at one.—Evening and afternoon employed in writing for my Commentary. Mr. Medhurst preached in Chinese in the evening.

"May. To teach the people *verbally* is a delightful work. O for more ability, more skill, and a better spirit for this work. But oh! when I look in, and see how little love to God and man is in my heart, what infinite reason have I to lie low before God. My dear lambs, my children, are a source of care. What shall I do to bring them up? How shall I best get the room of their dear mother supplied to them? Lord, look on us; bless us; provide for us.

"October 30th. Finished the translation of the Book of Job; being the *whole* of my share of the Old Testament; but none from the first of Chronicles, to the end of Job, has yet been revised; so that there will yet be a great deal of hard labour. I have, however, a great cause of thankfulness for being carried on thus far. Lord, make me humble; and direct my future labours.

"December 5th. Last week the Cholera Morbus visited our settlement; many died suddenly: sixteen died on the 2nd, and seven funerals passed our door on the 16th. To-day, five funerals passed. O how stupid is my heart!—With how little reverence do I contemplate God in his judgments. How unbecoming a Christian, and a Missionary, is such an apathy!—such indifference to the great things of God!

"A Kling man living in our compound died. This week eight persons died in Tambe Amat Saib's family, and himself; and, in another family, the mother, son, and a slave, all within about six hours of each other.

"Sabbath—as usual spent in the instruction of the

heathen.—The Lord open their hearts to the truth, and may this visitation be sanctified for the good of many, in producing a seriousness of mind, and fitness to entertain the Gospel. O that my heart could turn to the Divine promises with the delight of one who considers them his inheritance. O that I could perform every part of my public work like one really in earnest to see men saved—and whose object is, in a great measure, lost, where that is not the case.

"At this time, 'all faces gather blackness'—despondency seems marked in all countenances.—O that I could be so exercised as I ought, and that by a lively faith, I could contemplate death—disease—the grave—with some measure of composure. But alas! how strong my sins! how unsanctified my heart!" (At this time Dr. Milne wrote a tract for the Chinese, in order to improve this awful visitation.)

1820. "It has for some time become a matter of consideration with me whether it would be proper for me to marry again." ("Mrs. Milne," Dr. Morrison says, "in her last testament, desired her husband to marry again. Those estimable persons, so affectionately attached to each other, did not consider such a proceeding as at all implying a want of sincere love to each other.")—*Canton Memoir*. FOR IT, 1st. private reasons. 2nd. Could I get a suitable person, she would be a mother to my children. 3rd. My habits are of such a nature that I am in danger of neglecting my own person, clothes, property; and to leave my things in the care of servants, exposes to temptation. AGAINST IT, 1st. A fresh load of cares; 2nd. Danger of my not making her comfortable and happy, from my sedentary and abstract habits; 3rd. She may not be kind to my children; 4th. Subject me to some inconvenience; abridge my labours; another painful parting would have to take place.

"Let me beg of God his direction in this matter, as about how to dispose of my children for their education.

"Things to be guarded against.

" 1st. My besetting sins and all temptations, and inlets to them. 2nd. Passion, and fretfulness of temper. 3rd. Being carried away with the first view of subjects. 4th. All appearances of contempt or slight in treating my brethren. 5th. Excess of labour. 6th. Let me not suffer business, &c., so to disorder or engross my mind, as not to leave sufficient time and composure for attending to my children and my own edification. 7th. Let me not neglect to consider what impression my conduct in any one, or all particulars, may be likely to have on witnesses and bystanders—strive that it may be such as I shall wish it had been when I am dying.

"Now, O Lord, in whose hands the events and occurrences of every passing year are—I beseech Thee be with me through this year, or that portion of my life which yet remains. Leave me not for a single moment without the influences of Thy Spirit, or the restraints of Thy Providence. Let me take no rash steps. May I and my children be the objects of thy continued providential and merciful regard. Overrule all events for our good. Direct ever in a right way. Prepare us for all vicissitudes. Help me in every duty. Pardon my sins. At death, enable me to say that 'thy well-ordered covenant is all my salvation and all my desire.' Amen.

"1822.—O God! beside Thee I have no resource. If thou forgive not my past sins, errors, and backslidings, they can never be forgiven. But 'there is forgiveness with Thee that Thou mayest be feared.'— O Sovereign God, exercise it abundantly to me, the most unworthy of Thy rational creatures. Abandon me not, leave me not, I beseech Thee, this year; but guide me,—O mercifully guide me, in all things, by thy counsel; and whenever, and wherever my earthly career may terminate, then—O then receive this soul to thy glory. My soul and body—my beloved children, and all my concerns, I now try to commit to thy merciful, wise, and Almighty guardianship, during this year, and for ever and ever. Amen. " W. MILNE.

"January.—Met with an Armenian Bishop from Jerusalem, named Abraham, who is visiting his countrymen in all parts of India.

"Singapore, March 13th, 14th, and 15th.—During these three days I have spit up much blood; it seems as if the former large quantities of mucus were turned into blood. But I have not felt much inconvenience yet from this. Since Sabbath last I have not been much out, nor done any thing within, except writing several letters, and miscellaneous reading. Learnt that a rude attack had been made upon my character, in a book called 'The Mahratta and Pindaree Campaign of 1817—1819.' This work is thought to have been written by an officer in the staff of Lieutenant-General, Sir Thomas Hislop, Bart., G. C. B., and who had formerly been at Malacca and Banca." (This attack, on which Dr. Milne makes no remark, like many others of a similar kind, proves that he who made it was himself in the wrong. The military writer professes to be a Christian; and the books he (or the friend who gave the information) complains of receiving in too great numbers, were for the diffusion of Christian knowledge. As a Christian and a gentleman, in the case he refers to, it was evidently easy for him to send to the Missionary a civil note, desiring that either a smaller number of the books, or none at all, might be sent to him. This proceeding would not have required any great effort of good nature and right feeling. However, instead of doing this, the circumstance is carefully noted down, and magnified, and compared to filling a ship with Bibles, and sinking it, in order to get rid of them; and eventually the fact, and the very judicious comment, are inserted in a page of a book on Sir Thomas Hislop's Indian Wars!)

"Another attack on Dr. Milne, as Editor of the 'Gleaner,' from a religionist, abusing him for a paper which he did not write, came to hand too late to gratify the spleen, and pride, and self-conceit of the writer. Dr. Milne's spirit had passed into the eternal world; and his body was laid in the grave." —*Canton Memoir.* Dr. Morrison adds, " Dr. Milne forgot the first attack whilst singing of mercy and judgment thus:—'Good news from my children— thanks to my God of all mercy. This day three years Rachel lay a dying by me at Clay-bang. Ah! what I have since passed through! But goodness and mercy have followed me. O that I had the assurance of God's being for me!' Then, 'who could be against me?'

"March 20th. This is the third anniversary of my dear Rachel's death—I have done but little in my work since last anniversary, and now it seems doubtful whether I be spared to labour more.—It seems my duty on this occasion, and daily, to pray, with submissive earnestness, that 'I may not be cut off in the midst of my days'—but that God may 'spare me a little, till I recover strength before I go hence and be no more.'—

"1. Until my own soul be better prepared for the heavenly world, and have more clear and satisfactory evidence of being in Christ.

"2. Until I complete, or put in a more favourable train, some Chinese works, either now in hand or, contemplated, for the benefit of the Church of Christ among the heathen.

"3. Until my children be made better acquainted with the Holy Scriptures, and disposed of for their education.

"Fully sensible that I deserve not so high a privilege as to be heard in these things, I have this day tried, with an humble and submissive heart, to solicit these blessings as free gifts from the Father of mercies and guide of all my ways.

"April 21st. Remained at home.—Saturday and to-day assisted Mr. Ince in revising a Scripture Catechism, which he is writing." (This is the *last* entry in his journal. On reading it, Dr. Morrison wrote thus: "Alas! my brother! Here Milne's account of his own feelings and occupations terminate. He never wrote again in his journal. Nature was fast decaying; he had yet, but a few days more to linger: and another hand must tell the brief tale. Apprehending, probably, his speedy dissolution, he was anxious to return to Malacca. The Penang Government very generously sent one of the government vessels on purpose to convey him thither. On his arrival at the Anglo-Chinese College, he was in a shockingly emaciated and weak state.") *Canton Mem.*

"Dr. Milne's death took place on the 2nd of June, 1822, at the hour of two in the morning. From the 24th of May, the day on which he returned from Penang, it was evident to all who saw him, that his useful and laborious life was drawing near a close. But the good man having begun several works which promised to be very useful both to the heathen and future Missionaries, was desirous, if it was the Lord's will, that he might be spared to finish them. But alas! for the cause, He who knows best, was pleased to call him away in the midst of his days; and we are bound to say, Good is the will of the Lord. From the nature of his disease, and the intense pain which he felt when he attempted to speak, those who were with him towards the close of his life, were deprived of enjoying the benefit of his pious reflections in the prospect of death, and of his views of the future prosperity of the great cause in which he had been engaged for several years. During his last illness he seldom spoke, but when it was necessary to settle his own affairs, or those of the institutions with which he was connected.

"The few words he uttered in reference to eternity were in unison with the principles which he held, and the doctrines which he preached when in health. He repeatedly said, that 'he had no hope of salvation but through the merits of Jesus; and that if sin was pardoned he was safe.'

"On the evening before his death he appeared more at ease than he had been for some days; but, alas! this appeared to have arisen from the exhaustion of nature; for at the hour already mentioned his happy spirit left this world of sin and sorrow, (and entered into the rest that remains for the servants of God) without a struggle or a groan. During the period that he was afflicted, he expressed a desire, that if his illness should end in death, his body should be opened, for the benefit of those who might be affected with similar disorders. Thus, the good man, in the prospect of dissolution, manifested a desire, that his body might be useful to his fellow-creatures after his decease. Accordingly, his body was opened; and it was evident, that his disorder had been pulmonary. The lungs, on the right side, adhered to the ribs; they had lost their natural colour, and were covered with small swellings, which, when opened, were seen to be full of matter. It may, perhaps, admit of a question, if his intense study, and much writing, did not help to accelerate his disorder, and hasten his death, as the lungs on the right side were in a much worse state than those on the left.

"On the 2nd of June, at four o'clock, P. M., his body was carried from the Anglo-Chinese College to the Dutch burying-ground, and laid in a vault which he had built for his wife and children. There the body of that faithful and diligent servant of God shall remain, until the great day arrives when God shall judge the world in righteousness; and it is sincerely to be hoped, that on that day, many of the poor heathens shall have to bless God that ever Dr. Milne was sent to these parts.

"The funeral was numerously attended. Messrs. Humphreys and Huttmann followed as chief mourners, A. Koek, Esq., Deputy Governor, in the absence of the Honourable Timmerman Thysseen, Governor; the resident of Rhio; the Members of the Court of

Justice; the Elders and Deacons of the Dutch Reformed Church, with most of the respectable inhabitants of Malacca followed the bier. There were also hundreds of natives, both Chinese and Malay, as spectators. The Chinese Séen-sangs, the Students in the College, with the Chinese Printers, and many of the youths from the schools, attended of their own accord; and thus showed their respect to the remains of him who had fallen a sacrifice in his exertions for their welfare." (This account of Dr. Milne's death and burial is, I believe, from the pen of Mr. Huttmann: but the following remarks are by Dr. Morrison:)

"The closing scene of this good man's life was peace; but not joy. Those who possess comparatively much knowledge, understand best how ignorant the wisest men are; and those who have thought most on the awful realities of eternity, are likely to meet death with the greatest awe. It is a serious thing to die. To stand before the judgment-seat of Christ, is an awful anticipation. And, as it is not every good ship that enters its final haven with a fair wind, and under full sail, so it is not given to every good man to have a joyful entrance into the spiritual world. In that haven there is indeed eternal rest; but storms and tempests below, and dark clouds sometimes gloom at the entrance.

"The stress that is occasionally laid on the circumstances of a person's death, does not seem warranted by Scripture; nor is the assumed doctrine verified by experience. Bodily disease, and constitutional temperament, operate very much on the mind of man. Of the good man, the last end shall, assuredly, be peace; but that peace may not be felt till he has passed the bourne, and left on this side, the pained and agonized, or the sluggish, comatose, earthly tabernacle. Hume, who essayed to subvert the cause of God and of Christ on the earth, died jesting: and Milne, who laboured to promote the cause of Christ and of God, died mourning. Shall the manner of a man's death then, be considered as a proof or disproof of the justice and goodness of his cause?" (Dr. Morrison's first reflections on the loss of his Colleague, deserve equally to be preserved.) "Yesterday, July 4th, nine years ago, Mr. and Mrs. Milne were received at Macao, by me and Mrs. Morrison. Three of the four—all under 40—have been called hence, and have left me alone and disconsolate! But good is the will of the Lord. They all died in the faith and hope of the Gospel; all died at their post. They have left their bodies in the field of battle. They were faithful unto death in their Saviour's cause. Happy am I that none of them deserted it! Even my poor afflicted Mary returned to die in China!"—*Original Letter.*

CHAPTER XVI.

THE MISSION FAMILY.

It has been already seen, that the Milnes and Morrisons lived, "as being heirs together of the grace of life." How much they loved each other appears also, in no faint light, in Dr. Morrison's Memoirs by his widow; a work rich in documents, which throw open the *heart* of the senior Missionary in all its love for his colleague. It is, therefore, both my duty and privilege to show how that love was reciprocated. "Dear Robert," and "Dear William," as they address each other, were emphatically brethren; and "Dear Mary," and "Dear Rachel," as emphatically sisters. All their mutual intercourse and correspondence justified, as well as illustrated these fond familiarities. This is peculiarly honourable to Dr. Morrison: for although he needed a *friend* in his Mission, who does not feel that he could have done without a *helper* in the translation of the Scriptures? He could have stood *alone* in that work, and he knew this too; and yet he not only allowed, but encouraged Dr. Milne to share the labour and the reward with him. Very few men would have displayed such magnanimity or disinterestedness. Dr. Milne was, indeed, worthy to share the honour. He would not have been employed in the work if he had not; nor would he have undertaken it, had he felt incompetent for it. But still, I doubt much if any other man, with Dr. Morrison's scholarship, would have accepted, much less sought for, a *partner*, in such an immortalizing work. In saying this, I am expressing Dr. Milne's opinions as much as my own. Robert and William were too "dear" to each other, and the cause of God to both, to have any rivalry or jealousies between them. And this is the more creditable to the piety of both, because the spirit of neither was unambitious, nor very accommodating. Each of them had to suppress a temperament, not easily kept under.

How they lived and loved will appear from the

following letters, which Dr. Morrison himself selected as specimens of Dr. Milne's correspondence with his own and the Mission family:—

"My own Dear Love,

"I wrote to you yesterday—I am quite well to-day; but as busy as a bonnet-maker, finishing Mr. Morrison's Grammar; I am in hopes of finishing it to-morrow, perhaps to-night, then I should like to complete the translation of his Catechism, and my journals and letters; after that I shall be at liberty to come down, and go to Java as soon as an opportunity offers.
" *To Mrs. Milne.*"

"*Malacca, 1st April,* 1819.

"My Dear Robert,
"Your various, long, and excellent letters by Captain Hummet, and Captain Snoball, came duly to hand. The Bengal Merchant is not yet come. But alas! how shall I commence the painful subject of this letter. If you saw me all in black, a dress which you know I abhor, you would conjecture that the hand of the Lord had removed some dear friend: yes, Robert—Rachel is gone! and what shall I say? The hand of the Lord has done it—I would bow with reverential submission. My loss and the dear children's is irreparable; to her, I trust, the change is gain. Rachel, my best earthly friend, is gone! Yes, I tenderly loved her, and well I might! But I will stop. Her demise took place on the 20th instant, at the country-house of Adrian Koek, Esq.,

about four miles from Malacca, whither we had removed three days before, for the benefit of the country air. Her death happened on the forty-second day after her confinement. She seemed to recover very well for the first ten days—but afterwards caught cold, which was followed by an inveterate dysentery, vomiting, and an affection of the lungs. The Dutch medical man denied any affection of the lungs, but I am quite convinced that in this he was entirely mistaken. Mrs. Milne, ever since her former illness, (in which you were her nurse; yes, she often spoke with almost tears of gratitude, of dear Robert's kindness) looked upon herself as not long for the present world. She had been making actual preparation, and though she said little towards the last, she in general expressed her entire confidence in the Lord Jesus. She dozed for the chief part of the last two days, and did not feel, she said, much pain, though her cough and the phlegm, and the matter from the lungs, were exceedingly troublesome. She often called me to read hymns, and pray with her. About nine, A. M. she expired, and her countenance, which had been affected by the few last pains, resumed its wonted aspect, as at times when she used to contemplate any subject with pleasure. You know I argue nothing from this in favour of her eternal state, but merely mention it as a subject on which the thoughts of a fond and bereaved husband dwell with a melancholy pleasure. I know you valued and loved Rachel—therefore I do not write as one fearful that what is said may be abused. I think I shall take some notice of her death in the 'Gleaner.' Though it is very delicate for me to say any thing, yet I think, by a general and short sketch, accompanied with occasional remarks, some good might be done in a certain circle of readers—and who knows but the attention of some of those ladies, to whose kindness our family is so much obliged, might be awakened to more serious reflection?

"The children, William and Robert, have now the measles—but are getting over them. I deeply feel for Mary's continued affliction, let us abound more in mutual prayer for each other.

"I assure you the many kind and encouraging paragraphs in your last two letters could not come more seasonably, had you known exactly the state of my family and mind.

"Ever yours,
"W. M."

"To Dr. Morrison.

"Dear Robert,

"Pull together."—yes, with all our hearts, and hands, and strength. Let us be decided on that. Let us not be over sanguine—let us not give up plans that have been long matured, to please any individual—let us concentrate our exertions—let our plans be proved on the broad scale. The Lord make us humble, and enable us to display due respect to our fellow servants. It is now midnight, I cannot sleep now a days often till two o'clock in the morning.

"Ever yours,
"W. M."

"R. Morrison, D. D."

"*Malacca, 25th June,* 1819

"Dear Robert,

"I feel myself exceedingly solitary at times. I work off the feeling by labour. O that I could live more in the enjoyment of divine consolations. Last night I was at Rachel's grave, over which the grass begins to grow.—I will send you a lock of her hair, and some token of remembrance both for yourself and Mary.—Grace and peace be ever with you.

"Yours, faithfully,
"W. M."

"*R. Morrison, D. D.*"

"*Malacca, 19th September,* 1819

"Dear Robert,

"I am at a great loss how to do about my dear Amelia—I doubt not but she will be sent for next year either to Bengal, London, or Aberdeen. She is so affectionate a child that I hardly think I should be able to part with her:—she often says, looking at my head, 'Papa is now old—I must stop and take care of Papa. I Papa—now, I no Mamma—I love Papa—William and Robert and Farquhar too, Mamma—stop, I grow large, and I then their Mamma.' You will excuse a fond Father, Robert, for thus relating sayings of a beloved child.

"Ever yours,
"W. M."

"*R. Morrison, D. D.*"

"*Malacca, 16th September,* 1820.

"Dear Robert,

"I disdain the idea of any man on this side of India being more attached to the Missionary Society's objects than I am. I know there is none more so—nor is there one who has attempted to do more (according to his strength and talents and opportunities) than I have done—and I am sure you can say the same. I do not, therefore, allow any one to say that we are not the Society's *servants*, without opposing it.

"How could you possibly think that 'I consider the College as a concern of yours, or that you have other feelings than those in union with the spread of the Gospel, by supporting it?'—No, Robert, it is not so; I do not think so; I never, for a moment, thought so. On the contrary, I daily admire your disinterestedness in all you do for the College; and your devotedness to the Gospel. Do not let any hasty note of mine disconcert you, Robert!—I consider the College as I do my own family concerns.—I feel myself bound by almost equal ties to seek its good.—It is my resolution to do so to the utmost, and to the last. Farther, I venture to say, I am not discouraged by all these reverses. The Lord be with us and bless us for ever.

"Ever yours,
"W. M."

"*Robert Morrison, D. D.*"

"*Malacca, 9th October,* 1820.

"Dear Mary,

"I was surprised and delighted the other day to hear from Mrs. Macalister, that you had gone to

China with the children. I was not at all prepared to hear of this, as Robert's letters intimated no expectation of your being out so soon. It is matter of gratitude to God that you have been so far restored as to venture on a voyage. Robert has been lamenting for you these five or six years. The Lord grant you his presence and blessing; and, if his will, many happy and useful days together. But why did you bring out the dear children so soon? Will they not lose by it?

"Ah! dear Mary! how are my family circumstances altered since I last saw you! The dear friend whom you loved, and who loved you, and often spoke of you, has been in the world of spirits for more than eight months;—of this you have, of course, long since heard. The will of our Father in heaven be done. May we ever be prepared so to say, and to feel as we say.

"You have not seen my dear William, Robert, and Farquhar. W., and R., and Amelia, are at school, with Mrs. Thompson, a very worthy good lady. Amelia can read tolerably well in any common book, and my dear William read, for the first time, at family prayer, yesterday, the first twelve verses of Matt. v., and my dear Robert, to-day, a part of the same chapter. They all three repeated, yesterday, the 5th question of my Chinese Catechism. These little things, I know, will be pleasing to you, who are a parent.—They almost daily speak of *uncle* Robert. Farquhar is a fine child, and just beginning to speak. They all live with me, and under my care; and all, even Farquhar, eat with me. I have two old Malay women, and a nurse for Farquhar.

"Write me soon—inform me what size your dear

children, Rebecca and John, are, and what progress they have made in knowledge. Whether healthy and strong. Kiss them for me. Amelià remembers you and Rebecca, she says, but that can only be from hearing me and her dear mother speak of you. I intend to send you some sweet-meats and a little sago, by this conveyance, if possible. Robert would not allow me to send him any thing,—but ladies and children need such things. How did you leave your aged father? I have my health tolerably well at present. I am writing largely to Robert. I trust God will deeply impress your heart with a sense of your obligation to be useful, now that he has restored you to a measure of health.

"Ever yours,
"W. Milne.
"To Mrs. Morrison."

The following letter to one of his sons, is very characteristic of both the father and the man. It is as full of tenderness as of order.

"Singapore, 10th March, 1822.

"My Dear Robert,

"How do you do? I hope you are a good boy; kind to Farquhar; learn your lessons well; and do what you are told. There are some bad boys in the world who run, and jump, and tumble till they tear all their clothes; wear out their shoes, and hurt themselves: then they become sick—the doctor must be called; and after all, perhaps they die. Some run about the mouths of wells till they fall in, and are drowned. Some run and play in the sun till their heads are pained, and they take fever and die; and some run up stairs and down stairs, till they fall and break their heads and legs. Don't you think, Robert, that these boys are very bad? O yes, indeed, they are; and you must remember never to do any thing so bad.

"How is the state of your bowels, my dear? Can you *go out* every day? If not, you must tell Mr. Humphreys. Now I'll tell you what a good boy loves to do:—1. He loves to pray to God. 2. He loves to learn to read God's Holy Word. 3. He loves to keep the Sabbath. 4. He loves to give his pice to the poor. 5. He loves to write, and learn all other good things. 6. He loves to keep his hands, and face, and clothes all clean. 7. He loves to obey his parents. 8. He loves to think, and read, and hear of other good children; what they did; who they were; and how they lived and died. There was a little boy named *Robert Good;* he was always sorry: 1. When he saw children who did not obey their parents. 2. When he saw brothers or sisters fighting and beating each other. 3. When he saw boys running after an old man, or a fool. 4. When he saw children growing large, who yet could not write, nor read, nor pray. Then he was very sorry. Don't you think he was a very good Robert? You must try to be like him.

"Now, my Robert, God bless you for ever. Amen.

"Your dear Father,

"W. Milne."

It was of this boy Dr. Morrison said, "I wish to adopt little Robert Milne as my son, and to support him with my own Robert. This *must* be arranged with the executors."—*Life*, Vol. 2, p. 164.

"*Malacca, 18th August,* 1821.

"Dear Robert,

"Since my last to you by the Royal George, Mr. Ward, Purser, I have been for ten days in the country, *labouring to be idle and to eat the wind!*—or, plainly, for my health. I had a considerable spitting of blood one day, which has not yet entirely ceased. It is probably from a small ulcer in the throat, as I have been troubled with a slight soreness in my throat for several weeks:—I hope it is not from the lungs: a slight cough brings it up, but I am not greatly incommoded with it; still, however, I feel as if I must relax a little; I wish the printing of the Scriptures was finished: I am revising my translations daily to get them in readiness.

"Tell Mrs. Morrison I have some curious *mats* for her."

Such ought to be, because such might be, the spirit of all Mission families. It is not, therefore, in compliment to the *first* Mission families in China, much less to swell out this volume, that these letters are introduced, but to furnish both a specimen and a proof of the possibility, beauty, and advantage of living as heirs together of the grace of eternal life, in all Missionary neighbourhoods. The Morrisons and Milnes did so: and again, I say, at all hazards of misconstruction, that they had to " rule their spirit," in order to realize the full sweets of friendship, and all the benefits of union. There is no *insinuation* in this remark. I intend it as one of the highest compliments which could be paid to their prudence, zeal, or piety; and should it be taken otherwise, my opinion of either its truth or tenderness will not be altered. I know what I say, and whereof I affirm; and do not choose to *veer* round to unqualified compliment, now that it is fashionable to forget old opinions on this subject.

CHAPTER XVII.

JEWISH WITNESSES IN CHINA.

Dr. Milne's attention was drawn to this subject, on the return of Dr. Morrison from Pekin, by the following note in his friend's journal. "Had a conversation with a Mahommedan gentleman, who informed me that at Kae-Fung Foo, in ' The province of Honan, there are a few families denominated, the sect that plucks out the sinew' from all the meat they eat. They have a house of worship, and observe the eighth day as a Sabbath?" On reading this, Dr. Milne's curiosity was awakened. He published, at Canton, the following inquiry. "What is their formulary of worship? What their numbers? If Jews, when did they enter China? The fact of their existence in the very *heart* of the Chinese empire is a very interesting one, and highly deserving of farther investigation."

This appeal does not seem to have drawn forth any information, and the College library was too scanty to furnish the means of judging. I have, therefore, attempted to answer the questions, which so much interested my friend; because the facts of the case give new interest to China, and may lay hold upon the heart of some future Missionary. Besides, our sacred associations with China are so few, weak, and vague, that we all need new links between it and our sympathies. I make no apology, therefore, for the prominence given to the Jews in this chapter, nor for the spirit in which it is written; but tell the story just as I found it, and as it affected me whilst searching it out.

Indeed, I should do violence to my own sympathies with the "seed of Abraham," as well as violate the principle on which Paul formed his "Great Cloud of Witnesses," were I not to include, in this work, some notices of the Jews in Asia, and especially of those in China, as witnesses for God against idolatry amidst the Heathen, and as vouchers for the truth of both Old and New Testament prophecy to all Christians. It is the more necessary to do this now, and in a work on Missions, because public sympathy with the Jews has not had much of either the spirit or the form of evangelical solicitude for their conversion at home or abroad, of late years. The Scotch Kirk is just beginning to wipe off this reproach from herself, and at a critical moment also. Her agents are examining Palestine with *Presbyterian* eyes, just after certain *Episcopalian* eyes had discovered that little more than Liturgical worship is wanted on Mount Zion, in order to charm the Jews into the Church. On this point the doctors are sure to differ; but their difference will do good, were it only to bring back the grand question of *duty* from the dreamy regions of poetry, into the fields of Scripture and experience.

Amongst the Dissenters and Methodists, the seed of Abraham are almost forgotten, except in prayer. There were good reasons, perhaps, for giving up the Jews' Society to the management of Churchmen; but the Jewish *cause* ought not to be given up even to angels, by any Church that would be faithful to her charter, or conformed to the image of her Head. If we were hardly right when we did *something* to "gain the Jews," we are fearfully wrong now that we do nothing! Robert Hall felt this dilemma so painfully, that he plunged into a speculation about the possibility of their salvation, apart from the belief of the Gospel. A paper of his on this subject was published in the "Baptist Magazine," some years before he died; and its extravagance excited suspicions, not of his orthodoxy, but of his mental composure at the time.

There was no mystery in it to those who, like myself, had uneasy consciences on the subject. His conscience was not at ease whilst he was doing nothing to gain the Jews; and as he saw no way of doing any thing at the time, he tried to relieve himself from self-condemnation, by applying to their case the words of Paul,—without the *work* of Paul,— "As concerning the Gospel, they are enemies for your sakes: but as touching the Election, they are beloved for the Father's sake."—Rom. ii. 28. This is, I believe, the real secret of that strange speculation, although his biographers overlooked both.

These hints will remind many of the friends of

Missions to the Gentiles of their emotions, when they first read Dr. Claudius Buchanan's "Christian Researches in India, respecting the Jews." Little did he or his readers think, a quarter of a century ago, that either the *white* or the *black* Jews in India, would be almost forgotten by Missionary Societies. Their numbers, the antiquity of their emigration from Palestine, their communicativeness, and the prevalence of Hebrew books in their houses, and of copies of the law in their synagogues, formed a talisman which seemed then to open all hearts: and now we hardly hear them mentioned in either reports or appeals!

This reference to Dr. Buchanan will render it unnecessary for me to describe the present state of the Jews in India. My object in this chapter is to glance at the time and extent of the DISPERSION in Asia, in order to account for the popular tradition of apostolic and primitive Missions in remote nations of Asia. Now "the white Jews in Malabar date their emigration to India from the destruction of the second Temple."—*Buchanan*, p. 305. The black Jews, however, preceded them. Their colour proves this. "It is only necessary to look at their countenance to be satisfied that their ancestors must have arrived in India many ages before the white Jews." —*Ibid.* p. 310. In 490, they had both patriarchal jurisdiction and certain titles of nobility, in Cranganor. This, Buchanan says, is confirmed by "the native annals of Malabar, and by Mahomedan history." Their charter of these privileges, signed by seven Indian kings, claims date in 490. A copy of it, from the original brass-plate, is in the public library at the university of Cambridge. It is thus evident that there were Jews enough in Malabar, in the first century, to account for even an apostolic Mission; and in the second, to account for the copy of St. Matthew's Gospel, in Hebrew, which Pantœnus saw there: for, besides these two bodies, there were also many fragments of the Ten Tribes in the country.

Dr. Buchanan received from the black Jews a list of *sixty-five* places in northern India, Tartary, and China, in which small colonies of Jews reside. These he did not visit; but many of these colonies were visited and described by travellers at a very early period; and they all gave a similar account of themselves. This, it will now be my object to prove and illustrate, that we may see how God placed Jewish witnesses against idolatry all over Asia, and thus gave the first heralds of the cross a two-fold reason for going far into that quarter of the world, agreeably to the Saviour's last charge to his disciples, " Ye shall be witnesses unto me, unto the *uttermost* parts of the earth."—Acts i. 8.

The Jews in China give a similar account of themselves as those in India, although neither Medhurst nor Gutzlaff go into particulars on the subject. The latter refers only to the *sources* of his information; Benjamin of Tudela and Gozani; and their " Itinerancies " are not very accessible to general readers. Gozani's account of the *Teaou-kin-keaow*, in the capital of Honan, or of " the sect that pluck out the *sinew* from all their meat," is so interesting and graphic, that it deserves to be preserved entire. I can only give the substance of it, however. He visited their *Li-pai-see*, (La-paesze,) or synagogue, at Kaefung-fu, in 1704, and had a long conference with them. Unfortunately, however, he could neither speak nor read Hebrew, and they could only communicate with him in Chinese. "They showed me," he says, " their KIMS, or sacred books; and permitted me to go into the most SECRET place, which they themselves are not allowed to enter; it being reserved solely for their *Cham-Kiao*, (or Chung-Keaou) or Ruler, who never enters but with the most profound reverence. On some tables there were thirteen kinds of tabernacles, with a vale before each of them; and within each of them, a copy of the *Kim-Mousa*, or Pentateuch. Twelve of the tabernacles represented the twelve tribes; and the thirteenth, Moses. The Kims were written on long pieces of parchment, and rolled around sticks. I prevailed with the Ruler to let the curtain of one of the tabernacles be withdrawn and one of the books unrolled. It seemed to be well written. There are also, in two other places of the synagogue, several old chests, containing *Takim*, or small tracts of parts of the law, which they use as prayer-books; and all are preserved with greater care than silver or gold." In the middle of the synagogue there is a magnificent pulpit, with a richly embroidered cushion. It stands very high. On Saturday, and the most solemn days, they read the Pentateuch, from this "chair of Moses;" and worship towards the west;— Jerusalem being west from China. There are no statues or images in the place but the *Van-sui-pai*, or picture, on which the Emperor's name is written. In the great hall of the synagogue, there are a number of *incense* vases or censers; the largest of which is for the Patriarch Abraham, and stands in the centre. Next to it are the censers of Isaac and Jacob, and the *Chel-cum-pai-se,* or Twelve Tribes. Then those of Moses, Aaron, Joshua, Edias, and several other illustrious persons, both male and female.

'In this hall, the Jews of Honan, honour both their ancestors and their *Chim-gins,* or the great men of the law, just, they say, as the Chinese honour Confucius and their ancestors. They told Gozani that they paid the same honour to Confucius also, that the Literati of China did. This is a remarkable fact; and it goes far to prove that the honour paid to the dead in China is not worship; for if it were, the Jews would hardly join in it. The Jesuits took this ground, when put upon their defence for allowing their Chinese converts to honour the dead agreeably to the laws of the empire. They used, indeed, a stronger argument in appealing to the Pope,—that his dominion would be lost there, if their liberty were denied. In 1707, however, even the Pope forbade the practice; and he is less squeamish about idolatry than the Rabbins. Thus we have two facts which balance each other. It is, therefore, evidently the duty of our Missionaries to lean to the *safe* side, until they are quite sure that no worship is intended by the incense burnt to the dead. Gutzlaff says, " The question whether the funeral rites are idolatrous or not is easily answered. The same honours and adoration are paid to the idols." Vol. i. p. 504. On the other hand, however, the Emperor, Kang-he, in 1700, solemnly assured the Pope that the custom was merely political; and the Jews said the same. Still, Clement XI. believed neither testimony, but forbade the ceremony, even at the expense of a quarrel with the Emperor, and of a libel on Infallibility; for Alexander VII. had sanctioned the custom. I will only add, that Medhurst takes the same view of the funeral rites as Gutzlaff.—*China*, p. 237.

Gozani had his own Bible with him when he visited the synagogue (or rather the temple) of the Jews in Honan; and as it had the names of the books of the Old Testament at the end of it in Hebrew, he showed the list to the Ruler, who pronounced them at once to be the names of the Chin-Kin, or the books of the Pentateuch. This led to a comparison of sacred chronology, genealogy, and names; and Gozani found that his version and the Ruler's had "a perfect conformity." He learned, also, that the usual feasts of the law were regularly celebrated, although without sacrifice or altar. These Jews said, that their ancestors came into China during the *Han* dynasty. Now this date embraces 206 years before the Christian era, and 220 years after it. Either period, however, gives the emigration great antiquity, and connects it with memorable events in the annals of China. Printing was discovered, according to du Halde, under *Vou-ti*, the fifth Emperor of the Han dynasty, just fifty years before the birth of Christ. This Emperor carried his conquests also as far as Bengal, and into the Mogul's country; and although the Chinese annals do not mention Jewish captives—because they seldom mention foreigners at all then—these Jews were most likely brought from the Mogul's empire, where, as we shall see, large bodies of the Ten Tribes were settled then.

By the way, this absence of all reference to the first appearance of Jews in China, furnishes a complete answer to the popular objection made to the

Nestorian reports of early Christian Missions in China. "There is no account of Christianity," it is said, "in the early annals of the empire." Neither is there of Judaism. Thus the cases are parallel. It is also a curious fact, that the two religions most opposed to idolatry are the only two whose first entrance into China is passed over in silence. Had Dr. Milne noticed this coincidence, he would not have wondered that neither *Choo-foo-tzse,* nor *Tzang-Tzse,* mentions the Nestorians. But this subject will occur again, when we come to analyze the Delai Lama of Thibet.

The first Jews in China, under the *Han* dynasty, may have been part of the grand dispersion, when Shalmaneser led the Ten Tribes into captivity, and thus they date far beyond the Christian era. Or, they may have been of the dispersion in A. D. 61, when the temple was destroyed; and thus contemporary with the white Jews in India. The earliest account we possess of them, is by two Mahomedan travellers who visited China in the ninth century. Renaudot translated this work into French, and accompanied it with his "Enquiry concerning the Jews in China." There is, I believe, an English version of the work, but I have never seen it. Indeed, the French one is scarce now. The two Arabians say, that in 877, during a revolution at *Can-fu,* 120,000 Mahomedans, Christians, *Jews,* and Parses, were put to the sword. They add, that the exact number of each sect was recorded, after the massacre. They also contrast with this, the liberty and prosperity of the Jews in Ceylon. Thus there were annals of Christianity in the 9th century in China.

Renaudot speaks very highly of these Arabian travellers; and confirms, from his own inquiries, the fact that both in his time, and anciently, there were "many Jews in several of the provinces of China." I will only add, that there is a truth-like simplicity about the statements of *Wahab* and *Abuzaid*, which speaks for itself and them too.

The accounts of *Peristol*, an Italian Jew, agree in the main with this view of the numbers of his countrymen in China; and as these round numbers sustain the assertion of *Josephus*, that "multitudes of the Jews did not avail themselves of the decree of Cyrus to return to their own land," even *Basnage* admits it to be "very plausible," that many remained.

Rabbi Benjamin, of Tudela, if the best known, is the least trust-worthy writer on this subject, although Professor Zacouth, the historiographer of the King of Portugal, calls him "the mighty luminary of Israel." Benjamin would have been a dangerous reckoner, when David "numbered the people." He saw *double*, or but *half*, the probable numbers, just as local policy required. He finds 50,000 Jews in Samarcand, and only a few hundreds in Rome. He places 350,000 "independent Israelites" in Themoi and Chebar alone, and only 392,215 Jews in all the other parts of the world. This was in the 12th century.

The fact is, he reckons some of the sections twice over, as in the case of the Jews in Poumbeditha; and his object evidently was to *blind* the Spanish Jews to Christianity, by emblazoning the state of the foreign Jews. Still, there are *facts*, in his itinerary, although Talmudized. It is impossible to believe with *Gerrens,* that the Jew of Navarre never travelled. His routes are indeed a "burlesque upon geography" occasionally; but even then, they prove that he was no *compiler* of travels. A *designing* man would not have fallen into Benjamin's blunders; for he buries Rabbi Akaiba, the martyr for Bar Coziba, first at Rome, and then at Leucha in Babylonia! His mistakes in history and philosophy are evidently from sheer ignorance; and his Chinese Griffins, which could fly away with an ox, are mere Talmudic extravagancies. I mention these characteristics of his work, because it is often referred to as an authority. It is not "a catalogue of lies," as Gerrens calls it; but, like other old chronicles, it abounds with fables; and ought not be quoted as Brerewood employed it.

Rabbi Mannasseh, a higher authority, states explicitly, that the Dispersion climbed the great wall of China; and he applies to them Isaiah's prophecy concerning "those in the hand of Sinan."

The only countryman of our own, who has examined this subject with much care is *Brerewood,* in his "Inquiries touching the religions of the World;" but the worthy *Greshamite* (he was professor of Astronomy in Gresham College, 1670) tired of tracing the wandering stars of Jacob, closed his "tedious discourse," as he calls it, by a dissertation on the dimensions of the Whale and Elephant of the Talmudists!—*Brerewood,* p. 132.

"It will both illustrate and confirm these desultory notices of the Jews in China, to mention the fact, that all the Jesuits were not so successful as Gozani with the Jews in Honan. Nearly a century before his visit, they had been visited by Father Aleni; but although he was called by the Chinese,

"the Confucius of Europe," he was not allowed to
draw a curtain, nor open a book, in the synagogue.
They told him of a bible at Pekin, in the Emperor's
library; but he could never find it. He suspected,
however, that the keeper of the Pagoda, where the
books of foreigners lay, eluded his inquiries. But
however this may be, the fact is, that the ruler of
the Synagogue, at that time, suspected the Jesuits.
His predecessor had offered Ricci the care of the
Synagogue, if he would eat nothing "unclean."
This is a remarkable fact. Ricci's letters to him
about the Scriptures, so surprised the old man, that
he was willing to resign all to the Jesuit. Ricci,
however, could not leave Pekin; and before Aleni
went to Honan, the old man was dead. I know of
no reason for discrediting these accounts. Locker
has endeavoured to represent Gozani and Ricci as
echoing each other. But the *dates* refute him. See
Vol. 18th *Lett. Edif.* and Locker's "Travels of the
Jesuits." Vol. 2.

CHAPTER XVIII.

APOSTOLIC MISSIONS IN ASIA.

Vast as the Roman empire was when the Apostles of the Lamb received their commission to evangelize the world, it was not "the world" to them.
They knew less of the nations which formed the
western empire than of the Asiatic nations which
were beyond the limits of the eastern empire. Those

of them who wrote to, and for, the churches in the empire, would, of course, call it "the world," agreeably to the *popular* use of the word: but all of them, as Jews, would naturally *think* of the Asiatic nations chiefly, when they thought of their own commission to "all nations." Their "kinsmen according to the flesh," were chiefly in Asia. Both the captivities and the emigrations from Palestine travelled eastward: and, in that direction, the curiosity and the tastes of the Hebrews leaned. Their *magnetic* pole was in Asia. So much was this the fact, that even Paul, although emphatically the Apostle of the Gentiles, had to be *kept out* of Asia, by a special prohibition from "the Spirit." Both Paul and Silas were evidently *set* upon going "far hence," amongst the Asiatic nations; and reluctant, at first, to come into Europe. The reason is obvious. Paul, although a Roman citizen, had no Roman partialities or tastes. He would, as a "Hebrew of the Hebrews," have felt most at home, and felt most for, "the lost sheep of the house of Israel," then scattered throughout Asia, as well as in Bithynia and Mysia. Besides, he knew that "a remnant according to the election of grace," was to be gathered out of all the Twelve Tribes at large, notwithstanding they were so widely scattered; and therefore, he *leaned* to Asia, because there he could preach equally to Jews and Gentiles at the same time.

Paul was not "suffered" to go thus into Asia. He has told us, however, that *others* did go. "Yes, verily, their sound went unto *all* the earth, and their words unto the *ends* of the world."—*Romans* x. 18. Commentators have no authority for confining "the feet of them who thus preached the Gospel of peace to Israel" then, to either Palestine or the Roman empire. Their feet were, of course, "beautiful upon the mountains" of Asia Minor and Proconsular, and both longest and oftenest there; but it is altogether improbable, to say the least, that the feet of *none* of the apostles or Evangelists ever stood upon the mountains of Central Asia. It is, indeed, tradition chiefly, which assigns Thomas, and Philip, and Andrew, to the *far* East; and tradition, like our weather almanacs, tells more *lies* than truths, in general. In this case, however, neither history nor Scripture *contradicts* tradition. How far they *confirm* it, I purpose to examine.

Now it ought to startle us, not a little, that we know nothing concerning the labours of some of the Apostles, if we reject the reports which prevail concerning their missions to Asia. But even this is not the most startling fact; God himself, according to *popular* opinion, kept the Gospel out of Asia, by a special interdict, even when Paul was bent on going there. This is not *like* God!—unless we suppose that Paul was not *wanted* there: and surely this supposition is both more rational and pious than to suspect God of partiality. "All souls are mine, saith the Lord;" and as there were incalculably more souls in Asia than in Europe, it is utterly incredible that Asia had no evangelists sent, or "suffered to go," into it. All that we know of the Divine character or administration, warrants, yea, binds us, to take for granted, that Paul was not *needed* there, when he was hindered from going into Asia; or that Asia had already its fair proportion of the Apostolic staff. This view of the matter is *like* both God and his ambassadors; whereas, the popular view of it impugns the equity of God, and leaves some of the Apostles under a cloud, as well as unaccounted for.

We could not, indeed, *blame* them for not going "into all the world," without passing a heavier condemnation upon ourselves for not doing so: but still, it would be strange, to say the least of it, if inspired men, newly commissioned, and noble-minded, had altogether overlooked Asia. This would be unlike themselves, or an anomaly in that character, which the baptismal fires of Pentecost purified and enshrined. We cannot, indeed, tell ourselves exactly, how they were to reach India, Parthia, or Tartary, at the time they are said to have gone there: but we somehow feel, that a few of them ought to have made the attempt; especially as they had the gift of tongues. We are unwilling, in fact, to believe that none of the Apostles set an example of a Missionary spirit, in harmony with the letter of their instructions.

'There is, I confess, only too much truth in the remark of the late Dr. Burton, of Oxford, that, on the general question, the only "alternative offered to us is, of either knowing *nothing*, or not knowing *what* to believe."—*Eccl. Hist. Lect.* xi. p. 352.

This is a painful dilemma! Not so painful, however, as that which we have just glanced at. For, as we do not meet with Thomas or Bartholomew upon Paul's "line of things," there is some reason for listening to tradition. It may say too much of their "line of things:" but as they had one of their own, and as it never crosses, nor is crossed by, the *Pauline* routes; and, as no church in the time of either Origen or Eusebeus had any temptation to assign Thomas or Philip to Asia, it is thus more than probable that they went into some parts of it. But even this is not the *strongest* probability. Neither the Greek nor the Roman Church appropriated these two Apostles as tutelar saints, in the way that most of the other Apostles are claimed. Both Churches place them in the Calendar; but not for "services rendered" within their *own* pales.

Is there, however, any Scriptural evidence, that any of the Apostles went farther into Asia than St. John did? Now we know that Paul and Silas wished to go into Asia, after they had gone throughout Phrygia and the region of Galatia, in Asia Minor,—"and were forbidden of the Holy Ghost to preach the word in Asia."—*Acts*, xvi. 6. They then "assayed to go into Bithynia, but the Spirit suffered them not."—v. 7. These are remarkable facts! Why this two-fold arrest? It brought, indeed, Paul into Europe; and thus we may well be thankful for it. He was just the man to gauge and to grapple with the European mind of his times. This was a valid reason for keeping *him* out of Asia. It does not follow, however, that he was given to Europe— at the expense of Asia. The probability is, that Asia could spare him, or dispense with his services; from having the services of some of the other Apostles at the time. This is a more natural supposition than to assume that God, in mysterious *Sovereignty*, kept the Gospel out of Asia. It is, also, a more *pious* mode of solving the difficulty. Besides, it is the fact, that in no other way, can we account for one *half* of the Apostolic staff at the time. For if they were not in Asia, where were they? They were not dead. We cannot trace them in the spheres of Paul, Peter, or John. We cannot believe that they were idle, or less faithful to their commissions, than their brethren. We cannot suspect Luke of either partiality or prejudice, in writing the Acts of the Apostles.

Thus nothing is so probable as that most of the apostles, whom we cannot trace in the wide circle of what we call apostolic churches, were in spheres beyond that circle, and especially in the Asiatic spheres, throughout which portions the ten tribes were scattered, and other Jews located. Now it was the *duty* of all the apostles to *begin* with " the lost sheep of the house of Israel," wherever they went preaching the Gospel. Accordingly, they not only began at Jerusalem with the "men of *Judea*," but also with the "men of *Israel*," who were from "*every* nation under heaven;" saying to both alike, " unto you first, God having raised up his Son Jesus, sent Him to bless you." (*Acts* ii. 5, 14, 22.) It is also the fact, that the Epistle of James is addressed to "The *twelve* tribes scattered abroad." Peter's First Epistle also is addressed to the scattered strangers in "*Asia*," as well as to those in proconsular and lesser Asia. Now if epistles could be *sent* to the remnants and sojourners of the twelve tribes in greater Asia, apostles could *go* to them. The fact that epistles were sent, involves the fact that teachers had gone before them, as well as the converts of Pentecost, who returned from Jerusalem into Asia: for, I repeat it, some of the apostles even, cannot be found at all, in the Roman empire.

All with whom great *principles* are of more weight than precise dates and names, will feel now, that no failure in specifying persons, places, or conveyances, can invalidate the Scriptural fact, that Christianity was known to portions of the ten tribes in greater

Asia, as well as to the Jews in lesser Asia, in the time of James and Peter. Geographical criticism upon the words, Asia, India, Parthia, &c., must pass for mere quibbles or impertinences, with every man who believes that *all* the apostles were faithful to their commission; or, that God did not evangelize the Roman empire at the *expense* of all the rest of the world. It is unworthy of Dr. Adam Clarke, to say, that the Asia Paul was kept from, must be the Proconsular, because it was not Asia Minor; or to explain the restraint laid on Paul, by saying that the place was not "sufficiently prepared to receive and profit by" the Gospel. India was as much civilized then as Cappadocia or Bithynia. "Even before the age of Pythagoras, the Greeks travelled to India for instruction; and the trade carried on by the Indians with the *oldest* commercial nations, in exchange for their cloth, is a proof of their great progress in the arts of industry. We may also trace the origin of most of the sciences in the history of that country." (*Raynal's Indies*, Vol. i. p. 44.) Rollin's account of the commerce of India, from the time of Solomon, is too familiar to be quoted here. Besides, Dr. Clarke had before stated, on Matt. xxiv. 13, that the Gospel had been preached previously to the destruction of Jerusalem, "as far east as Parthia and India, as well as in lesser Asia."

But Dr. Clarke is not the only commentator who forgot himself on this point. Dr. Doddridge, quoting from Dr. Arthur Young, with approbation, says, that Jude preached in Persia; Philip and Andrew in Scythia; Bartholomew in the northern and western parts of Asia, and Thomas in several eastern parts; "in most of which places Christian Churches were planted in less than thirty years after the death of Christ." After this statement, we expect him to say, that Paul was not wanted in Asia: but Dr. Doddridge was as inconsiderate as Dr. Clarke, and said, "that the reason for hindering Paul was, perhaps, that the people of those places were remarkably *conceited in their own wisdom.*" Had this been the reason for not suffering Paul to go into Asia, it must have kept him out of Athens and Rome also. Neither the Indians nor the Persians, nor even the Chinese then, were so conceited in their own wisdom, as the Greeks and Romans. Thus, the popular reasons for supposing that none of the apostles went into Asia greater, and that others of them were kept out of it, will not bear critical, philosophical, nor theological investigation.

"These hints will receive, perhaps, both illustration and confirmation from a passage in the apocalyptic visions of the great Apostle of Asia Minor, John. After he had seen "Heaven opened," and heard the "new song," and been pointed to the "White Horse," on which one "went forth conquering and to conquer," he saw "an angel ascending from the EAST, having the *seal* of God, to seal the servants of God." *Rev.* vii. 2, 3. This Angel, John says, sealed an equal number of each of "the twelve tribes of the children of Israel;" or, in round numbers, twelve thousand of each; in all, a hundred and forty and four thousand. Now this sealing took place, not in Judea, but in the east; and there only, perhaps, could *equal* numbers of ten of the twelve tribes have been found, at that time. For although many, perhaps most, of the captivity returned to their own land, all history, and especially their own historians, prove that "multitudes preferred to remain" in the east. Thus the Apostles had a powerful motive to go eastward, when they began to act upon their wide commission, as the Evangelists of the world. Is it not, therefore, highly probable, that the *sealed* in the east were the seals of the Ministry of those of the Apostles, who cannot be traced in "the field" at all, except by the traditions which assign them to Asia? This supposition, to say the least of it, is more respectful to the character of the Apostolic body at large, than the gratuitous insinuation of some modern writers, that they lingered as long as persecution would let them in Jerusalem, and only went abroad to preach when they could no longer stay at home in safety. This charge has always appeared to me wanton as well as unwarranted. It was got up, indeed, when the advocates of Missions were called upon to explain, why we were so *late* in taking up the cause of the heathen? The delay admitted, of course, no apology: but something must be said; and therefore *precedents* were brought forward; and amongst them, the lingering of the Apostles at Jerusalem. Paul had a different opinion of the body at large, and said of them, "verily their sound went forth in all the earth, and their words to the ends of the world." Or if this be figure, take fact from Paul's pen: "other of the Apostles saw I *none* at Jerusalem, save Peter and James." *Gal.* i. 19.

"The chief difficulty with modern writers on this subject seems to be, to find a *way* for any of the Apostles into the far east, and especially to India. But we have seen that the Jews were there before them; and Apostolic Missionaries were surely as likely to make their way there, as the exiles of the Dispersion. Besides, it is acknowledged that Pantœnus visited India within 'a hundred years afterwards;' (*Burton*, p. 31;) and then, neither roads nor conveyances were more numerous than before. Dr. Burton had no occasion to throw any doubts around the visit of Pantœnus, on the ground of such an assumption as 'that the Hebrew or Syriac copy of St. Matthew's Gospel, which he found in India could be of no use there.' It was just the copy to be useful to 'the remnant,' whom the Apostles of Asia went after. Neander judged better when he said, 'The matter of the Hebrew Gospel is no proof that Pantœnus did not mean India properly so called; for we may suppose that the Jews who now inhabit the coast of Malabar had already settled there: and the words of Eusebius well suit the notion of East India proper."—*Neander*, vol. i. p. 76. In like manner, Giesler throws no suspicion upon the words of Eusebius, or the visit of Pantœnus, although he supposes, with Dr. Burton, that the Thomas of India was a disciple of Manes. Vol. i. p. 54. Again, therefore, it may be said, that an Apostle of Christ was just as likely as a Manichæan to adopt the maxim, '*inveniam viam, aut faciam*.' Mosheim also harmonizes the accounts of Eusebius and Jerome, concerning Pantœnus; although he maintains that they mean by India, Arabia Felix. *Comment*, vol. ii. p. 7. He has, however, no other way of getting over what Jerome says of 'the Indian Brahmins to whom Pantœnus preached Christ,' than by charging ambiguity on the word, 'Brachmanus,' and assuming that Jerome 'had no other than his own fancy for what he said;'—(*ibid.* p. 7;) a mode of reasoning, happily rare in Moshiem, which would upset his own conjecture: for even his appeals to Tillemont's life of St. Bartholomew, although they prove that Arabia Felix was called India by the ancients, and that Bartholomew preached in Arabia, do not prove that the Apostle went no farther into the east. It is, I am aware, a serious matter to differ from Moshiem. He differs, however, from himself at times, as we shall see, when we come to his hitherto untranslated work on the church in Tartary.

In the mean time, we are not altogether unprepared now to listen to other authorities, on the subject of apostolic Missions in Asia. Their probability is already strong, and the traditions of them we shall find to be equally numerous and harmonious. Indeed, I am not quite sure that the annals of the Syrian Church, ought to be called traditions. Her first and great Missionary College at Edessa, which produced the first and best version of the New Testament in Syriac, certainly in the second, if not in the first century, and from which all the first Missionaries to Asia went forth, was not likely to be ignorant of the route or range of either the twelve apostles or the seventy disciples. One thing is certain, and it deserves special attention, that the Syrian Church sent her Missionaries, not into the fields of those apostles and evangelists which the ACTS enable us to trace, but chiefly into the quarters of Asia, to which all churches assign those apostles whom the ACTS do not embrace. This fact proves, at least, that she had entire faith in the EDESSAN TABLES, which account for those ambassadors of Christ we cannot otherwise find. Both the Greek and the Roman Church believed the same thing concerning the distant spheres in Asia, to which some of the apostles' went: but they did not, like the Syrian Church, follow them by Missionaries, until a late period. Edessa and Nisibis, not the schools of Constantinople or Rome, sent forth the Missionaries who were "baptized for the dead," in Tartary, China, and India.

Now according to the Edessan Tables, and the works of the Syrian patriarchs, as they are characterized by Asseman, a Syrian, whom all scholars venerate and almost love, because he moved about in the Vatican library, amongst the parchments of antiquity, as carefully as he had followed his sheep on Lebanon, when, like Milne, a shepherd boy,—" St. Thomas was not only the apostle of the Syrians and Chaldeans, but also of the Parthians and Indians; and with him was joined Jude afterwards." In the epitome of the Syrian canons, Thomas is called "the apostle of the Hindoos and Chinese." The Syrian chronicles call him, "the first bishop of the East;" and Ebedjesus says, "India, and all the regions about received the priesthood from" him. Amru also, the best of the Syrian historians, traces both Thomas and Bartholomew, through Arabia and Persia into India and China. And all the Syrian writers quoted by Asseman, agree in stating that a few of the twelve, and many of the seventy disciples, "went far into Northern Asia, preaching the Gospel." Now even Moshiem acknowledges that, "at a little later period" the Gospel was carried to China, Seres, and Tartary;" and admits that it was proclaimed there "by the first teachers after the apostolic age;" as will be seen in the chapter on the origin of Christianity in China. He doubts very much, if not denies, however, that Thomas, or any apostle, went so far. And yet, the very testimony which he admits to be both valid and conclusive proof "that the first teachers after the apostles" went thus far, maintains that some of the apostles themselves also did so. Now, although I will not affirm that they did, I will question the logic of either denying or doubting it, if the Syrian vouchers be allowed to have substantiated the fact, that disciples of both the twelve and the seventy did so. Besides, it is, as we have seen, quite as likely that some of the apostles, as they had certainly as much opportunity and more reason, would do so, as that any of their disciples would attempt the enterprise. However learned, therefore, it may appear, and however fashionable it may be, to throw doubts upon the traditions which Eusebius has preserved, and the Syrian fathers chronicled, it is not unreasonable for plain men like myself to ask even the most learned, why the apostles could not range Asia as well as the Roman Empire? It was not, indeed, so easily done in the apostolic age; but it was done by the Nestorians afterwards, when there were no greater facilities for travelling, and far more difficulties in acquiring the Asiatic languages. I am neither able nor anxious to separate the pure gold of sober truth from the dross of extravagant tradition, on this subject. It does appear to me, however, only another kind of extravagance to set against the uniform voice of antiquity, a few verbal criticisms upon geographical names, and to give unknown men credit for doing what well known men had it equally in their power to accomplish, and more in their heart to try. Besides, there is neither proof nor probability, from history or tradition, that none of the apostles made their way "far hence amongst the Gentiles" of Asia: whereas, there is every reason to believe that those of them whom we miss in the Acts, were as much Missionaries as those we find, and neither idle nor unenterprising in Persia, Tartary, or India, when their more known brethren were jeopardying their lives in "the high places" of the imperial field.

Whether Wilberforce took this view of the matter I do not know: but he said one day to Dr. Olynthus Gregory, whilst anticipating the progress and success of Missions in the field of the world, "I should not wonder if some Missionary discover in central Asia, traces of Apostolic men, and even a primitive version of the New Testament." Neither hope is altogether visionary. Early traces of Apostolic men, as we shall see, were found even in China by the Jesuits; and what is the Lamaism of Tartary, but Heathenized Christianity, in one sense?

In a word, I wish to plead for nothing beyond an intelligent regard to the vestiges of the ancient Syrian Church in Asia, as vouchers for the zeal and enterprise of the Apostles, Evangelists, and Primitive Missionaries. Dr. Wilson, the Bishop of Calcutta, calls the Christians of St. Thomas by their right name when he says, they are "an ancient Church preserved in the midst of idolatry, from the days of the Apostles." This will be their "name and memorial for ever," in spite of all verbal criticism. Mar Thomas, of the fifth century, can never be proved to have been the founder of "the *Surians* of Malabar," as the Portuguese called them, when they found a hundred and ten native churches in the country, "wholly ignorant of the great Western apostacy and its peculiar errors."—*Dr. Pearson's Swartz.* HYDER himself knew them better than some modern writers, when he called their chief city, "*Nazarene Ghur.*"

Most cordially do I echo the wish of Bishop Wilson, that Prebendary Gilley, who has thrown so much light upon the ancient Christians of the valleys of the continent, would do the same justice to the Syrian churches of India. They had, indeed, no influence upon the reformation here, or in Germany; but the great Syrian Church of Asia at large, which, *Utriac* says, eclipsed, even in its decline, both in numbers and purity, the Greek and Roman Churches put together, in the middle ages, will be found, I suspect, to have had no small influence in checking some of the corruptions of both Churches, for centuries before.—*Brerewood,* c. 10. True, the Syrians were chiefly Nestorians then; and that is the name of rank heresy in most of our Ecclesiastical works, although Luther first, and Baxter afterwards, opposed and denounced the calumny. The fact is, the Nestorians were the first *Protestants,* as well as the most active Missionaries, in the world. Rome, not Edessa, nor Nisibis, was the real school of gross heresy. I have endeavoured to throw some light upon this subject, in a subsequent chapter.

I sympathize deeply with all who feel, on reading this chapter, that it is almost as painful to think of lost apostolic labour, as to think of vast nations which had no apostolic visit. Persia, Tartary, and China, and even India, retain so few and faint traces of Christianity, that we are hardly gratified, at first, to find any trace of it. In this dilemma we must just do what we are compelled to do, when we think of the seven churches of lesser Asia,—wonder and weep. How soon "the sweet influences" of John, "the beloved disciple," were lost there! How little reformation, even the Apocalyptic threatenings, produced there! The Syrian churches of India are not so corrupt as the Greeks or Romanists of Asia Minor. Even the Lamaism of Tartary is hardly more Heathenish than some of the forms of Christianity which have prevailed for ages, where all the Apostles laboured, and even Emanuel himself preached. And yet, "Thy land, O Emanuel," is "holy ground" in our estimation, not only because Thy presence graced it, but because Thy Gospel was first preached in it! Yes; "the Apostles of the Lamb" help to render it sacred in our estimation, and touching to our sympathies. This is as it should be. It is not wrong, therefore, to allow our sympathies to go forth eastward, wherever there is the shadow of a probability that either Apostle, Evangelist, or Disciple, went. Tradition is, indeed, an *ignis fatuis*, which can never be followed far with safety or pleasure: but incredulity is a dark lantern, which is as useless as it is unseemly. Those are more nice than wise who spurn all tradition. It deserves, indeed, no quarter when it clashes with the New Testament, or abets Ecclesiastical usages, subversive of, or at variance with, the spirit of the Gospel; but it is not unworthy of all confidence, when it locates the Apostles, or maps the seats of the primitive churches. Then, as Moshiem says of Tertullian, "it puts on a little (a great deal?) of the rhetorician;" but still, its rhetoric is too eloquent and uniform to be altogether visionary, or deceitful.

CHAPTER XIX.

THE ASIATIC NESTORIANS.

It is not one of the least of the benefits which America is yielding to Europe, in helping on the evangelization of the world, that she is not the *dupe* of names, and especially not of nicknames. A Nestorian is not necessarily a heretic in her vocabulary; nor does she sympathize with the wrecks of the Nestorian churches in Asia, chiefly because of their episcopacy. She sees them with the Scriptures in their own hands, or desiring to have the Scriptures, and hating popery; and she loves them "for the truth's sake which dwelleth in them," although they do not understand much of that "truth as it is in Jesus." In this, America caught the spirit of Melancthon, who looked at once to the Syrian Patriarch, when allies were wanted by the Reformation, against Rome. Melancthon knew, and Luther proclaimed, that the Nestorians were Protestants in the fifth century. The Lutherans, indeed, found no response to their brotherly appeal, from the Patriarch of the Syrians, at the time of the Reformation; but the American Missionaries in Persia have the Nestorian Bishop at their *Moonshee*, now that they are translating the Scriptures into modern Syriac. Mr. Glen, who is now at Tibris completing the Persian translation, expects a *revival* of religion amongst the Nestorians of Persia, through the labours of the American brethren. I state this fact on the authority of one of Mr. Glen's sons, who is just about to sail for India, as a Missionary to the Mahometans. I thus bespeak some attention, and sympathy too, to both the modern and ancient Nestorians of Asia.

"The *Nestorian Heresy*," is a phrase of "great swelling words," which is not so true as it is proverbial. It began to be a current phrase in England, in the thirteenth century, when Matthew Paris, and Roger Bacon, were our only chroniclers of Asiatic Nestorianism; and whilst the pope was trying to follow in the train of Gengis-Kan, in order to gain the subjection of the Nestorian Churches in China, Persia, and India, to the Holy See, just as the Tartar had subjugated these nations. His Holiness had heard, somehow, of the influence which the Nestorian Bishops had with the Tartar Princes; and as he was blowing the trumpet of the Crusades without awakening any echo in the Palaces of Europe, he turned his attention to Asia. This is the secret of Friar Bacon's attacks upon the Nestorians. "He follows, also, Rubriquis, who hated them," says Marsden, the learned editor of Maro Polo.

They were not such heretics as Rome said. Accordingly, even Mandeville says of them, "They believe well in the Fadre, Sone, and Holy Gost." There could not be much heresy, as to doctrine, where the Trinity was well believed; and it was not likely to be either ill believed or ill expressed, by the disciples of Nestorius. He was, certainly, an ill-tempered Trinitarian, but not an unsound one.

It is of some importance to clear up this point, in order that the reader may sympathize somewhat with the Asiatic Nestorians, as well as discern the real causes of their decay and extinction in China.

And that they deserve a share in our religious sympathies, will be believed at once, when I say that Baxter has thrown his mighty shield over the Trinitarianism of Nestorius and his disciples. "Nestorius," he says, "defended his priest, Anastasius, for saying that the Virgin was not the mother of God. This set all the city (Constantinople) in a division; suspecting him of denying the Godhead of Christ. But he was of no such opinion. He would not call Mary the mother of God, nor the mother of man; but the mother of Christ, who was both God and man." Baxter adds: "For my part, I again say, past doubt, that he was not heretical, *dere*,"—*History of Councils*, "*by Richard Baxter, a hater of false history*," p. 87, 94. Lond. 1680.

Dr. Hale, also, the learned chronologist, praises Nestorius for opposing "the extravagant veneration of the Virgin Mary, whom the Orthodox, in their disputes with the Arians, styled *Theotokos*, the Mother of God: which, he contended, should be changed into *Christotokos*, the Mother of Christ."— *Hale, on the Trinity*, Vol. i. p. 18.

Neither scholars nor theologians need to be informed that Hale was a rigid judge of heresy. He so hated Arianism and Sabellianism in all their forms, that he forgot his loyalty to the Episcopate of Constantine, in his love to Athanasius; and revived the old heathen sarcasm of Ammianus Marcellinus, and added the testimony of *Hilary* to its truth,— "that the Bishops, galloping in troops to attend councils, jaded all the post-horses, and wore out all the public carriages of the empire."—*Ibid*. p. 16.

Similar complaints are paid to the substantial orthodoxy of Nestorius and his adherents, by Dr.

Gregory, in his history of the Christian Church.— p. 276.

I mention these well-known champions of orthodoxy first, that the general reader may feel confidence in the testimony of less known authorities, and thus rid himself of the prejudices and suspicions which the proverbial phrase, "Nestorian heresy," has thrown around the Nestorian church. Both Baxter and Hale call the Nestorian church in Asia, "the purest of the Greek churches." This, I confess, does not amount to much; but still, it is enough to prove that much evangelical truth, as well as many superstitions, was embraced in Tartary and China; and thus, enough to interest us in the Asiatic converts of antiquity; many of whom deserve the same sympathy which we so cordially extend to the first Albigenses and Waldenses of France, the first Hussites in Bohemia, and the first Lollards in England. Neither the first nor the last Nestorians in Asia, had, indeed, any influence upon the Protestant reformation; and thus they can never lay hold upon our national sympathies, nor be associated in our memory with "the witnessing remnant" of the dark ages. The time will come, however, when Protestant Missionaries will plead with the Asiatics, by appeals to the memory of their Nestorian fathers: some of whom they will place in "the cloud of witnesses," just as we add to it the Waldenses and Lollards. Barsomus will blaze like Wycliffe in that cloud!

Nestorius himself, however, will not be placed in it. His name will never become a watch-word, nor a talisman, in Asia again. For he was, what Baxter calls him, a firebrand," although no heretic. "Give me the earth weeded from heretics," he said to the

Emperor, "and I will give thee heaven. Help me against the heretics, and I will help thee against the Persians." Thus the Monk of Antioch rattled the Peterine KEYS, when he was made patriarch of Constantinople! That patriarchate gave Nestorius great power. Like that of Alexandria, Ephesus, and Cesarea, it was not subject to the Pope. See *Bingham's Ecc. Antiq.* b. 2, c. 18. The new patriarch began his career by ordering the church of the Arians to be pulled down. To prevent this, they themselves set it on fire, and perilled the city by the flames. He then attacked the Novatians, although they seem to have been heretics only in discipline, at the time."— *Gregory*, Vol. i. p. 136. In a word, he " raised stirs in so many places," that the Emperor, Theodosius, Junior, was obliged to curb him, and to call him before a General Council at Ephesus. He was thus put into the hands of his personal enemy, Cyril, the patriarch of Alexandria, who presided under the twofold sanction of the Emperor and the Pope. Cyril, and his party charged Nestorius with blasphemy, for refusing to call Mary the Mother of God; which was, they said, a denial of the union of the human and *divine* nature in Christ, and an assertion of two persons in one nature. He meant, however, two natures in one person, after their union; and, therefore, said to the Council, "I will not acknowledge that the *divine* nature was ever two or three months old: I am now clear from your blood: I will come before you no more!" In this spirit he retired, and some of the bishops followed him. Cyril summoned him to appear again; but in vain. The Council, therefore, proceeded to examine witnesses, and to read his sermons; and then they anathematized and deposed him, as a blasphemer against Christ.

All this was done by the Council, before John, the Patriarch of Antioch, arrived with his eastern bishops. When John, therefore, found that he was treated as *nobody*, by the court, he formed a court for himself; and, with Nestorius and Theodoret, deposed Cyril, and Memnon of Ephesus. Then came the tug of war! Cyril summoned John: John refused. Cyril's synod deposed John's synod: John's synod deposed Cyril's. Then the Emperor's commissioner deposed the heads of both deposing parties;—declaring their acts null, and commanding them to begin anew.

At this crisis, the legates of Celestine arrived from Rome, and joined issue with Cyril. This junction tempted the emperor to revoke the deposition of Cyril, and to confirm that of Nestorius. It is creditable to Nestorius, that he retired quietly to his original place in the monastery of Antioch, where he lived four years, both honoured and beloved. During that time, however, his friend John was won over to the decree of the Ephesian Council; and Nestorius was soon banished to Oasis, in the Egyptian desert, where he died in want and wretchedness.

These facts, although they cannot engage much of our sympathy for the intolerant patriarch of Constantinople, account for the deep sympathy which the Nestorians felt for both his creed and himself. For we shall find, even in the remotest parts of central Asia, that, a thousand years afterwards, Nestorius was venerated as a saint, and Cyril detested as a heretic and a firebrand. They also kept up the renunciation of the Council of Ephesus, which the Nestorians of the fifth century began, just as the old

Seceders of Scotland, half a century ago, made it a term of communion to renounce "as a work of the *deevil*," the awakening produced at Cambuslang by Whitefield. Accordingly, Brerewood says, "Even at this day, beyond the Tigris, they say as Nestorius himself said, "You may say that Christ's mother is the parent of God, if you expound it *well:* but it is improper and dangerous." They renounce the Council of Ephesus, and all that owned it. They communicate in *both* kinds. They use not auricular confession, nor confirmation, nor crucifixes on their crosses; and their priests have liberty for first, second, and even third marriages."—*Brerewood's Inquiry*, pp. 139—144. Barsomus, however, has the chief influence in all this.

It was necessary to bring out with some distinctness the characters of both Nestorius and Cyril, in order to account for the zeal and fidelity with which Nestorianism was espoused by some of the oriental bishops, in spite of Cyril, and perhaps in spite *to* him. Besides, there are few points in ecclesiastical history we are less familiar with, than the introduction and triumphs of Christianity in Asia. The iniquitous phrase, "Nestorian heresy," has diverted all, but students, from caring any thing about the reputed heretics of the fifth and sixth centuries. It is, therefore, necessary to disabuse the public mind on this subject; that any reader may know, now that China is becoming a field of Protestant Missions, what China was taught when, in the year 636, the Syrian Nestorians sent OLAPAAN there, under the sanction of the Emperor, to preach the Gospel.—*J. Reinhold Foster's History of Voyages*, Chap. iii. p. 108.

This must be my apology for going a little farther into the opinions of Nestorius. His general character, as given by Socrates (Scholasticus,) may be depended on: "he was eloquent, self-conceited, not very learned, and but very little versed in the fathers: but to avoid all extremes, he would only call Mary the mother of Christ." Dr. Gregory calls Socrates, "the excellent and accurate" historian; and prefers him to both Sozomen and Theodoret.—*Ecc. Hist.*, Vol. i. p. 292. I quote this testimony because it can easily be verified by Parker's translations of these ancient historians. The third edition of Parker, in 1729, should, however, be consulted by the reader.

The best accessible authority, on the orthodoxy of Nestorius, is the learned Frenchman, *Dorodon*. He quotes the explanatory letters, which Nestorius sent to Cyril, Celestine, and the Council of Ephesus: and from all of them, it is self-evident that the patriarch meant only to guard against the impious absurdity of imputing growth, suffering, or death, to the *divine* nature of Christ; and to check the idolizing of the Virgin Mary. Dorodon labours to prove also, that Cyril, Celestine, and the Council, were the *real* heretics! Baxter, however, although he laughs at Cyril for imagining that Christ's natures were two *before* the Incarnation, maintains that Nestorius and Cyril only differed about words; or that "the one spake of the concrete, and the other of the abstract." "I need no other proof of my opinion, that they were agreed in *sense*, than that Cyril and John (who had deposed each other) professed, when *forced* by the Emperor, that they had meant the same, and knew it not! But it will be said, they all condemned Nestorius. True; to quiet the world, and please the court. Socrates saith, "the Emperor, who excelled all the priests in meekness and moderation, and could not away with persecution, was more against Nestorius because he was a persecutor than because of his opinions."—*Baxter's Hist. Councils*, p. 95.

It will relieve the attention of the reader, although at the expense of his gravity, to be reminded that some of the Bishops of the Council at Ephesus, could not write their own names; but had to subscribe thus, " I, such a one, have subscribed by the hand of such a one, because I cannot write." Or, "Such a Bishop having said he cannot write, I, whose name is under written, have subscribed for him."—*Jortin*, Vol. iv. p. 77. It is still more humiliating to remember, that 'the Emperor Theodosius, well meaning as he was, was weak enough to importune poor Simeon Stylites to bring the Bishops to unity by his influence with Heaven.—*Bin.* p. 928; *Baron*, p. 432. I mention these pitiable facts to prove that such men were not very competent judges of Scriptural Orthodoxy, and ought to have no influence upon our judgment of Nestorianism. Besides, they hated Nestorius himself, rather than his creed. LUTHER was the first Protestant who proclaimed this fact; and he proclaimed it in thunder. See *Moshiem*, Vol. ii. p. 70. *Note* 9. Moshiem himself says of the Nestorian commentators of the sixth century, "that they were careful in exploring the true sense and native energy of the words employed in the Holy Scriptures."—*Ibid.* page 126. Their expositors were numerous; and yet he ranks these reputed heretics amongst the best; and says of their opponents, "we can scarcely name a single writer (of the time) whose opposition was carried on with probity, moderation, or prudence."—*Ibid.* p. 131. Of the Nestorians in general, he says, "We must observe, to their lasting honour, that, of all Christian Societies established in the east, they have been the most careful and successful in avoiding a multitude of superstitious opinions and practices, that have infected the Greek and Latin churches.— *Moshiem,* Vol. i. p. 248. What they are at present in India, the Bishop of Calcutta, who lately visited their Matran, shall tell: " I trust I may say of them, that they have kept the word of Christ, and not denied his name. The errors which have crept into their Liturgies, are not drawn into articles of faith, nor fixed by General Councils."—*Dr. Wilson.* Bishop Heber, unfortunately, was there whilst a *schism* prevailed amongst the Syrians.

A thousand things more ought to be said of the Nestorians, but I have not room to enlarge. I cannot conclude, however, without again stating, that Barsomus, not Nestorius himself, had the chief influence in the spread of Nestorianism. It was the Bishop of Nisibis, not Nestor, who was the real father and founder of the Nestorian Church in Asia, as well as of the Mission-School at Nisibis. This will not surprise those who remember his influence with Pherozes, the Emperor of Persia, in the fifth century.

See Gibbon, and Moshiem, and Mr. Campbell's Missionary Work on "British India," just published by *Snow.*

CHAPTER XX.

THE SYRIAN MISSION-SCHOOLS.

Had any English writer done for the Schools of Missions, what Stanley has done for the Schools of Philosophy, Edessa and Nisibis would be names of renown amongst Christians, just as the Academy and the Lyceum of Athens amongst scholars. Edessa's celebrated water-springs, which won for it the name "Callir-hoe," would be often employed as emblems, if not of purity, yet of the copiousness and rapidity of those streams of knowledge which it poured over the length and breadth of Asia. We have no Mission-Schools to compare with Edessa and Nisibis. The enterprise of all our colleges and universities united, does not amount to a tithe of their doings and darings, in order to spread the Gospel. Even the college of the Propagandi is not to be compared with them. What Narione says of Barsomus, that he was "*Libus al hudeed,*" clothed in iron, is characteristic of the spirit also of their Missionaries. They dared and endured all manner of perils and privations without flinching. The sands, and snows, and seas of Asia, could not intimidate them. The wild Tartars and the wily Persians; the effeminate Hindoos, and the ferocious Abyssinians; the orderly Chinese, and the rude Bactrians, were all alike to them. They followed roaming tribes, and domesticated themselves for life in settled nations. They went out from Edessa with no bank-credit at Babylon or Alexandria, and upon no term of limited service; but to live and die with the churches they might raise. And as they consulted not with their own flesh and blood, so they would "Know no man after the flesh; but forced their way to the thrones of both kings and khans, as ambassadors of the King of Kings; and into camps and cottages, as heralds of salvation.

Edessa had another distinction. It was not only, as Dr. Burton says, "a kind of metropolis of Christians in that part of Asia in very early times; but there is every reason to believe that the *old* Syriac version of the New Testament was translated there; for even if it date back to the first century, it is not, perhaps, too old for that school."—*Michaelis Introd.* c. vii. s. 8. Dr. Marsh denies this early date of the *Pishito,* and would, refer it to the fourth century, or at farthest to the time of the determination of the Canon. This does not affect, however, the *source* it issued from. Besides, as the Philoxinian version was made in 508, the old Syriac, if made in the fourth century could hardly have become so obsolete as to require a new *Shito* then. It is also acknowledged by all who can judge (I cannot) that the old Syriac version is far superior to the new one, although the latter was collated in the Alexandrian library by Thomas of Heraclia.

The best account of Edessa, that I know of, is *Bayer's:* and as he addresses his preface to *Asseman,* the scholar who, of all others, could judge best, and feel most upon the subject, he has thus given us the best pledge of his fidelity. It is also a proof of his competency, to all who know Asseman! for neither

a Sciolist nor a dreamer would have appealed to him?
Besides, Bayer illustrated his history of Edessa by
fac-similes of the coins and tiaras of its ancient *Ab-
gars*, or Kings, and shows from these vouchers, the
early prevalence of Christianity in that kingdom.
The Heathen *symbols* gave place to the cross on its
crown and coinage, under Abgarus Bar Manu, about
A. D. 165; not A. D. 200, as Bayer says.

As this work is not translated, and but rarely to
be met with in this country, I have ventured to characterize it thus, that general readers may have confidence in the testimony of Bayer. And he deserves
this the more, because it is not the ecclesiastical, but
the political history of Edessa, which he chiefly gives.
He refers to its library, churches, and Missions; and
thus confirms Asseman; but his chief object is to illustrate its vicissitudes as a bulwark of the Romans
against the Persians, and as the victim of Mahommedan cruelty afterwards. The only ecclesiastical
question he goes largely into is, the credibility of
Eusebius in regard to the letters which, tradition
says, passed between the Saviour and Abgarus
Uchomo. Eusebius says that he himself found
these letters in the archives of the church at Edessa,
and translated them into Greek. Bayer, like Moshiem, Neander, Giesler and Burton, acquits Eusebius of fraud and pretence in the matter. Perhaps
Neander hardly does so; for he says, "Eusebius *suffered* himself to be deceived."

Now whatever Neander meant by this remark,
Eusebius could suffer himself to be made a tool. His
story of Constantine's vision of the cross was evidently not credited by himself, but told in obedience
to imperial authority. The courtly Bishop, had he

believed it, would not have left it out of his church history, nor put Cæsar "on oath" for a fact in his own life.—*Henley's Dissertation, and Maclaine's Note on Moshiem.*

The introduction of Christianity into Edessa, cannot, perhaps, be precisely dated. "We find it established there," says Giesler, "as early as the middle of the second century." Bayer proves that the Church of the Christians in Edessa was destroyed by an inundation in A. D. 202; and Neander, that the marks of Baaltic worship gave place to the Cross, by the influence of the Christian sage, Bardesanus with the King.—Vol. i. p. 74. But even the latter date would not sustain the guess of Michaelis, that the old Syriac version was made in the first century. Still, that would not have been an insignificant nor obscure edifice in Edessa, in A. D. 202, the destruction of which became a matter of history, although it stood, as Asseman says, "between the great rivers, Euphrates and Tigris." Such a building was not the work of a few years then, and not likely to have been the first Christian temple: for, as Bardesanus had influence enough at the Court of Edessa in the middle of the second century, to abolish the rites of Cybele and the symbols of Baal, by regal edict, he was not likely to have had less influence with his fellow-citizens. Eusebius says of him, "he was a man of great abilities, and a powerful disputant in the Syriac tongue. As a powerful asserter of the Word, he had many followers. Amongst his works there is a most able dialogue on Fate, addressed to Antonine. This man composed also the dialogues against

Marcion."—*Ecc. Hist.*, p. 149, Bagster's London Edition.

Now all this could not be the work of a *young* man. Accordingly he is usually called, "the Christian *sage*, Bardesanus," from the time he wrote to the Emperor; and as he was born in Edessa, of Christian parents, we are thus thrown back nearly to the beginning of the second century for the origin of Christianity in Edessa. Nor is this all. Mesopotamia, in which Edessa stood, is named by Tertullian, as one of the early seats of the Church.—*Adv. Jud.*, c. vii. p. 212. Besides, "the dwellers in Mesopotamia," are specially named in the list of the people who heard the Gospel on the day of Pentecost.—*Acts* ii. 9.

Thus we arrive, with certainty, at the fact, that the Syriac version of the New Testament *may* have been translated at Edessa in the first century, according to the guess of Michaelis. And this is not an uninteresting fact. It throws much light upon the subsequent popularity of Edessa, as a "school of the prophets," and the grand Missionary College for Asia. The place which gave birth to a Canon of the New Testament, and to which the Saviour was supposed to have sent a letter, was likely to be popular, as the seat of a Christian academy. All this accounts also for the fact, that the Church in that city was "classed by the Arabs amongst the *wonders* of the world."—*Bayer*. It had also some other popular distinctions. Pliny says it was called Antioch once. Isidore says it was founded by Nimrod. Giesler proves that some of the first and last apologies addressed to the Roman Emperors issued from it; and from the specimens he has given of those by

Bardesanus and Tatian, there was evidently enough of pure truth in the midst of their Gnosticism, to draw Christian students to Edessa; so that Moshiem might well hesitate to join in the sweeping assertions of either Eusebius or Beausobre against the sages of Edessa.—*Comment.*, Vol. ii. p. 367.

All this may weary a reader who feels no interest in the first Missionary college, which the world saw, or the church patronised. It did not, however, weary me to trace it out through many a heavy page; nor will I believe that the friends of Missions will take no interest in the Gosport of Mesopotamia. Romish writers say, indeed, of both Edessa and Nisibis, that they sent, " as by a *canal*, poison and mud into India and China;" but we know what this means. They would say the same of all our Mission schools, and libel Milne or Williams, as they did Barsumus and Olapaan. Julian, the apostate, however, did not deem Edessa a false or feeble ally of Christianity. He both feared and hated the Syrian seminary.

My limits do not allow me to sketch the history of these schools farther. Besides, my object does not require details. The fact that the Syrian church, which was the grand Missionary church of the world, had Academies for training her evangelists, is the point of interest to us. This precedent, so *primitive* as well as rational, ought to be generally known and studied by the churches, that they may sustain best the colleges which do most to cherish a Missionary spirit amongst their students. The ancient schools of the Christian prophets were not exclusively, nor chiefly, for *home* service. Even the great Syrian monasteries of later times, such as Beth-Abensis in Assyria, whilst they supplied pastors and teachers at home, might both be challenged and picked by the patriarch, in common with the colleges, whenever he wanted peculiarly qualified students for foreign service. Such was the control which the churches had then, through their patriarch, over their colleges. And they had a *right* to it all; for all their schools were founded and sustained by themselves. Besides, they were sure not to impoverish themselves, whilst providing for the heathen. I find no instance in their history of any lack of supplies for their own pulpits, nor of any such *rush* of students into Asia, as weakened the ministry at home, even when the Missionary spirit of Edessa and Nisibis was at its height. Neither have I found, although I searched diligently, that the *mixture* of students for home and abroad, in these colleges, unsettled the minds, or distracted the studies of either class. Really, Missionary men made their purpose their fate, and stuck by it, unshaken and unmoved, by their popularity; and the *pastoral* spirits, from contact with Missionaries, carried both fire and fond recollections into their home spheres, which made their churches zealous.

CHAPTER XXI.

THE ORIGIN OF CHRISTIANITY IN CHINA.

Dr. Milne entertained strong doubts of the truth of the reported Nestorian Missions in China. But he ought not, perhaps, to be held responsible for his opinions upon this subject, as he had but a small library to consult, and not much time to spare for such researches. His opinions had, however, the sanction of Dr. Morrison, and are held by other Chinese Missionaries. Not one Protestant Missionary, so far as I know, has thrown a single ray of glory upon the path of the Nestorians in China. Even Gutzlaff, with all his enthusiasm, dismisses his illustrious forerunners thus summarily:—" The introduction of Nestorianism in the seventh century, is almost proved: yet the influence it had upon the Chinese, and the purity with which it was promulgated, must have been very slight, nor can it have extended beyond the *western* frontiers."—*China Opened*, Vol. ii. p. 229. It is, however, highly creditable, in one sense, to our Missionaries, that they have cared so little about an ancient church in China, which left so few traces of either its influence or existence in that empire. They have employed themselves better, than in studying Amru, the Assemans, or Le Quien. I feel this deeply, and gratefully acknowledge it. Still, I do not think myself ill employed, in trying to create public sympathy with the old lights of China, as well as for its present darkness. It most likely had the light *before* Britain, and had certainly *more* of it in the fifth century than Augustine brought here at the end of the sixth century. Christianity lasted longer also at Cambalu (now Pekin) than in some places where the Apostles themselves planted it; and remained whilst it lasted in the northern capital of China, purer than it was then or is now in Rome. This was nothing to our ecclesiastical history, whilst ecclesiastical policy cared nothing about Missions: but it is *something* to the church of Christ, now that she "cares for souls," and "watches for souls," as one who must give account to him who says, "all souls are mine." All who feel thus, must feel also that China is emphatically the LAND OF SOULS!—and thus, that "the land of Bibles" owes more to it than a translation of the Bible, and the *smallest* of its Missions, even although the former be the greatest boon we ever gave to a people.

It will also, to say the least, do our future Missionaries no harm, to know that even central China is not untrodden ground, although no traces of the first Missionaries be discoverable now. They will not soon outrun or overtake OLAPAAN, were China fully open to them; nor easily rival SUBACHABESUS, were they as welcome at court as either Schaal or Ricci, Verbiest, or Corvinus. In like manner, it cannot but do the Churches of both Britain and America good, to be aware that the Syrian Church, with fewer resources than they possess, eclipsed them, as it did both the Greek and Roman, in Missionary spirit; and poured from Edessa, Nisibis, and Bethabensis, far more Missionaries, in a far shorter space of time, over Asia, than all our Societies have given to the world. Their Missionaries, indeed, cost them less. But what must have been the *spirit* of the Syrian Churches, when it could create men, who either created their own supplies, or cared nothing about privations? The tone of piety which did this, must have been very high; especially amongst the parents, who gave up their sons to such Missions. And these young men, who went so readily "on the forlorn hope," so far as all earthly comfort was concerned, must have been trained by old men of eminent piety and devotedness: for the youth of a

Church seldom rise above the *level* of its pastor and leading members. Every voluntary Church, at least, begets children in its "own image." So long, therefore, as privations and hardships are held to be serious evils, and especially while the comforts of life are more prized in the Churches than the consolations of godliness, there will be but very few young men born in the *Pauline* image, or willing to "suffer the loss of all things," in order to win Christ, or to win souls. For my own part I am both astonished and delighted, that young men are found ready to make the sacrifices they do, whilst *comforts* are so popular at home. I dare not, however, conceal the fact, that we can never evangelize the world, until both Churches and Missionaries make more sacrifices than they do, so far as the East is concerned. Both India and China were, no doubt, less perilous and expensive to live in, when the Syrian Missionaries went there, than now. There is a new state of society, as well as an altered state of climate; and therefore it would be bad policy and base cruelty, to risk the life or influence of Missionaries, by a niggardly support. We must not, however, forget either apostolic example, or the imitations of it which the history of the first Syrian Churches and Missionaries presents. Both had some way of going to work in Asia which we have yet to learn.

I will now disentangle from Moshiem's Tartarian Church History, the substance of what he affirms and admits concerning China. This will best accredit any additions or illustrations which my own researches furnish. Now Moshiem, although he rejects the tradition of an Apostolic visit to China, and discredits the opinion of both Kircher and Ortelius, that the Gospel was preached there in the first century, acknowledged that at a "*little* later period" it was carried "to China, Seres, and Tartary." "It may be *proved*," he says, "by the Syriac records, that at the beginning of the fourth century Christianity was *flourishing* in the provinces of Chorasan and Mavaralnahara; and from a variety of learned testimonies, we may admit that although the Gospel was not introduced into China by the Apostle Thomas himself, it was yet proclaimed there by the *first* Christian teachers after the Apostolic age."

His reasons for this belief are the following:—"Arnobius, who flourished in the third century, expressly mentions the Seres amongst the people who had then embraced Christianity; and it is universally acknowledged that the Chinese nation is meant." I may just add here, that Arnobius describes, not an infantile, but a confirmed state of Christianity, or such as Persia then presented.—*Book* 2, p. 50.

Again; Moshiem says, "The antiquity of Christianity in India is proved by La Croze in the clearest manner;" and then he argues, that as the archiepiscopal See of China was originally conjoined with that of India, the metropolitan seats must have been chosen at the same time. "But," he asks, "why should a metropolitan have been appointed, unless the religion of Jesus had been spread far and wide, *long* before; and unless there had been many Bishops? These things could not have been accomplished in a *short* space of time. The Chinese, it is certain, were converted long before Salibazacha created metropolitans."—*Hist. Tartary*, p. 8.

Moshiem's object, be it remembered, is not to settle the question of the origin of Christianity in China, but to base upon the fact, that "its healthful doctrines" having been preached there in the earlier ages, this argument,—" If China itself was so *soon* illuminated by the light of Divine Truth, why should not TARTARY have shared the blessing, seeing some of its provinces bordered on Syria, and thus were nearer to the source from which the glorious light emanated?"—p. 9. Thus Moshiem is not making out a case for China, but appealing to ascertained and acknowledged facts. And incidental appeals of this kind are often the most valid proofs in history.

The only great public monument of the early Christianity of China, which has yet been discovered, is that which Dr. Milne calls "the stone tablet of See-Gan." This "Syro-Senic monument," Moshiem calls "a matter of greater moment" than any of the *coins* which have been found. It was discovered at Sigan-fu, in the seventeenth century. The inscriptions upon it are partly in Chinese and partly in Syriac; and contain certain doctrines which prove, says Moshiem, that the Nestorians erected it, A. D. 781. The Syriac compartment of the stone records the names, *seventy* in number, of the first Missionaries from Syria to China, whose names had not perished.

This "valuable treasure of antiquity" has not, as might be expected, passed unquestioned. It created a *sensation* in Europe, when Kircher published a fac-simile of it in his Prodroma-Copto. The Jesuits, of course, were suspected of forging it, and certainly their *character* was no pledge for its authenticity. Moshiem, however, acquits them of all fraud in this matter, as he well might: for it brought no glory, but that of discovery, to their own church; and neither she nor they would have forged a compliment to "the Nestorian Heresy." It was, however, said to be invented, in order to prove to the Emperor of China, the antiquity of Christianity in his country; and Moshiem, although he "fearlessly acquits" the Jesuits on this point also, hardly answered the objection, by saying, "that they had showed clearly, before the monument was discovered, that the name of Jesus had been known to the Chinese," much earlier than the date of the stone. This is Le Compte's argument. But the date itself is better proof, that the tablet was not got up by the Jesuits for this purpose. Had they invented it to prove the antiquity of Christianity, it would have been dated back to apostolic times, according to their own tradition that St. Thomas went into China.

The next proof of the prevalence of Christianity, in the ninth century, in China, to which Moshiem appeals, is, that on the revolt of a certain Baicher, many Christians were martyred in the city of Canfu or Canton. In this century, also, Ehn Wahab, an Arab, had an interview with the Chinese Emperor, who showed him paintings of Noah, Moses, and of Jesus Christ, riding upon an ass; saying of the Saviour, "He was not long upon the earth: all his deeds were done in the space of thirty months."— *Reuandot's Translation.* Golius, also, mentions another ancient Mahometan traveller, who heard of a Monk in China, A. D. 978. Marco Polo, it is well known, found many Christians in China, in the thirteenth century. Even in the seventeenth century, "Ricci was told," says Purchas, "by some Mogore strangers, that in the Xensian province, were white men with long beards, who worship Jesus."—*Pilgrim.* p. 378.

On reviewing these things, Moshiem says, "If they be well considered by the pious mind, the infinite goodness of the Supreme Ruler will be worthily magnified, because he suffered not the truth to be unknown even in the most distant countries of the earth, but made the name and glory of the Divine Redeemer to be proclaimed abroad at all times." Having said this, Moshiem goes *back* upon his ground, as if he suspected that he had not given the best proofs, or felt that "the pious mind" deserved more. He, therefore, introduces the celebrated Nestorian Missionary, Subachabesus. This man was the first scholar of his age, and the glory of the Nestorian school of Beth-Abensis, in Central Assyria. But the patriarch of the Syrian church wanted a bishop for his churches in Gelo and Dailmistæ. He, therefore, ordained Subachabesus, that he might ordain presbyters wherever they were needed. But the Missionary would not merge himself in the prelate. The moment he had done with episcopizing, he began to evangelize beyond the limits of his diocess, and proceeded to the extreme boundaries of Tartary, Cathay, and China, converting many people. This was in the eighth century. "But this apostolic Missionary," says Moshiem, "reaped not the reward of his labours from men: on returning to Assyria, he was murdered by the barbarians." Little as we know of the details of this martyr-missionary's labours, it is impossible not to sympathize with Subachabesus, somewhat as we do with Heber. Like Heber, he was an elegant scholar, naturally fond of retirement. He had, also, a heart for *home* scenes and society, and yet he laid all its yearnings upon the altar of Missions, as a "living sacrifice" unto God. If he did not leave the cloistered cells and shades of Beth-Abensis without a struggle between taste and conscience, yet, judging from Asseman's account of him, he nobly forgot them all, when once "far hence amongst the Gentiles," except when he remembered that they sheltered, in inglorious ease, companions of his youth, who ought to have been partners of his labour. It seems to have been in order to draw them into China and Cathay, and to rouse Beth-Abensis from study to enterprise, that he bent his steps homewards again. He was not abandoning his Mission, nor yielding to home sickness, nor playing the fearful game of "limited service;" but, like *Williams*, returning to strengthen his Missionary staff, and to pledge the churches, with their patriarch, to new efforts. It was in this spirit Subachabesus was coming home. Perhaps this was known to be his errand wherever he came, and thus led to his martyrdom: for as his own labours had converted many idolaters, the "craftsmen" were likely to say to the mob, "This Paul hath persuaded away much people from the gods which all Asia doth worship."

What shall we say to these things? It seems *hard* that "burning and shining lights" should be thus suddenly extinguished, just when most wanted. The fact is, *more* of them were wanted in China, Cathay and India, at the time than the living voice of Subachabesus could have called into the field. God, therefore, called, by the voice of the Martyr's blood, at the doors of all the cells in Beth-Abensis; —and not in vain! The Patriarch "substituted for him, Kardagus and Jaballaha," says Moshiem, "with fifteen others from this famous monastery. Some of them were sent into China; and one of them, David, as its Bishop. Jaballaha died, although not by the hands of the barbarians, by hard labour for them." Timotheus was the Nestorian Patriarch, under whose auspices these undertakings were accomplished. See also, *Asseman*, Vol. iii. p. 489.

The first successful effort made by Rome in China and Cathay was at the close of the thirteenth century, when John de Monte Corvinus was sent into Asia. He went boldly to the great Chan at once, and proffered religious instruction to him. He succeeded also in building two churches in Pekin, under the sanction of the Emperor, who delighted to hear the children chanting the Litany. He also translated and published the New Testament and Psalter in the Tartar language, "in a very beautiful form," says Moshiem; who argues thus from the facts: "it is evident from these excellent endeavours of Corvinus, that he burned with a sincere desire to convert the heathen. Had he desired only to make them Romanists, he would not have translated the New Testament into the Mogul language. But he wished to make them Christians, and set before them the law of Christ." I find amongst my memoranda, but without the name of the authority, the pleasing fact that Corvinus, besides baptizing 5,000 children in Pekin, bought also 150, in order to educate them at his own expense. This school was, no doubt, the chanting choir which Moshiem mentions.

He adds, that the Pope commanded Aegedius Romanus to prepare a Catechism of Christian doctrine, as a help to Corvinus in spreading the Gospel. My notes say, that his holiness, Clement, had the Catechism filled with *pictures*, that it might be more popular than the Missionary's version of the New Testament. Be this as it may, the other helps sent to Corvinus from Rome, did not long sustain his influence. It almost died with him, although at one time it was so great, that to confirm it, the Pope commanded the suffragan Bishops, whom he sent out, to be as subject to the Archbishop of Cambalu as to himself.—*Moshiem.* His holiness at the time, however, was availing himself of the influence of Corvinus, in order to win over to his own side Timur, the great Chan of Tartary.—*Appendix,* No. 38.

In the beginning of the fourteenth century, Odoricus, de Portu Naonis, a ranscistan, spent some years in Pekin. In 1330, he came home, and wrote an account of his travels. He did not go out, he says, at the command of the Pope, but of his own accord, to improve his mind. What improvement his *mind* acquired, I do not know; but his *manners* must have undergone a considerable change; for he had to meet the Emperor at all the royal feasts, and to pronounce the benediction. He says, also, that "through his instrumentality, many of the great nobles of the court were led to embrace the Christian faith."—*Dr. Halde,* c. iii. Altogether, the accounts given by Odoricus, as related by Bolland and Henschen in the Actis sanctorum, led Moshiem to say, "Thus *flourishing* appears to have been the state of the Tartar and Chinese church in that age."

It deserves particular notice that, at this time, the Franciscan Missionaries in Asia were skilful physicians. They had not, however, the honesty to ascribe the cures they performed to the real cause,— the power of medicine: they called them *miracles*, of course; and such all extraordinary cures would seem to a barbarous people. Accordingly, almost every patient who was cured, became a convert. This fact is instructive, now that medical Missionaries begin to form a part of our agency in China. The want of the " gifts of healing " there, was early and deeply deplored by both Morrison and Milne: but the American Missionary Board was the first to understand them, and Dr. Parker, of Philadelphia, the first to respond to them. Sir Henry Halford understood this question before we did. We have, however, followed the American example, at last, and sent out Messrs. Lockhart and Hobson; men of equal piety, talent, and science. So far we have done wisely. Should the experiment succeed, however, and medical skill acquire, in China, any thing of that popularity which mathematical science once had at Pekin, we shall do well to remember that the French Missionaries were insnared by their science, and the French nation so fascinated by its influence, that their zeal for the Gospel became a mere thirst for national glory. Colbert made mathematics the *glory* of both Church and King, in his management of the French Missions in China; Le Compte himself being judge. Avril says, that when Couplet returned to France, he was quite the *lion* of Paris, for a time. And it is just possible, that there would be a rush of medical candidates, were any physician to acquire the fame of Schaal, Verbiest, or Couplet. In the mean time, however, the pretended miracles of the Romanists in China, are not unworthy of being studied as *medical* facts, by those who feel interested in this question. They are, indeed, "*lying* wonders;" but still some of them are truly wonderful, as cures. And their fame lives yet in China, and leads to imitations. Even so late as 1807, a Chinese impostor was executed in Tonkin, for attempting miraculous cures. " He gave out that he could cure all evils," says Guerard, "and many thousands of deluded wretches flocked around him. He died, prophesying that he would rise again in three or ten days."—*Report of Chinese Missions for* 1809.

CHAPTER XXII.

THE ASIATIC PRESTER JOHN.

This was once a name of renown in Europe. Popes and princes vied with each other to discover Prester John. He was so much talked of in the middle ages, that it became proverbial, even amongst the common people, to call a happy lot, "a place in Prester John's land." And yet, neither popes nor the people knew well, then, where this great Christian prince dwelt. The first embassies in search of "this second Crœsus," as Moshiem calls him, were sent into Æthiopia. He dwelt at Caracor, the capitol of Tenduch, or Tanguth, a region in Tartary, adjacent to China: but the ambassadors of the king of Lusitania found him, as they thought, in the emperor of Abyssinia; who, because he also was a

Christian Crœsus, must, of course, be Prester John! This was in 1487. But in 1308, and in 1177, the popes pretended to have had messengers from him. Alexander III. played him off, as his friend and ally, against the Emperor Frederick, who had driven his holiness from the Vatican to Venice; and Clement V. promised the Prester's help to the crusaders. And at all these periods, his was a name to conjure or conquer with; for, besides the mystery which surrounded it, sixty-nine Christian kings, besides five Mahometans, were said to be tributary to it, and one hundred and twenty-seven archbishops, with twenty bishops under each of them, bowed to it. This was his fame at Rome.—*Dr. Geddes's Eccl. Hist. Ethiop.* p. 22. And it was not less at Constantinople, in the twelfth century. The "glorious John" of that age, sent a letter to the emperor, still more astounding than these reports. According to his own account of himself, his state had no parallel. Princes and prelates were his ordinary servants, and the stars of heaven the only fit emblems of his power and glory.—*Asseman's Bibl. Orient.* Vol. iii. c. 9.—*Moshiem's Tartary*, App. No. 1. Extravagant as all this is, there is not a little truth in the fame of Prester John. Dr. Geddes, if I understand him, must have forgotten some of the books he mentions, when he said, that "the whole story of this enchanted Asiatic Christian empire was invented and kept up by the trumpeters of the holy war; no such empire having been discovered in Asia even to this day." This is as far below the truth as the popes went above it.

Moshiem has carefully investigated the matter in his history of the ancient Tartaric Church, which I shall chiefly follow, except when I can refer to more accessible books, or quote subsequent discoveries. The reader must not, however, expect here all the information his curiosity may wish for. My object is, simply, to interest him on behalf of Asia, by telling as much of the little I know, as shall awaken sympathy for those vast regions which the Nestorians so nobly penetrated, and so long influenced. There is, indeed, reason to fear that the Nestorian Missionaries of "Prester John's land," were neither so spiritual or orthodox as we have seen some of their brethren in other quarters, at an earlier period. They were, however, quite equal to both the Greek and Latin priesthood of the middle ages.

The first Prester John of Tartary arose with the eleventh century. Whilst merely a king, he lost himself one day in the depths of a forest, where he had been hunting. A celestial being, he said, (or as Moshiem conjectures, a venerable Eremite or Anchorite) found him, and offered to place him in the right road again, if he would promise to confess the name and doctrine of Christ. He agreed to the terms; and on his arrival at home sent for some Christian merchants who were in his camp, to learn from them the way of salvation. Having heard them, he began to worship the Saviour, and sent to Ebediesu, the nearest Nestorian bishop, a request for baptism, coupled with some objections against abstaining from flesh on fast-days. Ebediesu was then the metropolitan of Maru; a name well known to the readers of Asseman. He submitted the whole case to the Nestorian Patriarch, accompanying it with high eulogiums on the character of the prince. The result was, that this Tartar king of the *Kerits* was baptized by the name, John. Missionaries, also, were sent into his kingdom; and soon 200,000 Tartars followed his example.

This "benefit to the Christian religion," as Moshiem calls the conversion of the Keiit-Tartars, explains, I think, the real origin of the title *Prester;* a word which has occasioned "no small stir" amongst the learned. I. C. Scaliger derives it from the Persian word, Presteghani, which signifies *apostolic;* a title very appropriate, and likely to have been given to a king who had set such an example, and who must have used much influence amongst his people in favour of Christianity. I do not know whether Scaliger reasons thus from the etymology he has given. Moshiem does not, although he seems to prefer Scaliger's to all others. Purchas also, although he calls John, indisciiminately, Presbyter, priest, and precious John, prefers Prestigian, as the true etymology, because, he says, "Scaliger is the *Alpha* of learned men in our age."—*Pilgrim,* p. 560. Besides, it will readily occur to any one, that Presbyter or Priest would hardly have been a compliment to a powerful Lama, as well as Chan, in the eleventh century, whatever it was in the fourteenth when Prester John's land was tributary to the Mogul emperor.

The next Apostolic John, of whom we have any authentic account, is probably the one who wrote to the Greek Emperor, Alexius, in the twelfth century. He is said to have warred against Persia, and to have taken Ecbatana itself. He determined also to succour the Christians in Syria and Palestine; or, as Purchas says, "to free Jerusalem from Saracenic servitude;" but, after encamping on the banks of the Tigris, he abandoned the enterprise suddenly, and returned home. Purchas says, "because he could not find a passage" for his army. Moshiem, however, says, on the authority of Gabulens, that "from some unknown cause he was obliged to return."

The last of the great Prester Johns was subdued by Zenghis Chan, and slain by Taianus. The conqueror, however, married the daughter of his victim, although he knew her to be a Christian, as well as to be under the influence of the most popular Nestorian monk in Tartary.

It will throw some light upon the knowledge which the Chinese had of Christians at *this* time, as well as prove the extent of Christianity in Tartary, to state here, that the Emperor of China sent an embassy to congratulate Togrul, the last Prester, on his accession to the title. Then the Emperor addressed him, as the Aunak-Chani, or great Chan of Tartary. Moshiem, Asseman, and La Croix, state this fact. It was also to him, according to Baronius, that Pope Alexander III. wrote from Venice. Whatever exaggerations, therefore, may characterize the name of Prester John, it had then weight enough to win public honours from the Emperor of Germany in his designs against the Pope. Zenghis Chan, also, the conqueror of Asia, evidently deemed it an honour to obtain John's daughter in marriage. All this, I am aware, proves nothing in regard to the purity of Christianity in Tartary then, or the spirituality of its priests and people. Neither, however, could well be lower in Tartary than they were in Europe; and therefore it is saying not a little to the credit of the Nestorians, that they had as much religious influence in the barbarous nations of Asia, as Popes or Patriarchs in Europe. Another thing also is certain, if the visit of the Pope's legate to the last Prester John be a fact,—that Rome obtained no concessions to her supremacy, or her peculiarities, from the Nestorian pontiff.—*Moshiem's Tartary*, p. 28. If the Aunak-Chan listened to Philip as the Pope's physician, he had no ears for him as the Pope's legate, Baronius himself being witness.

Neither the fame nor the family of the last Prester died with him. In the thirteenth century, Marco Polo found a descendant of the family, reigning over the kingdom of the Kerits; and up to the beginning of the fourteenth century, others of them reigned in Tenduch, India, and Cathay. By that time, however, they were hardly Nestorians. John Monte Corvinus says, that he found one of them who " had *been* a Nestorian," and succeeded in converting him to the Catholic faith. Whoever this was, he had not forgotten the ecclesiastical rank of his Fathers altogether; for he took orders from Corvinus, and assisted at mass in his regal robes.

Some of the family of Zenghis Chan also became Christians. His second son, Zagatai, the viceroy of Samarcand, publicly professed the doctrines of the cross, and founded the church of John the baptist on the occasion. Marco Polo says, that the roof of this edifice was supported by one pillar, which rested upon a *sacred* stone taken from the Saracens; and Moshiem thinks that this foundation was the famous "black stone" of Mecca. However this may be, it seems certain that the Saracens managed to remove the stone, without bringing the roof on their heads.

Some of the Emperors of the Mogul dynasty in India, also, retained something more than mere curiosity towards Christianity. Akbar was again and again, "almost persuaded to be a Christian," by the Goa Missionaries. He despised the Koran, but venerated the New Testament, and erected an altar to Jesus Christ in his court. But his *harem*, he said, "tore Jesus Christ from his heart." He added, "in a word, the Gospel is too pure, and my manners too corrupt." The struggles of Akbar between conviction and passion, are best told in *Catrou's* translation of Dr. Manouchi's Memoirs of the Mogul Dynasty. An English edition of this work was published in London, in 1826. It well deserves to be studied by young Missionaries for India: for it was compiled at the court of Delhi and Agra, whilst Signor Manouchi was physician to the imperial family; and thus throws new lights upon Indian Mahometism. Even Tamerlane, it appears, was no Mussulman at heart. He turned his arms against Bajazit, and marched to combat a Mussulman whose sect he hated, in aid of a Christian Prince whose religion he respected.—*Mogul Dyn.* p. 15. Moshiem also admits that Tamerlane, like Zenghis Chan, had no great faith in the Koran, but denies that he had any faith in Christianity.

But although all the descendants of Prester John retained some *leaning* towards Christianity, and many of them continued Christians, none of them seem to have attempted to renew his pontificate. The strangers who visited Rome in 1482, and told the Pope that they were sent by Prester John for a Romish bishop, were evidently from Æthiopia, and not from Tartary. They did not, however, tell a falsehood: for their princes had been long known in Europe by that name, and their land was the first that was searched for that potentate.

Odoricus, of Naon, who visited Tartary in the beginning of the fourteenth century, found the original domains of the Presters reduced to a narrow compass: " I went from Cathay," he says, " into the land of *Pretesoan,* which is but a hundredth part of what was formerly called by that name." He then went into Thibet, and visited the grand Lama, as he is now called. Odoricus, however, calls him the *Abbassi,* and says that the name signifies Pope.— *Act. Sanct.* Vol. I. p. 983.

Thus the Nestorian Church, in Tartary, like its regal pontiffs, gradually passed away. But the Tartars remained. What, then, did they become when they ceased to be Christians? This is a natural question, but it is not easily answered. We know too little of Prester John's land now to be quite sure that all the Tartars became either idolaters or Mahometans. There may be some fragments of Christianity there still, which a future Dr. Buchanan may bring into the same notice which he obtained for the Syrian church. This, however, is not likely. But it is still more unlikely that either such an office as Prester John's, or all the customs of a people who had been Christians for ages, would be allowed to pass away at once, as if they had never been; for, to say nothing of principle, habit and superstition must have upheld some of the old rites and forms of Christianity for a long time, whatever other system the people were led or lashed into. All Druidic rites are not yet banished from our country. Our language will perpetuate the memory of Baal, and the names of the old British gods, unless, like the old style, they should be abolished by act of parliament. To whatever altars, therefore, the Tartars went when they apostatized from Christ, they were sure to carry with them not a few of their old ceremonies, and even some of their Christian sentiments. But that subject will come before us in the chapter on the Lamaism of Tartary.

It is not altogether without reason that I have hinted at the probability of some future Buchanan finding in Tartary some Nestorians yet. "Even in the beginning of the last century, Moshiem says, a man arose in Russian Tartary, claiming to be a descendant of Prester John's, and was soon followed by vast multitudes, who venerated him as a god descended from the skies. "The Russians have not yet," (1730,) he adds, "been able to allay the excitement" created by this impostor.—*Eccl. Tart.,* Note, p. 19.

Thus, long does the power of a regal name last, in connexion with a nominal Christianity. Kings can prolong forms, however unfit they may be to defend or perpetuate the faith. The first kings of a new creed, especially, will leave an example for good or evil, which will live to be old. Both the Tudors and the Stuarts have ecclesiastical influence in England yet. The glorious revolution did not dethrone many of their maxims in the church. It becomes, therefore, a grave question for both Missionaries and the Societies which regulate and sustain them,—and especially for the churches which sustain both,—how far kings, queens, and chiefs, in Africa and the islands of the Pacific, should be identified as such, however pious, with the Christianity of their dominions. The London Missionary Society especially, must now look at this question in all its bearings, because its catholic principles leave its Missionaries at full liberty to introduce the *government* of whatever church they came from;—Independent, Presbyterian, or Episcopalian; and, thus, one may give too much, and another too little, power, somewhere, to the civil magistrate. Contrasts of this kind, happily, have not arisen yet. Our Missions, however, are watched. Professor Lee ascribed their success in the South Sea islands, to the aid of the civil power.—*Lett.* ii. p. 57. Mr. Williams answered as became him, without ceremony or circumlocution, "Now this assertion, it is not founded in truth: I am, moreover, happy in being able to contradict the assertion of Dr. Lee." —*Missionary Enterprises*, p. 190. This is just the style in which to answer the worshippers of " nursing fathers and nursing mothers," when they ascribe conversion to human laws; but Missionaries must have the *spirit* of Williams, if they would continue to be able to say with him, "I can safely affirm that, in no instance has the civil power been employed to propagate Christianity.—*Ibid.* p. 191. It is quite as possible, however, to underrate kings, as to overrate them, even in connexion with Christianity. They owe to it, if they believe it, all their influence, just as any one else does. But how that influence should be employed, except in protecting its peaceable adherents, I frankly confess I cannot tell, although I am quite sure that Christianity scorns all their penal sanctions, however she may admit or welcome some of their laws, in her favour.

CHAPTER XXIII.

THE LAMAISM OF ASIA.

We are so much accustomed to the effrontery of the Pope in claiming almost divine honours, that we rather smile than weep, when we remember that the Dalai Lama, or chief priest of Thibet, is worshipped as God. Thus the moral sense gets blunted, by familiarity with idolatry, except the forms of that idolatry be revolting to *humanity* as well as to reason. We could not otherwise laugh at the *Lamalamalu* of Tartary, whilst we weep because of the grim and grotesque idols of other heathen nations: for the *Saviour* once held that place in Tartary, which the grand Lama now holds in Thibet! Until Zenghis Chan subdued the last Prester John, Christ was, nominally at least, "crowned Lord of all," by the principal Tartar nations. But now, a wretched mortal is worshipped as Lama-Congiu,—as well as Lama-Lamai; or as "the everlasting father of heaven," as well as "priest of priests;" and yet no one thinks the melancholy fact worth mentioning! Like his pretended immortality, it is laughed at; although, to aggravate the enormity, the court of China pays divine honours to him. That court has, indeed, exacted homage from him, and made his godship *Kotu* almost, in Pekin: but they returned him the compliment in 1784, if not since then. He thus falls properly within the circle of my Asiatic researches.

The latest accounts we have of modern Lamaism

are by *Turner* and *Bogle*, who visited Lassa on behalf of the East India Company. They say, "the religious forms of it are so like Popery, that a Capuchin might easily hail a brother in a priest of the Lama." This will remind the reader of poor father Grueber's complaint,—that the devil must have taught the Lama to imitate holy mother Church and his holiness the Pope. Even Andrada was astounded at the resemblance; and wiser men, La Croze and Bayer, studied it deeply. One of the late Princes of Denmark obtained so much information about the ancient manuscripts in the college of the Lama, that he applied to a learned friend of mine to visit it, in order to ascertain their bearings upon Christianity and masonic mysteries.

I thus bespeak attention to the subject, in a half-playful, half-plaintive tone, that I may not be expected to give a formal account of the Lamalamalu, nor be blamed if I fail to account for some of his peculiarities. Moshiem is against my opinion of the modern Tartarian pontiff: and, therefore, I feel no small hesitation in saying that I have an opinion of my own on the subject: for highly as I think of both Bayer and La Croze, I am afraid to lean to their judgment, even when Moshiem deliberately calls it in question. My difficulty, if not my diffidence also, is increased by the consciousness that the works of neither are familiar to general readers; and thus all parties come to be suspected of either credulity or speculation.

It is, however, no fancy, that the Lamalamalu has great influence in China. This is my apology for bringing him into notice in a work on Chinese Missions. Adam Schaal (and I am not ashamed to plead the precedent,) endeavoured to unmask him to the Emperor, during the palmy days of Jesuitism at Pekin: but although the Emperor confessed the Grand Lama to be a grand impostor, he was afraid to treat him as such. The fact is, the Bogdoi Tartars, who conquered China in 1644, are subject to him, and wear his cross. The emperor knew this, and paid him great honours, as well as made him splendid presents.—*Avril's Travels.*

It is owing, most likely, to this intimate connexion between the Lamas and the Emperors (for it was *originally* a connexion with Prester John,) that none of our Missionaries can find in the public annals of China, any reference to the ancient Christianity of China. This absence of all memorials of either Judaism or Christianity, is only what might be expected, when the Tartars conquered China. It was then their policy to suppress and erase whatever belonged to a religion which their fathers had abandoned.

I will now assume, for the sake of inquiry, that the Dalai Lama of Thibet, is, in one sense, a corruption of Prester John; stating known facts, in order to ascertain whether *this* be a fact. I prefer this process to affirming, with Rees' Encyclopædia, that "the Grand Lama is but a corruption of Prester John;" or with Gibbon, that "Prester John evaporated in the monstrous fable of the Lama;" or even with Marsden, in his Notes on Marco Polo, that "nothing is so likely." This is more easily said than proved. It is, however, more probable than the popular legend, to which Gutzlaff refers,—that an apostate Nestorian bishop "had himself deified." —Vol. i. p. 275. I know of no authority for this tradition. I have seen, in some Encyclopædia, I think, a quotation from Albericus, which says, that in 1145, a Nestorian priest usurped the throne of Asiatic Tartary, on the death of Kem-Chan: but it says nothing about his deification. Besides, we have seen that the first Prester John arose with the eleventh century; and that in 1165 a second corresponded with the Greek Emperor. Unless, therefore, Albericus be misquoted, he must have misunderstood the origin of the Presters, and thus of the Grand Lama too. What, then, are the facts of the case?

Now there was so much absolute *heathenism* in the religion of the Grand Lama, in the sixteenth century, that even the Emperor of China, although he revered him, refused to send *Gherardini*, a Christian painter, to take his portrait, "lest the artist should be shocked at the Pontiff's idolatry."—*Jartoux*. Had the Emperor known that the Grand Lama was but a corruption of Prester John, he could not have done the Jesuits a greater service than send them to see what a pope, or a patriarch, might become in course of time. But for the REFORMATION, the Pope of Rome would have been like the Lama of Thibet by this time.

Few chapters in ecclesiastical history are so curious as the transformation (if it be true) of Prester John into the Grand Lama. That chapter, however, has yet to be written in our language. Would that I could tempt some real scholar to write it! I can only throw out desultory hints; and these only in their bearings upon the claims of Asia, and the duty of Missionary Societies.

Anthony Andrada, the Jesuit, who resided some

years in Thibet, found many traces of Christianity in Lamaism. It owns a Trinity, although it worships idols. It maintains that the second person shed his blood for the salvation of mankind; his body being pierced with nails; and yet the *name* of Jesus is not retained. The Grand Lama administers bread and wine, as a sacrament, to his priests. He wears the tonsure, like the Romish priesthood, only larger.

These seem to be fragments of Nestorianism, which survived the conquests of Genghis Khan, and could not be suppressed by Budhuism. The Tartars took no more of the Indian heathenism than suited them. They embraced transmigration, and eat *raw* beef as usual! Even their priests, when they are in Pekin, feast and dress, *Gerbillon* says, like the Chinese.

La Croze, after examining the prayers of Lamaism,—some of which he has translated,—was of opinion that many of the best petitions are fragments of the ancient Christian liturgy of great Tartary, although the system is "now direct heathenism." And certainly some of the petitions are remarakable. For example,—"let our prayer be to God! Thou who art raised above all creatures, give us wisdom. Thou, true Lord, be merciful, and bless me, as thou hast promised. Send my guardian Angel at every hour, every day. Be ever with me: never withdraw thyself. Send, Lord, according to thy *promise*, thy Angel to our whole assembly. May the blessing promised to God's assembly be upon me. May the blessing of the *strengthening* Angel be upon me. May my prayer overflow and diffuse like water in spring!" This is not like heathenism. The *adorations*, however, are in the true "unintelligible sublime" of India, as Locker calls them.

Gutzlaff, as might be expected, heard enough of the Grand Lama in China, to awaken his curiosity; but found nothing to gratify it. "Is the Dalai Lama," he exclaims, "the fabulous or real Prester John of ancient times? Or is all this affinity only accidental?" This uncertainty about Prester John embarrassed the inquiries of Gutzlaff: otherwise, he was in the right track, when he suspected that the Shamanist Budhuists, when they fled beyond the Himalaya, derived some of their rites from the "depraved Nestorians of central Asia."—*China Opened*, Vol. i. p. 275. Moshiem himself, traces Lamaism to the Sammanœ, and labours to resolve it all into Budhuism. "Nothing is more certain," he says, "than that it is the same system as that of the Bonzes of China," Siam and Japan. There, however, the system has no striking features of real Christianity in it, and was never suspected of deriving any thing from corrupt Nestorianism. Only in Tartary has it any such vestiges of positive Christianity. It is a serious matter, however, to differ with Moshiem. He seldom speaks strongly, without strong reasons; and, on this subject, his researches were extraordinary. Still, it is the fact, that Lamaism is the only form of Budhuism which, by his own acknowledgment, presents any thing that ever any one has suspected of a real Christian origin. So far this is an anomaly. Bayer and La Croze felt it to be so; and Moshiem himself was not a little *afraid* to differ with them.

We have seen, in the former chapter, that whatever the Tartars became after they ceased to be Christians, they were sure to carry to their new altars some of their old rites, and thus to give a *mixed* character to the idolatry they embraced. Moshiem requires us to recognise this principle of our common nature, when he is explaining the corruptions of Christianity in primitive times. These, he says, were inevitable when the Schools of Philosophy gave converts to the church. This is true. It is, however, equally true, that idolatry would be somewhat refined, if not a little Christianized also, when a church gave converts to heathenism. Moshiem ought, therefore, to have given Lamaism the benefit of his own general principles, especially as he found nothing else in Asia bearing such marks of Christianity.

Besides, it is both unnatural and unprecedented, that a great religious power should be allowed to pass away from one system, without some bold man trying to revive it on behalf of another system. Prester John's rank was just as likely to be appropriated by the high priest of the Shammanist Budhuists, in Tartary, as the Pope's authority in England was by Henry VIII.

We thus obtain a natural clue to the labyrinth of Lamaism. This form of Budhuism was in Tartary, as Moshiem says, long before Prester John arose. But we never hear of it during the dynasty of the Presters. We hear of five Mahometan kings which were subject to John; but of no Shammanist. The sect must, therefore, have either remained independent, or too small to be noticed, whilst the Presteral Church was dominant: and in either case, its chief priest was sure to grasp at power whenever an opportunity occurred. An opportunity did offer itself when that church was expiring. Accordingly, Odoricus, in the beginning of the fourteenth century, found the chief priest of idolatry reigning over the Thibet portion of Prester John's land, under the name of the *Abbassi.* Now, to say nothing of the resemblance this name bears to the title of the Ethiopic Prester John, (although the coincidence is curious)—Odoricus says that it signifies Pope, and that this priest was " head of all idolaters." Whatever, therefore, be the precise meaning of the name, Lama, or more properly the name, *Lamalamalu,* it was not the first name assumed by the pontiff of idolatry in Thibet. At least, it was not the only name. See *Purchas,* p. 363. The modern historians of China, following De Guignes, can hardly be blamed for saying, that the Chinese Emperor, Ming-ti, sent to "the Grand Lama, at Lassa," when the prediction of Confucius—that "the Holy One would be found in the west" was supposed, in A. D. 65, to be fulfilled. One name is as good as another for the high priest of Lassa, whilst it is merely a name. I can find no evidence, however that this was the original name of the pontiff of Fo or Budh. It is not the name of his priests in India, nor is a cross their chief badge. Besides, it is only the name of the spiritual Prince of the country. The title of the temporal Prince is "Deva."—*Avril's Travels.*

My reader will now sympathize with old *Purchas,* in calling these questions "misty mysteries," and perhaps apply to me the older proverb, "Catch a Tartar if you can." I myself feel with Purchas, that "it is religion in *us* to suspend our discourse of this religion," as soon as possible.—*Pilgrimage,* p. 359.

What, then, seems to be the fact on this subject? Now, taking all things into the account, it appears to me that the *first* Prester John, before he became a Christian, had been the LAMA of the Shammanist Budhuists in his own territory; and that their Lama, when he saw the *last* Prester extinct, availed himself of the fall of the Christian dynasty, to take measures for the restoration of the idolatry which the first Prester had abandoned. This would naturally lead the *aspirant* to make all the concessions and approximations he could, to the most popular Christian superstitions of the Tartarian Church; that thus he might conciliate its adherents to Budhuism, as well as secure his own pontificate; for he could hardly look for John's power, apart from all John's ritual.

Marsden, in his notes on Marco Polo, has assumed part of this theory, in order to account for the first Tartar Chan taking the title, Prester John, at his baptism; and not without reason; for it was customary amongst both the nobility and the Chans to combine the priestly office with the civil, or to be Lamas as well as chiefs. This is the case still in Tartary, and one reason why the Emperor of China pays so much deference to the Grand Lama. The first John was not likely, therefore, to lay aside his *sacred* rank, when he became a Christian; nor the Nestorians to wish him to cease from being both priest and king; and thus he was baptized Prester, or apostolic. This accounts, also, for the influence he had at once over 200,000 of his subjects, who followed his example in embracing Christianity at once. It was their high priest, as much as their king, they obeyed and copied. Accordingly, whilst their kings remained Presters, the Tartars, to a great extent, remained Christians. When, however, Christianity lost the last Nestorian prince, and Zenghis Chan created a vantage ground for idolatry to rally upon, it was as easy as it was natural for the old Budhuist party to deify their high priest, as well as to accommodate his ritual somewhat to the prejudices of the Christians. Gutzlaff thinks that the Budhuists of Thibet "borrowed many ceremonies from the Nestorians," even in the seventh century.—*China Opened*, Vol. ii. p. 218. In fact, Budhuism has been a *plastic* system every where, out of India. Gutzlaff says, that the Chinese moulded it into a shape to suit themselves; and it is evident from Xavier's discussions with the Japanese, that they had adopted the Chinese version of it. "Go to China," the Bonzes said; "we got our religion from them, and cannot change until you bring them under the yoke of Christ."—*Turselline's Life of Xavier*. La Loubere maintains that he could find no trace of "a Divinity" in Siamese Budhuism.—*Asiat. Res.* Vol. viii. p. 400. Thus it was just as likely to accommodate itself to such Christianity as prevailed under the last Prester, as to the taste of China and Japan. In like manner, the deification of the Grand Lama is no anomaly in that system. Budh, or Fo, is merely a *Sanaam*, or saint, who appeared from time to time as a reformer, and disappears in the supreme felicity of *Nurupan*. There is a remarkable paper on this subject in vol. ii. of the Bombay Transactions.

Now, we can account for the remarkable specimens of Lamaic *prayers*, which La Croze translated, and deemed parts of an ancient Christian liturgy, as well as for all the Popery which Grueber blamed the devil for teaching at Lassa.

Lamaism, however, is still at Lassa, and is a formidable enemy to Christianity in China,—whatever may be thought of any man's theory of its origin. Moshiem seems wrong, and no one may be right, as to the rise and progress of this idolatry: but it reigns in Tartary, and has sway in China; and thus it has to be *fought* some day by our Missionaries. Both Missionaries and the churches, therefore, ought to know something of this "mystery of iniquity," that they may be prepared for the contest with it. It is an influential form of evil in China, whether they think so or not. The Jesuits, who were no mean judges of either human nature, or national prejudices, dreaded the influence of the Lama, quite as much as that of Confucius. Verbiest reckoned it "a kind of miracle," that the influence of the Lama over the Queen-mother at Pekin, did not defeat his own influence with the Emperor. Her priests, he says, assured her that Lamaism had no bitterer enemies than the Christians. The Emperor himself could not overcome her repugnance to Verbiest, when he made him his own companion in a visit to Tartary. "You are not *expected* to pay your court to the Queen," was the excuse of the monarch for excluding the priest. The result of Verbiest's observation in western Tartary was, that Christianity would not easily prevail whilst the Lamas stood.—*Travels of the Jesuits*, Vol. ii. p. 146.

CHAPTER XXIV.

A VOICE FROM THE TOMBS OF MORRISON AND MILNE, TO THE SCHOOLS OF THE PROPHETS.

It is not by accident, nor by human concert, that there should thus cross your path, just as you are going to "*serve at the altar,*" challengers for China and the East, who interpose a flaming sword in your way, until you judge righteous judgment between the claims of Home and Foreign service. "*This is the Lord's doing,*" and, therefore, it ought to be both marvellous and providential in your eyes: especially as the Altar at which you are about to consecrate yourselves is, itself, consecrated to the service of the world at large, and destined to enlighten all the dark places of the earth.

Not thus were Latimer and Knox, Watts and Doddridge, arrested and adjured, by loud voices from the living and the dead, when they began to ponder their ordination vows, and compare the claims of destitute churches. A destitute world was not thus forced upon their attention, whilst they were judging of the path of duty. Their prayerful inquiry, "Lord, what wouldst thou have me to do?" if it glanced at all beyond the land of their fathers, could have no reference to "*the land of Sinim,*" or to the shores of *Ophir*. No star had arisen in the east then, to reveal its darkness, or to guide wise men to its help. The Orient was almost unknown, and altogether unpitied by Protestantism. But now,

> "The world is all before *you*,
> Where to choose."

Neither the Reformers nor the Puritans had any choice, but amongst the British vineyards. They were "shut up" to Home, because shut out from all the world besides, except as exiles.

This insulated position must, of course, have greatly simplified both their deliberations and prayers, whilst searching for the path of duty. All the lamps of Providence shone then upon

> "A little spot enclosed by grace,
> Out of the world's vast wilderness."

You cannot ascertain the path of duty so soon or easily now. It is both more wide and more winding than in the days of old; and must be examined under all the new lights which Providence has been kindling and accumulating around the church.

Do you regret this? Would you prefer a state of things at home or abroad, in which you could lay your hand on the Altar, and swear ministerial allegiance to Christ, without one *Missionary* feeling or recollection? Heaven would not register such vows, now that the whole earth is crying out for help! The groans of creation would prevent your vows from becoming a memorial before God, if they breathed no sympathy with the bondage of creation. Take care what you vow, whilst voices from all nations are thus ascending to the throne of God, and thundering around the church! The cry "*Come over and help us*," is gone forth upon the four winds of heaven, and it cannot be stopped nor outspoken by any claim or cries of home affairs. All the interests of the church are now at stake, upon the evangelization of the world. She must go *back* and go *down* in all her influence, if she do not go " *into* all nations," and preach the gospel. She must act out her commission now, or vacate her claims: for the compulsory principal dare not, and the voluntary principal will not, sustain her, *under any form*, apart from action and enterprise. She must set herself to " save others," if she would save herself!

You have not " fallen on evil times," (whatever church you belong to,) because you cannot take your place at the Altar so easily as your fathers did. The times are, indeed, past, when it was enough, in order to prove a *call* to the work of the Ministry, to be able and willing to preach the gospel any where at home. That was sufficient proof of being " *called of God as was Aaron*," whilst God had not thrown open the world to the church: but it is not enough, now that great and effectual doors are opened in all nations, and outstretched hands and streaming eyes are entreating help. This is as much and as certainly the voice of Providence, as any opening in, or invitations from, the British Churches. It is, therefore, not Providence at large, but a part of the shadow of it, that you are watching, if you are weighing only calls and prospects at home. There is, indeed, much Providence in them. Yea, it may be *your* imperative duty to stay at home, just because so many are wanted to go abroad. So far as you are individually concerned, there may be nothing personally providential in all the aspects or appeals of the Heathen world. They cannot regard all the sons of the Prophets; and, therefore, they may have no direct bearings upon you. They do bear, however, directly upon some, yea, upon many; and you may be *one* of the "chosen vessels" whose duty it is to bear the name of Christ "far hence among the Gentiles." It is, therefore, at your peril to go up to the Altar as a Minister until you have fairly and fully met the question,—What is my duty in this day of Missions? You often and honestly say to God, when you think of going to his Altar to take his vows upon you, "*If thy presence go not with me, carry me not up.*" You cannot bear the awful idea of running unsent, or of studying unaided, or of labouring unblessed by God. No wonder! You will have to review through all eternity your ministerial choice and career. Judge, therefore, now, whether the Divine Presence is *likely* to "go with" you at home, whilst the Divine Command is calling for so many to go abroad?

Again I say, it may not be your duty to quit your native shores: it is, however, your immediate duty to look this question fully in the face. It will force itself upon you before you die; and when you are dying, it will flash out upon your spirit, as the forerunner of all the audits of your stewardship. At that solemn moment, next to the humble consciousness of being "in Christ," nothing will be more soothing than the conviction of having been in your *proper* place; or at least of having done all in your power to ascertain the will of God, as to your sphere.

Have you, then, done so? Will you do so now, "without partiality, and without hypocrisy?" Any one may skirt the confines of Omniscience, or bear the question within the outer "rings" of its heart-searching light, without ascertaining either the will of God, or the real bias of his own will. This is but complimenting Omniscience; not consulting it. You cannot be impartial or sincere, unless you penetrate to the very farthest and brightest point, at which the "LIGHT FULL OF GLORY" is accessible. Place yourself in the full blaze of divine scrutiny, if you would be successful or honest. There,—lay open your whole soul, and the whole case of the heathen world; and keep both open, until you can appeal to him who knoweth all things, that you have no will of your own. "Dwell in" "this *secret place of the Most High*," until you can come out of it in a spirit which could meekly go before the universe, or up to the eternal throne, to avow its motives.

Are you afraid of this process? Do you suspect that it would overturn the anticipated fabric of your ministerial happiness? Is there any *place* or *person*, for whose sake you shrink from coming to the light thus fully? "If your heart condemn you, God is greater than your heart, and knoweth all things." Besides, he *disposeth* all things, as well as knoweth them: and, therefore, whatever you are willing to give up, for his service, he can take away. Do not, then, peril your fondest wishes, by consulting them first or chiefly.

Perhaps you are already so placed and pledged, that it seems too late now to reverse your choice, and thus useless to review it in the orb of Omniscience. It cannot, you think, be honourably altered; and, therefore, it should not be unsettled. You did not mean ill when you made it, and as it is not bad in itself, you hope it may turn out well in the end.

This is a delicate subject: but still it is not so difficult as it seems. Engagements are, indeed, solemn things, and should be held sacred. To revise them is not, however, to violate them. In this case, it may confirm them: for it is not yet certain that you are called or qualified to go abroad. Or if you strongly *suspect* that your path of duty would have lain there, had not these engagements shut you out from it, why should not the reasons of this suspicion, if fully gone into, weigh as much with others as with yourself? If there be reasons which would alter your choice, were you free to yield to them, is it not just as likely they would sway another? At all events, it is your duty to submit them to every one concerned in your movements. Hush not up, hurry not over, a question, which, if not honestly dealt with now, may, embarrass, if not imbitter, your ministerial life through all its stages.

If, however, you be quite free from all pledges to any place or person; and thus at full liberty to weigh, in the balance of the sanctuary, the comparative claims of China and the churches, I congratulate you, even if you have no leaning towards foreign service yet. I do not appeal to you, assuming that you have either a Missionary spirit or bias already. If, indeed, you have, so much the better: but still, all that I want is, to obtain from you a fair hearing to foreign claims. Let them make their own impression, and produce their legitimate effect upon your spirit, as it is. Real Missionary spirit is the fruit of Missionary study. A sudden flash of zeal, or flow of sympathy for the Heathen, is no test of call or qualification to teach them, now that our Societies know what there is to do and endure abroad. *Mind* is wanted, as well as emotion: *physical* strength as well as devotional feeling. And in regard to China and the East, the *order* of mind most wanted there, is not to be called forth by mere spirit-stirring appeals, however holy or heroic. Sober facts and solid arguments, can alone draw out the *kind* of men suited to these spheres. The Chinese are not a barbarous people, except so far as Europeans and Americans brutalize them by opium. Even in India, it is the shrewdness and sensuality, more than the sanguinary horrors of Hindooism and Budhuism, that are to be grappled with now. Suttees are vanishing; but subtleties are increasing in number and ingenuity. Idols are at a discount; but skepticism bears a high premium. Education is popular; but it is prized only for selfish reasons. Men of mere *feeling*, however ardent, are not adapted to this state of things. Any man can weep at a Pujah, or thrill with horror at a funeral pile, or hang his harp upon the willows of the Ganges and the Bhurampooter, whilst their waters and alligators are glutted with suicidal sacrifices, and their eagles and vultures with infant victims: but he must be a reasoning, a resolute, a prudent, as well as a holy man, who can gauge the *springs* of these enormities, and grapple with the *motives* of these infatuations. So also in China: there is neither such craft or cruelty, such pomp or sensuality, in their idolatry itself, as to stir up the spirit to indignation or horror. There is enough to *wind up* a great and good spirit to all the heights of solemn sympathy and patient enterprise; but nothing to enlist sentiment, or to enliven curiosity. Countless numbers, and cold delusions, and universal self-conceit, and heartless formality, make up "the image and superscription" of China: and, therefore, his eye must be far-reaching and keenly scrutinizing, as well as "single," who can read the natural character, so as to discover its valuable points, and devise lines of practical operation for its improvement.

The man also, who sees no glory in the power of the press to move China; or no sublime efficiency in the calm and dew-like descent of Bibles and Tracts on "the land of Sinim;" or no moral grandeur in directing and gratifying the national taste for reading; is not the man for China. Yea, if his spirit cannot be stirred in all its depths, and fixed at all its heights, by the prospect of watching the mighty chaos of the Chinese mind, just in order to fathom its everlasting channels, and to discover its *ground stream*, that thus he may open a passage for future Missionaries, and pave the way for the moving of the Spirit of God upon the face of the dark waters, he is not the man for China. Yea, unless he can discern unspeakable glory in the *foundation stone* of the spiritual temple, which Morrison and Milne, as "wise master builders," laid, and thus can shout, "Grace, grace unto it," as the sure pledge and prelude of the *top stone* being brought forth with the shoutings of the universe, he is not the man for China. He must, too, be able and willing to work *under ground* there, who would work well. Not that he will be unseen or unnoticed. Both the church and world will have their eyes upon him: the former in admiration and hope; the latter in curiosity and surprise. No name will be more waited for or welcomed than his, at the boards of Missions and on the platforms of meetings, when glad news come from far countries. Labourers in China will soon be the great *land-marks* of the Bible Societies, of both the old and the new world. And on no spot, more especially than on that where Bible Missionaries are laying the foundation of

Christian Churches, will angels watch, or Providence smile. He is not "a wise master builder" whom this cannot both inspire and satisfy. The work is under ground, but its reward is on high: and all that is now doing above ground by others, in other places, will be improved by it, and identified with it, for ever.

Dr. Morrison understood this; and it sustained him, under all the Herculean labour of translation and compilation: under all the solitude and sorrow occasioned by bereavements: under all the annoying restrictions of a jealous Government, and a monopolizing Factory: and, even, under all the mortifications which arose, when some of his favourite plans were thwarted or ill sustained. Yea, he so understood both his work and his reward, that he *returned* to pursue them, after seeing that the British Churches had no sympathy with him, except as the translator of the Scriptures into the Chinese. Whatever else he had lived and laboured for in China, they would hardly look at.

He came to them with "*the burden of China*" pressing upon his spirit and absorbing all his thoughts; and thus reckoned that he had only to mention its countless millions and his own loneliness, in order to bring all the Churches to the help of the Lord against the mighty; but no man appreciated or understood his solemn appeal, in its *intended* sense. It was interpreted as a mere call for a COLLEGE! Even as that, it was all but confounded with certain Indian speculations, by the generality. He saw all this, and keenly felt it all: but it never unsettled his purpose. It dimmed his eye, and made him "dumb with silence;" but it did not alienate his heart from China or Britain.

You will now ask, how all this bears upon my argument! Thus:—all this *died* with Dr. Morrison! It cannot happen again. The danger is on the other side now. Another Morison would be almost idolized. See how public hope and sympathy hang upon his son! He is understood, and appreciated, and responded to, at once and universally. Could Mr. Morrison only say, that China Proper was "open," he might command the Churches and pick the Colleges of both Britain and America.

I know what I am about in thus dealing with facts: see to it—that you deal as honestly with them. Would that I could *act* upon them, as freely as I argue from them! But, alas, it is too late to think of acting: I can do nothing but write. You, however, can do more.

In all this, I have not forgotten the question, "Is China open to the Gospel?" nor the command, "Open China." China Proper is not open: but around it, there is free access to at least *fifty* millions of Chinese, who keep up a regular intercourse with it. This door has been open for many years: and if we refuse to enter it, why should Providence open others? In fact, it is well that others are not yet opened: for who is fit to enter them? Consider this. The existing state of things in that empire is just what it ought to be, whilst the existing state of things in the churches remains what it is. God is "the God of order, not of confusion;" and, therefore, He will not throw open such an empire, until he can throw into it efficient agents, in something like sufficient numbers. The good shepherd "gently leads those that be with young;" and, therefore, he will not task nor tax his churches beyond their ability. The unwilling and the unwise may insist on China being open to the Gospel, *before* they open their hearts or hands to China: but Providence is not thus unreasonable or unkind. He has too much regard even for their comfort, and too much pity even for their weakness, to bring on a demand upon their families or property, which would either impoverish them, or tempt them to desert his cause entirely. He knows such men too well, and loves better men too much, to hurry on a crisis which would be fatal to the half-hearted, and overwhelming to the simple. He will stir up no crusade for China, which, like that for Palestine, would drain the resources or the strength of the British churches. Accordingly, Providence is making no demand, at present, beyond their ability. They are able to occupy posts of observation and action, all around China. They are able to furnish and sustain as many agents as there are stations. They are, also, willing, waiting, yea, longing, to be led out to the help of the Lord in "these quarters." Already they are whispering his own question, "who will go for us?" and, ere long, they will thunder it, in a voice which will make " *the posts of the doors* " of all COLLEGES " *move!*"

He must have something more of ISAIAH in him than the evangelical spirit of that Prophet, who is warranted to say at once, in answer to this question, " *Here am I, send me.*" In general, they are not the fittest to go, who are the *first* to offer. An immediate answer to a rousing or melting appeal on behalf of China or India, ought not to be accepted or given, unless it be the explosion of a " secret fire," which has been long pent up in the spirit, and only waiting for an opportunity to explode. Then, it cannot be too promptly given, nor too readily accepted. Morrison responded at once to the appeal of Bogue, when Hardcastle appealed to the Mission College at Gosport, on behalf of China. He did right. His promptitude was prudence of the highest order. His spirit and the Society's purpose were evidently made for each other, like Adam and Eve; and, therefore, the moment they met, "they kissed each other." China, and the first thing that could be done there, (the translation of the Scriptures,) formed the precise element which his spirit, although unable to define it to itself, had long been "feeling after," with all the steadiness of an instinct, and all the cravings of a latent taste: and, therefore, whilst he moved into that element at once, he did so with as much deliberation as delight. It had been the vision of years, and the object of all his prayers, although he could not *name* it, until it was brought before him as a reality. Then, "*Adam called his wife's name Eve.*"

Is there any great object, beyond the Home Ministry, which thus, vision-like, floats around, or flashes across your spirit; disturbing or diverting it, whenever it tries to settle under any vine or fig tree in the British vineyard? Do you often feel as if any home sphere would, like the cave in Horeb, expose you to the question put to Elijah,—"What doest thou here?" This may be a "heavenly vision," although yet dim and undefined. Deem it not so, however,—if your health be delicate, or your nerves weak, or your spirits constitutionally low, or your tact for acquiring languages small, or your fear of dangers great. It is not "heavenly," in the sense of a call to go abroad, if your physical or mental powers be but questionably adapted to foreign labour. It is, however, heavenly in a sublime sense: for God is thus moulding your spirit to the love and espousal of the Missionary cause now, that, when you begin your ministry, and whilst you continue it, you may sustain that cause by your advocacy, and extend it by your example, at home. And, next to a high tone of spiritual mindedness, you can carry nothing more healthy into your future sphere, than the " holy fire " of Missionary zeal. Your flock, wherever it be, will certainly quarrel or decline, unless you fill their hearts and hands with as much of God's work at home and abroad, as they can hold. He must now "feed swine," (I mean Antinomians,) who will not make the sheep, and the lambs too, *useful* to the great shepherd. Let it be seen, wherever you go, that " *it was in thine heart* " to build a house unto the Lord, " not upon another man's foundation." David was not permitted to build the Temple; but no man contributed more to its erection than he did. His property or influence might be traced, in splendid forms, from its foundation to its top stone, and from the holy of holies to the court of the Gentiles. Thus any of you can make up, at home, for what you cannot do abroad. But you are not all placed thus. Some of you are fit to go, and free to go. Both your frame and your aspect bear the stamp of enterprise. Only mark how they thrill to the thrilling cry of Morrison, in his "*parting memorial:*" "Alas, my brethren, how long shall the millions of eastern Asia inherit lies!"

"To every tone, with tender heat,
 Your heart-strings vibrate, and your pulses beat."

Who then, will be baptized for the dead? Remember; they are emphatically "the MIGHTY dead:" so mighty, that a double portion of the spirit of Morrison and Milne is sure to rest upon their first successors; and if the tomb of Xavier, on the Island of Sancian, could call forth the flower of the Papacy to baptism for the dead, shall the tombs of the first Protestant Missionaries, at Macao, appeal in vain to Protestant Colleges? God forbid!

Be not afraid of the Chinese language. It is, indeed, peculiar, even unique; but it is also fascinating. The Hieroglyphics are not all arbitrary. What can be finer than the symbol of friendship?—*two pearls of equal size and purity;* showing how rare and valuable it is. Besides, the language was acquired by many, even before Dr. Morrison published his Dictionary. Hear what his son says on this subject:—

"It cannot be learned in a day, but demands long and attentive study. I say not this to discourage any one: for the number of those (not by any means men of great natural abilities or quickness of parts) who have attained a useful knowledge of the language, is a sufficient guarantee for the practicability of acquiring it." Add to this fact, the experience of the Popish Missionaries. They never failed to master the language. They went out young, and well-grounded in the classics, and making their purpose their fate; and they were soon able to speak in courts or cottages. So may you. It is not desirable, however, that *all* who go to China should contemplate the study of its *classics,* to any great extent. The majority ought, certainly, to prepare themselves to wield, with ease and power, the mighty energies and facilities of the press: but some ought to set their hearts quite as resolutely upon acquiring the vernacular, with an express view to *preaching* the Gospel. Indeed, were I not too old and infirm to be worth the expense of being sent out, I, for one, (notwithstanding all my partialities to the pen), should feel it to be my duty to become a scholar in one of the Chinese day-schools for boys, that I might obtain just the same instruction which the natives give to their children. I certainly could learn what their children are taught: and that, with what I could acquire by frequent and friendly intercourse with the people, would soon enable me to tell them "the wonderful works of God, in their own tongue." I throw out this hint, because some of you may be hindered by the suspicion, that great proficiency in the written language of China is essential to usefulness. But this, although the general rule, admits of exceptions. Indeed, exceptions ought to be forced and fastened upon that general rule: for it is itself an *exception* to the general rule of Scripture. Preaching the Gospel is God's ordinance; and, therefore, no present peculiarity of China can be safely allowed to set aside preaching. All other methods of doing good "are lawful," yea, obligatory, whilst this is impracticable: but to make this practicable, ought to be the grand aim of all preliminary operations.

And now, beloved young friends! who will be baptized for the dead? The eyes of the Churches—of the Societies—of the Chinese—of the World, are upon your ranks. The eye of Omniscience is upon all your hearts! Shall God have to say, "I beheld, and there was no man to answer," when I asked, "Who will go for us?" What, no man among all the sons of the prophets! It may not, must not, cannot be, that prophets should not be found for China! Angels wait for your decision. The souls under the altar chide your delay. Hell will say, "Aha; so would we have it;" if you all refuse.

Redeem the character of Protestantism: for, hitherto, Popish Colleges have furnished most Missionaries for China.

CHAPTER XXV.

THE SYRIAN CHURCHES IN INDIA.

"INDIA," says old Turselline, in his life of Xavier, "is a country of Asia, somewhat in proportion to a man's *tongue;* being almost twice as long as broad;"—"and there be very certain proofs, that St. Thomas, the apostle, not only preached there, but also watered the same with his blood, bringing very many therein to the *faith* of Christ." The "certain proofs," Turselline leaves his readers to find out as they can. Other Jesuits are more accommodating. Father Bohurs specifies the little mount near Meliapore, and the *grot* too, where St. Thomas retired to pray, and where the spear of a Brahmin slew him. This is not all. There is a marble tablet in one of the chapels, he says, which was found by the Portuguese, when digging up the ruins of the old city, "whereon is a cross with characters graved round about it, which declare that St. Thomas came to Meliapore with a palmer's staff in his hand, built a Church there, and won the kings of Malabar, Coromandel and Pandi, with many other nations, to the law he preached. The marble having on it divers stains of blood, the common opinion is, that he suffered martyrdom upon it. But however that may be—the marble was placed on the altar when the chapel was built; and the cross distilled some drops of blood in the sight of all the people, the first time that a solemn mass was said there; which also happened many times in the following years, on the day when St. Thomas' martyrdom is celebrated."—*Bohur's Xavier.* No wonder Protestants should be as "slow of heart to believe" any thing whatever about Thomas having been in India, as Thomas himself was in believing the resurrection. Traditions which have such trash grafted upon them, may well disgust any sane mind. "A sound mind," however, will not overlook the fact, that the Indian tradition about Thomas must have been both rife and popular at Meliapore, before the Portuguese would have dared to graft such pretences upon the weight of his name. They had, however, secular as well as ecclesiastical reasons for *overdoing* the Syrians, in venerating the apostle. There were a hundred and ten Syrian Churches in Malabar then; and although the clergy no longer ranked next to the Nairs, or nobles, some of the laity along the coast were the principal merchants of the country; and the Portuguese wanted to monopolize the influence of both, if not to supersede them entirely. Besides, it became a point of honour with Rome, to subjugate the

Syrians of India to her yoke. The Pope would have allowed the mass to be said in Syriac, at Travancore, Dr. Buchanan says, if they would have owned the supremacy of Rome. And strange as this seems, there must be some truth in it; for the Doctor himself once heard a priest perform mass in both Syriac and Latin. Wrede, a distinguished writer in the Asiatic Researches, vol. vii. p. 373, states that one of their bishops was created a cardinal at Rome, in 1567. He died, however, just after this disgrace.

These concessions to this ancient church, as well as the coercions employed to subdue her, prove that his holiness thought she would be "a *feather* in the cap" of his triple crown. Now, although I do not admire his policy towards the Syrians, in any of its forms, I do both wonder and regret that only the Missionaries of the church of England, in our times, have taken any deep interest in them. I do not recollect to have ever heard or read any kindling appeal on their behalf, or any kind notice of them, by the Missionaries of other societies, until my friend Mr. Campbell, of Bangalore, in his noble work on "British India," just published, devoted a chapter to them. This is not as it should be: for, in one sense, that church is emphatically " a *lily* amongst the thorns." A torn and tarnished lily, I readily grant; which breathes but little of the fragrance of " the Lily of the valley." But still, it bears His name, and was torn for his sake. No other lily, planted in Asia by primitive hands, has lasted so long amidst the thorns of idolatry, or suffered so much. Although, therefore, I would not sentimentalize over her antiquity, and have no sympathy whatever with her, because of her approximations to *patristic* episcopacy,

I do love her, and wish to see her loved, "for the truth's sake," which has dwelt in her so long. What Henry Martyn calls "the devil with *four* faces"—(or Heathenism, Mahometanism, Popery and Infidelity)—has not been able to make the Syrian church deny the name of Christ. In a tithe of the time, during which she has kept the faith; and with none of her temptations to abandon it, the English Presbyterians became Socinians, and the Prester Tartars Lamaists. I do not wonder, therefore, whoever else does so, that Dr. Buchanan called the boundaries of the Syrian churches in Malabar, "the delectable mountains." John Bunyan would not have objected to this application of his graphic phrase. It was a noble scene on one of these mountains, when Buchanan challenged a comparison between his Syriac Testament, and the ancient copy from Antioch, which had been preserved so long at Angamalee! Well might Buchanan exclaim, when he saw the prospect of giving currency to the word of God in its first Indian sphere,—"God led me from *Cambuslang*." He evidently thought of *Whitefield*, at this hallowed moment. And no wonder. Had Whitefield never been at Cambuslang, Buchanan, humanly speaking, might never have been in Malabar. It was the memory of Cambuslang Christians which inspired his memorable saying, "I wish to be a pure *Namboory* (of high caste) amongst Christians."

We want a little of Buchanan's sympathy with the Syrian church. It would do her good, as well as ourselves. She is now complimented, if not flattered, at the expense of purer churches; and thus in danger of attaching more importance to her nominal apostolicity, than to vital godliness: for what can she think when she sees or hears of Protestant Missionaries and their churches, who, to say the least, are quite equal in piety and talents to their diocesan brethren, but are treated as schismatics, while she is hailed as "a little sister?" She has most likely forgotten that Aghæus, "the *silk weaver*," as the Syrian churches call him, was one of her founders: and thus she is likely to undervalue Missionaries who have been mechanics, when she hears them spoken of as uneducated "pretenders to holy orders." The only influence which this slander can have upon her priesthood, must be to divert their attention from that personal Holiness, without which no man has any right "to bear the vessels of the Lord," to that conventional holiness which any man may inherit or buy; and which, as an *heir-loom*, they inherit through a longer and purer channel than the British hierarchy can pretend to. One of the ornaments of that hierarchy, the Bishop of Calcutta, has just said of them, "How readily should we acknowledge what is good in the Syrian churches,—without requiring of them conformity to our liturgical worship, or our western notions?" This is a noble sentiment, and worthy of Dr. Wilson's best days: but whilst churches equal to his own in all moral goodness, and immeasurably superior to the Syrian in both faith and practice, are denied the benefit of his maxims, the Syrian Churches cannot become what his piety wishes them to be. For the very preference thus given to her, were it no reflection upon *her* betters, or *his* equals in piety, must make orders appear to her of more importance than ministerial character or qualifications. That others, therefore, may tell her, with equal sympathy and kindness,—that her ministers "must be born again of the Spirit," before they can be ministers sent of God,—I will remind the friends of Missions to India of the history of the Syrian Church, since Europe knew of her existence.

Our own Alfred must have known something of them; for he sent an embassy to the shrine of St. Thomas. But the first news of the Syrian Churches of India was brought to Europe by Pedralvares Cabral, a Portuguese adventurer, who had landed at Cranganor, in 1500. He met with several of the Christians of St. Thomas in that part, and even prevailed on two of them to accompany him to Lisbon. They were brothers; Matthias and Joseph. The former soon died in Lisbon. Joseph, however, visited Rome and Venice, and gave an account of the Church of Malabar, which was published in Latin. This tract is printed at the end of "Fasciculis Temporum."

Vasco da Gama was the next negotiator with this Church. On his arrival at Cochin, in 1502, as the admiral of a Portuguese fleet, a deputation of native Christians waited upon him, begging to be protected from the native princes, "because his master was a Christian king." Dr. Geddes says, they presented the admiral with the sceptre of one of their own ancient Christian princes, as a token of homage to the King of Portugal: but the Dr. doubts if they ever had such princes in Malabar. "It rests," he says, "on no very good grounds, so far as I can perceive." The fact, however, is unqualifiedly asserted in the appendix of the seventeenth Report of the Church Missionary Society. "They had kings of their own, from 920, until the legal power passed over to the infidel kings of Odiamper." They were, however, under subjection to the King of Cochin, when the Portuguese found them. Dr. Pearson says, " The Syrian clergy ranked next to the *Nairs*, or nobles of the country."—*Swartz's Life.*

Vasco da Gama could only give the oppressed natives fair words, and commend them to the Portuguese friars and merchants in India; and these, says Geddes, "neglected for forty years a Christianity which was under their very *noses.*" This is not a Protestant slander on the first Portuguese Missionaries to India. One of the ministers of Philip IV. told him to his face, " that the Indians who had nothing to say at Goa, but ' Lord *open* to us,' were not thought fit to enter into the kingdom of heaven." So much were the Romanists absorbed in amassing wealth and territory, that Manuel de Faria, the author of " Asia Portuguesa," says of them, " It is shameful that the church, even under the eye of the bishops of Goa, should continue a century without reducing the Christians of St. Thomas to the Romish faith. But the truth is, they are such merchants as Christ *whipped* out of the temple."—Vol. iii. Charges of this kind became so clamorous in Portugal, that Albuquerque, the first archbishop of Goa, found it necessary to bestir himself somewhat on behalf of the poor Syrian Christians. He sent a Franciscan Missionary to Cranganor, to preach Popery to them, and erected a school for training their children in the usages of the Latin Church. This he *blazed* over Europe as a grand specimen of Missionary spirit! The fact is, the Christians of St. Thomas would not listen to Friar Vincent's Popery. They sent some of their sons to the school; but when they found them innoculated with Popery, and speaking Latin, they would not let them preach in their Churches, but treated them as apostates from the true faith. A *Syriac* College was then tried; but Popery would not go down even in the language of their native liturgy. Transubstantiation, purgatory, images, oils, and the Pope's supremacy, were abominations to them. Even their sons, who became priests of Rome, would pray for their own patriarch at Babylon, when celebrating mass! This was wormwood and gall to the GOA fathers. They had, however, to digest it as they could; for at the time they were not powerful enough to persecute the Syrian Churches. They began, therefore, with their Bishop, Mar Joseph, whom they brought from Cochin to Goa as a prisoner, to be sent direct to Rome. But on his arrival at Lisbon, the Queen Regent was so charmed with his meek spirit, that she sent him back to Goa, with letters patent to resume his bishopric; he having given some promise to the Pope's legate to use his influence in India for the Roman Church. His own Churches, however, took the alarm during his absence, and sent to the Patriarch of Babylon for another bishop. They took also precautions to elude the vigilance of the inquisitors at Goa, whilst bringing the new Bishop into Malabar, and with success. Mar Abraham reached his seat in safety, and was welcomed with acclamations. This was too much for Goa to bear meekly, especially as it was followed by the return of Mar Joseph upon their hands. What could the Fathers do in this dilemma, but play off the *old* Bishop against the *new* one? Accordingly, they offered Joseph a band of Missionaries to assist him at Cochin, in reclaiming his place, and fulfilling his pledge to the Queen. But the *wily* Syrian had a revelation, he said, forbidding him to take such help! The Archbishop of Goa saw through this pretext, and called Joseph "a wolf in sheep's clothing." So he was, in one sense. There was no one else, however, who could divide the Malabar crozier with Mar Abraham; and therefore Joseph was allowed to go alone into his old diocess. But the flock, too, had begun to suspect their shepherd, and the greater part of the churches sided with Abraham. Him, therefore, Joseph soon denounced at Goa; and the Viceroy as promptly demanded him to be sent there a prisoner, that he might be forwarded as a heretic to Rome. The Goa fathers did not know Abraham, when they thus called in the power of the Viceroy. Abraham escaped to Ormus to get new powers from the Patriarch of Babylon, and then *went* to Rome to get them confirmed by the Pope! There he abjured his ancient faith, and gave in his allegiance to Pius V. During his absence, Joseph abjured whatever Popery he had embraced at Lisbon; and thus he became popular again in Malabar. Thus "diamond *cut* diamond" for a time. But Popes could not be trifled with long then, even in India. Joseph was sent to Rome a prisoner, and never seen again in Malabar. Abraham also was kept in the *shelf* at Goa, until his new orthodoxy should perform quarantine. He contrived, however, to escape from the inquisitors, and to resume his place. Gregory XIII., on hearing this, summoned him to a provincial council at Goa, under a promise of safe conveyance. Abraham went, and *again* abjured his ancient allegiance to the Nestorian Church.

How refreshing it is to look away from these equal

rogues of literal and mystical Babylon, to the Syrian Churches they wished to govern! Neither the threatenings of Rome, nor the prevarications of their rival Bishops, moved or modified their ancient faith in the least. They would not even *name* the Pope, unless to disclaim his authority and denounce his heresies. La Croze says, " They excluded from the pulpits of the churches their own sons, who apostolized, even before they shut out the Popish Missionaries.

These facts, so far, may be found in *La Croze's Hist. du Chist. des Ind.*, p. 55, *et seq.* But, although no work on this subject deserves more confidence, I prefer illustrations drawn from Popish writers. La Croze was originally a Benedictine of the Abbey of St. Germain, in Paris: but he became a Protestant, and was appointed librarian to the King of Prussia. His life, by M. Jordan, of Berlin, was published at Amsterdam, in 1743.

The spirit of the Mission-house of Goa shocked even the Mahometans of India. The prince who besieged Goa in 1570, in order to expel the Portuguese from the country, told both his soldiers and the viceroy, that he took arms to resist tyranny over conscience! He wrote to the viceroy thus, " I am confident that Jesus Christ, the God whom you adore, cannot be well pleased with *forcing* people to change their religion. This is a thing I stand amazed at; and am in duty bound to see remedied." To his captains he said, " It is more than time for the natives to look about them, and to join in extirpating tyrants who compel the Indians to change their religion." This tyranny was such, that even De Faria closes his " Asia Portuguesa " thus:—

"Even men when made wealthy by money, could

not build up a family by it, in any one instance. For, instead of any regard to religion, they pursued only the ends of a sacrilegious covetousness, by tyranny and all sorts of insolence." Faria is, indeed, speaking of the goyernors and merchants: but they made the *creed* of Goa the banner of their crusades. Father Venagre was associated with Admiral Galvam, who discovered that the cloves of India belonged to the king of Portugal, because the clove has five points agreeing to the five wounds of Christ, which are stamped on the royal arms of Portugal! Well might the Portuguese historian say, " we lose places by our insolence, which we gained by our valour." Gemulia, a native of rank, told them to their face, in the island of Ito, "You preach Christ crucified unto us, and yet crucify those who believe on him."

It was by such men that the Syrian Churches were harassed; and it was to circumvent such men, as well as to gratify his own ambition, that Mar Abraham perjured himself so often. The Syrian bishop was certainly a thorough Vicar of Bray, "and something more;" but still, he had to deal with even more unprincipled Bishops than himself. Soon after his return to his churches, a letter he wrote to his patriarch was intercepted by the spies of Goa; in which he excused his prevarication thus: "The Bishops of the council were over my head, like a *hammer* over an anvil."

No excuses, however, could reinstate Abraham in the confidence of his Churches. They called for an assistant Bishop from the patriarch, and carried their point. Mar Simeon was sent, and Abraham professed to welcome him. He was, perhaps, sincere; for he was now old, and had suffered much at Goa. But when Simeon, who had never seen Popery before, saw its inroads and designs on the Malabar Church, he rallied the faithful against the temporizing of his senior, and shook the last pillars of his throne. As might be expected, he was denounced at Goa by Abraham; and Goa soon sent him to Rome. He was sent, indeed, to be confirmed in his Bishopric by the Pope; but like Mar Joseph, he was never seen again in Malabar! These results smote Abraham to the heart. He felt that he had betrayed his brethren to Rome, and misled his flock. Under this conviction, the old man, when summoned to another council, refused to obey the Pope's brief, and returned to the simplicity of his own Church. Then the vatican began to thunder! But its doomed victim died before its bolts could reach him.

These are melancholy facts! They are, however, instructive; and the lessons they teach are wanted yet. Rivalry can still arise between separate Missions, and even between brethren of the same Mission. Indeed, it is well that there is neither a vatican nor an inquisition in London or New York to appeal to: for if there were, there is now and then a fiery or an envious spirit who would appeal. Mar Abraham is occasionally imitated in "a small way" by some one, in every Missionary Society. Happily, this occurs but seldom: but still, all Missionary Societies have seen enough of it to teach them prudence in the selection of their agents; and as much of it, as should make each of them take care how it treats the others. Rivalries have occurred both in Africa and India, which, if repeated, will not be so gently dealt with by the public, as those of Graham's Town and Tinnevelly have been treated. They will occur again, however, unless systematically watched against. "The spirit *lusteth* to envy," both at home and abroad; "and envy," says Bishop Hall, "is like fire in billets of *junipers*, it lasts more years than one." Bishops, boards and brethren do well to remember this!

The triumph obtained over the Syrian Church at the Synod of Odiamper, by the tricks of the Archbishop of Goa, Menezes,—"that unprincipled prelate," as Dr. Adam Clarke calls him, is too familiar to require notice here, even if I had room for the narrative. His triumph, however, did not last long, except on the coast. In sixty years, the Dutch "turned the tables" on the Portuguese, and then the Syrians turned them on the Pope.

I thus make no secret of either my dread or hatred of Popery; and no apology for expressing both, as personal feelings. I do *feel;* and feeling, like fire, will spread; not because it is mine, but because it is as honest as it is warm. Besides, it is wanted, now that Rome has assailed some of our Protestant Missions, and is menacing them all. The London Missionary Society began a year ago to arm its South Sea Missionaries, and is now arming all its Missionaries, for the onset, by furnishing them with the best refutations of Popery which our theology contains. This is as it should be. Let not, however, the friends of Missions strip their shelves at home, in order to help any of the societies. Our own children may want our *old* books, before long, although we may never need to study them again. Besides, many of these works are unfit for Missionary stations; and the most *learned* of them worse than useless, both at home and abroad; because they shift the battle of the Reformation from the table-land of the New Testament, into the ravines and defiles of tradition, where Erasmus became a coward, and Grotius an apostate, and Austria a slave. M'Gavin's " Protestant" will do more in Missionary stations, both for defence and attack, than Chillingworth or Faber. What is said of Shakspeare is true of M'Gavin:

"One wild Shakspeare, following Nature's lights,
Is worth whole planets filled with Stagerytes."

And as to the mode of warfare which "The Protestant" would inevitably originate, wherever Jesuits may be *smuggled* in by France, or wherever (to use their own phrase whilst in China) they can "*screw* themselves in," it can hardly be more unpolite than their own tactics. The vices and follies of a Church may be fairly thrown in her face, whenever she has the insolence to call upon any people to believe the vagaries of the fathers, or the trash of tradition. Then the *rogues* may be warrantably played off against the *fools*, without ceremony. Had the Syrian Church in Malabar, instead of arguing with Menezes, the Tippoo of Goa, in the synod of Odiamper, kept to her own version of the Scriptures, and bearded Rome with the abominations of the Popedom, she might have suffered more, but she would have sunk less.

I owe it to Truth, however, and most willingly I pay the debt, to exempt Xavier from identification with the policy of Goa. He was of another spirit. The fact is, he was one of "the first fruits" of the Reformation. This assertion will surprise many.

Not more, however, than the discovery surprised me, when I stumbled upon it in the course of my researches. But Loyola found it such hard work to convert Xavier; and Bohurs lets out so much about "the knowing Germans," who poisoned the mind of Loyola's pupil; and old Turselline, his first biographer, blinks so much the question of Lutheran influence, that my suspicions were raised. The result was, that I wrote a sketch of the Life of Xavier for this work, which proves, I think, that he was converted to God at the university of Paris, by the German Lutherans, whom Francis I. brought there for literary purposes. I have not room for the chapter on Xavier, although he was the first European who planned and prayed for China. I may, however, publish my sketch of his life in another form, some time. In the mean time, Carne's Life of him, in his "Distinguished Missionaries," well deserves attention.

CHAPTER XXVI.

THE OPIUM CRISIS.

So far as I can ascertain, Dr. Milne was the *first* writer, who denounced the Opium trade, as the curse of China, and the disgrace of the East India Company. He was not long in China, before he equally pitied the *smokers*, and despised the *smugglers* of Opium. But although he soon wrote on the subject, he wrote in despair. "The vast consumption of opium on this side of India," he said, "is the source of so many evils to the people,—and yet of so much *gain* to the merchants,—that I utterly despair of saying any thing on the subject, which will not be treated with the most sovereign contempt. I cannot but regard it, however, as one of the many evils which hinder the moral improvement of China."— *Retrospect*, p. 318. Malacca, 1820.

This was a bold appeal, although a hopeless one, at Malacca, then; for he stood alone, in making it. A few others, indeed, held his opinions of the enormity, and sympathized with his emotions; but they were not in a condition to speak out as he did. The appeal was, for a time, " the voice of *one* crying in the wilderness," and it awoke no echo until Sir Stamford Raffles began to plan for the welfare of the Ultra-Gangetic Nations. That philanthropic Governor, who was an honour to his country, as well as an ornament to his family, was the first man who set on foot statesman-like inquiries into the tastes and habits which sunk and kept down these nations. He saw, at a glance, that something prevailed, fatal to national improvement; and which, if not counteracted, would defeat all his benevolent designs. He began, therefore, by consulting Missionaries, as men whose designs were still more hindered by vicious habits than his own, and whose office bound them to investigate the sources of crime and misery. His first application was made to Dr. Morrison; and he, as may be supposed, was neither slow nor reserved in communicating to the Governor the results of his own observation, as well as the opinions of Dr. Milne on the subject. Both Missionaries denounced opium and gambling as the *bane* of China; and Dr. Milne was so much delighted with the philanthropy of Sir Stamford Raffles, that he dedicated to him his translation of the great "Imperial Edict," quite as much from feelings of esteem, as from personal gratitude. Thus the opium question arose. These men were the *Clarkson* and *Wilberforce* of it. I did not know this fact in 1835, when the Treasurer of the Home Missionary Society and myself made the first appeal to the British churches against "the infernal drug," in a pamphlet entitled, "No Opium; or Commerce and Christianity working together for good in China." We did not wittingly withhold the palm from its rightful owners; and whoever may achieve the abolition of the trade, without compensation to the contrabandists, need not be ashamed to follow Milne, Morrison and Raffles, nor grudge them their meed of honour. It ought, indeed, to give both confidence and inspiration to the leaders of this question in either House of Parliament, that such men were their forerunners. That senator does not know the moral *pulse* of the great missionary confederacy of the British Churches, who cannot make this TRIAD a talisman, which shall open millions of hearts, and raise millions of hands, for the abolition of the trade, and against all compensation to the traders, except the award of the same odium to the smokers and smugglers of Opium.

Amongst political writers who deserve well of their country for originating this question, the late *Majorribanks* merits the first place. He wrote with the warmth of a philanthropist, if not always with the wisdom of a philosopher. He was the first to prove to merchants and manufacturers, that the Opium of the East India Company was the *dead-*

weight upon our commerce with China, and a worse evil than the old Charter of Leadenhall Street. He was, however, the advocate of negotiation

"At the *Cannon's* mouth;"

and, as such, a dangerous friend to a question of morals and humanity. But still, he meant well, and he will be named with honour " on the Rialto," when merchants congregate to make China a new world on the map of Commerce; for he was the *Columbus* of the discovery, whoever may give a name to the results of it.

It must be a gratifying reflection to the friends of Missions, that Missionaries were the first to investigate and unveil the Opium " mystery of iniquity." Medhurst and Gutzlaff spoke out nobly, when they knew that we sympathized with Milne and Morrison on the subject. Had, therefore, the Chinese Missions done nothing else than raise the cry "No Opium," to its present pitch and prospects, they would not have been unworthy of their place or expense. That cry will lay the *moral* wall of China as flat as the walls of Jericho soon; and, eventually, the Ark of the Covenant will even be welcomed into Pekin. "The ram's horns" of that Ark may be laughed at in Leadenhall Street now; but, like the apocalyptic vials of Babylon, they will make the Court " howl," and the merchants " weep," before long.

Amongst the many interesting appeals made to the country on this subject, of late, the letter of the viceroy of Canton, to our gracious Queen, is by far, the most interesting. Its power and pathos would do credit to the pen of Wilberforce. The man might be an eminent Christian;—such is his quick understanding, and keen sense, of the evils inflicted upon his country, by the trade of this country in Opium. His letter would prove that the Emperor had acted on *principle* in demanding the Opium to be given up, even if the destruction of the poison were not begun yet. I did, I confess, fear that two millions of property might prove a temptation to the TARTAR DRAGON, until I read that letter; for had he appropriated the drug, I saw not how he could escape punishment. But it is now self-evident, that he acted on moral grounds. For, although his viceroy felt that he was pleading with a gentle Queen, and thus speaks to her heart as well as to her understanding, he evidently speaks from his own conscience, and with his master's sanction. He feels as we should do, were any nation to avail itself of the suicidal mania of our times, to pour in tempting forms of Prussic or Oxalic acid into the country. That outrage on humanity would shock even Opium dealers. Let them know, therefore, that British Christians see no difference between swift and slow poisons, which are equally fatal in the end to soul and body; and will no more agree to compensate Losers in the Opium Trade, than they would reimburse a company that lost money in manufacturing new poisons for *suicidal* purposes at home. It is of no use to mince this matter. There is no difference in the results of the drugs, whatever difference there may be in the intentions of the growers and venders. The Opium dealers may mean no harm to China, and be conscious of no crime towards God or man: but their intentions do not alter facts, nor prevent the ruin, for time and eternity, of their infatuated customers.

Besides, why should the land of our fathers be pilloried all over China, as barbarous and mean enough to make "merchandise of the SOULS of men," merely in order to save the *poppy fields* of the East India Company, and the pockets of Contrabandists? Britain never had a high character in China, and therefore she will not sink it lower for the sake of a party, whom even the Chinese mob as well as the court at Pekin, call "devils." This may be a very unfair designation of the party; but it is their name, and they have done some devilish things in China; and therefore have no right to implicate their country in their transactions, or involve it in their infamy. The British Commissioner at Canton staked the honour of his Queen and Country quite far enough, when he saved the Opium merchants' *heads* from the sword and the range of the laws. What then would all China think and feel, were Britain to reimburse as well as save these men? How could the Ambassador of the QUEEN look the Emperor in the face, if he had to say that Britain had paid for the Opium which the viceroy had destroyed? And an embassy which would dare to call on the Emperor to compensate the merchants, now that he has kept the *moral* grounds of his edict inviolate, might, indeed, fight; but negotiate they could not, even if all the compensation they asked for was only—that all the Chinese Opium smokers should wish them to do so. Why then allow it? This is wishing they would give up their pipes for the benefit of the impoverished smugglers.

I offer no apology for writing in this style. I know the mind of tens of thousands, throughout England, who think and feel as I do, and who will speak the same things in a voice of thunder, whenever the question of compensation is mooted. Government has only to keep the ground it has taken, when Parliament meets, in order to call forth, if needed, a "No Opium" cry, as loud, long, and hearty, as the "No Slavery" cry was once: for it will come from all the Churches and Chapels of the land which love Missions. In the mean time, this cry is rising as *prayer*, calmly, but fervently, before the eternal throne, from thousands of pulpits, vestries, hearths and closets, as a preparation for an appeal to the British throne. And who can wonder,—when a heathen viceroy appeals thus to a Christian Queen? "How can we consent to stand tamely by, and see the life's-blood of the central land corrupted with a deadly poison? Therefore it is that in our own country, we punish the seller and smoker with the utmost penalty of the law, in order to cut off for ever the transmission of his curse to all generations. Now, though we are aware that in several places tributary to your noble country, depraved men clandestinely grow and manufacture opium,—yet we cannot suppose for a moment, that it is your SOVEREIGN, or your honourable country, who causes it to secure life to yourselves, by involving others in the pit of death. Such conduct rouses the indignation of mankind, and the reason of High Heaven will assuredly never permit it. On the other hand, if you forbid the drug to be prepared, both countries will enjoy mutual peace and happiness. We most anxiously stand on *tiptoe* waiting your reply."—LIN, Viceroy.

"To The Queen of England, that she may cause the growth of, and traffic in Opium, to cease."

Lin is right: the *growth* must be stopped, if the traffic cease. Some people will trade in the drug, even if we cease to do so, so long as the Company are allowed to manufacture it.

THE END.

Lightning Source UK Ltd.
Milton Keynes UK
UKHW022157120922
408763UK00006B/1369

9 781373 396716